The Paxil Diaries

© 2013 mcgrew

All commercial rights reserved. No part of this work can be used or reproduced for commercial purposes in any manner whatsoever without written permission of the author, except for brief quotations and other fair use purposes. You are free to share electronic versions of this book so long as no money or other goods change hands, and are free to post it on web sites so long as the page it is on contains no advertising and it is posted in its entirety with a link to mcgrewbooks.com. For permission to copy for other than private use contact publish@mcgrewbooks.com

ISBN 978-0-9910531-3-1

Printed in the United States of America

Table of Contents

Forward: Paxil 1
1: What a long, strange trip 3
2: Sweet little Anorexia 9
3: loser+.5 15
4: Different bar, same results 21
5: It's Sunday again, fellow sinners 27
6: More music more music more music 33
7: Fun with offline trolls... 37
8: Blindness, envy, and jail 43
9: No music no music no music 49
10: Good time last night 55
11: Fuck Frankie 61
12: Real Poetry from a Real Poet 65
13: Vielie's Planet: Bummer 69
14: Two bands at Dempsey's! 75
15: Heather and Anne 81
16: Amy and the Teeniebobbers 89
17: Ginger and the Mickey 93
18: Family 97
19: Revelations 101
20: Am I too picky? 105
21: Is Ted Turner gay? 111
22: Mr. Opporknockity 117
23: Hey, Q! 125
24: Secrets of the Q revealed 129
25: The Q - continue, um... 135
26: Independence Day 141
27: Fifty Cents (Believe it or not) 149
28: Saturday, written as Science Fiction from the early 60s... 153
29: Friday night at home (and other dull stories) 159
30: Duffy's "Pub" 163
31: Brothers 169
32: Car Bombs 177
33: It's been such a long, long, long time 183
34: What a long, strange morning it's been 191
35: Bar Fight! 195

36: Court Hearing 199
37: I'm getting a final divorce decree for Christmas! 203
38: I'm back. And I hate technology. 209
39: The parts order from hell 213
40: Barfighting and other, less exciting stuff 221
41: Evil-X.. 225
42: 420 229
43: Patty's friend at K5 235
44: Redneck Friends 239
45: No Paxil for me, young man! 243
46: Stars and bars 249
47: July 4 - the lost diary 253
48: Bar stories 259
49: DOOMed 267
50: Crab racing at the saloon 275
51: Evil-X cheered me up 281
52: Little Feat 285
53: The Farmer And The Dell 289
54: Beer and Anti-Paxil 295
55: Child Support and other scams and bars and music and.. 299
56: At the bar... no, not THAT bar 305
57: The missing diary 309
58: Found: The Missing Diary 315
59: Evil always wins 319
60: Dempsey died 321
61: Killer 327
62: A Christmas Present from God 331
63: Racism on Martin Luther King's Birthday 335
64: The Angel's Mother – Chris at Christmas 339

Forward: Paxil

Way back in the last century there was a twelve year old girl who decided that she was going to marry the boy next door to the boy next door. The year was 1969, and the boy was a seventeen year old nerd who used a slide rule and had built a ham radio receiver, a guitar amplifier, and did all sorts of other nerdy stuff.

Unbeknownst to the seventeen year old nerd, all of the twelve year old girls thought this nerdy kid was really, really cool, including the one who swore that the seventeen year old would some day be her groom.

Of course, no seventeen year old boy wants a twelve year old girl. Not unless he's some sort of pervert child molester. This particular seventeen year old made his geek supply money at the drive-in theater, where he sold tickets, cooked, worked a cash register, and other sorts of mundane stuff that kids who worked at drive in theaters did.

I was that seventeen year old nerd.

After graduating high school, I went to college, where I dropped out after one quarter and joined the US Air Force.

This book is not about the Air Force. This book is not even about going back to college after the Air Force.

The summer of 1975 saw me mostly sitting in a lawn chair on my parents' patio, drinking beer and watching traffic drive down the street. Especially the girls on bicycles in their summer clothes. One in particular caught my eye. I didn't know who she was.

One day she was walking, and I decided that I would get in my car and offer her a ride. Half a block down I stopped next to her. She was frowning a frown that should have chilled my spine and made me run away screaming. But I wasn't that smart.

"Want a ride?" I asked. I had some pot rolled up and wanted to go for a ride to smoke it anyway, as I didn't want to smoke pot at my parents', or indeed even take it inside.

"Fuck off, asshole!" she replied. I drove away, and once out of earshot I told myself what a lucky fellow I was that this bitch had not wanted a ride. I had no idea how right I was, nor what a mistake even asking her was.

A couple of months later, that November, I was in a Pizza Hut with my old friends from the drive in theater years, laughing and drinking beer and eating pizza and having a good time when a very drunken young lady staggered over with a pitcher of beer. "Hey, I know you!" she slurred. I didn't recognize her, which was a very bad thing indeed. She was the one I'd offered a ride to and been so rudely put down by.

"Oops!" The drunken fool tripped on her own feet and spilled the entire pitcher of beer on me. "Oh my god, I am SO sorry," she said, wiping at me with napkins. I left to go change clothes, and when I returned she was gone.

The next day she called and invited me to a party. When I arrived I found that she was the only one there. We were married the next summer, the day before the US Bicentennial.

Twenty seven years after the spilled pitcher, after she had been unfaithful five times I knew about, and producing two daughters, I bought her a new wedding ring and a new car.

She was actually in the middle of affair number six (that I found out about) when I bought the car. She left me and the teenaged daughters for her new lover two months after I bought the car. The last night she slept in my house was Friday the thirteenth of September, 2002.

The daughters and I sought counseling, and were prescribed various antidepressants. Mine was Paxil. I recounted the aftereffects of the lost marriage and the subsequent Paxil use at kuro5hin.org ("corrosion", or "K5") as a kind of self-help therapy. The stories are known as "The Paxil Diaries" and are reproduced here as chapters in this book.

Chapter 1: What a long, strange trip...
Sun Apr 20th, 2003 at 08:13:36 PM EST

Sex, drugs, rock and roll...

*It's just a jump to the left
and then a step to the right...
It's a filthy drug and it will drive you insane
Lets do the time warp again!*

Only this time, the time warp needed no acid. Just the right bar, the right music, the right people...

My oldest daughter has spent the last month with her mother. My other daughter asked to spend the night with her friends last night, so I had the house to myself.

I put in a tape and watched an episode of *Star Trek*. Paramount would probably consider my taping episodes of their "property" for later use "piracy". They can go to hell. I imagine they probably will.

At any rate, sitting alone with the tube and a beer was boring as hell, so I decided to troll the bars and see if I could find conversation with female company. Maybe I'd even get lucky.

You can't throw a beer bottle in any direction in this town without hitting a bar with it. Actually, in the entire state, unless you live in a dry county. So I walked down to Duffy's, about four houses down the street. I'd been looking forward to it, since they were supposed to have some biker thing going on. And I like biker chicks. Most of the bikers look older than me by the time they're 30, and I like younger women. Runs in the family I guess; my dad's wife is ten years younger than him, and my grandmother, who married at 17, was eight years younger than my grandfather.

Duffy's was doing pretty good business, and there were some very attractive young ladies in there. Some rock and roll was coming from the jukebox, not very loud. I ordered a draft and started sipping.

The jukebox stopped. It was apparently redneck karaoke time. "Yeer walkin' own the fatin' sad o' meee... if you don't love it leave it..."

The place was nearly empty before he finished that first Nixon-era Pro-Vietnam propaganda song. About five old cowboy wannabes were all that was left. I didn't even finish my beer. "I think I'll find some place where the music doesn't suck so bad," I told the pretty bartender, and walked on down to the Track Shack.

I like the Track Shack. There's always good music coming from the jukebox, and pretty girls usually wind up sitting next to me. I wish I could remember how to pick them up... I was married way too long.

But last night it was pretty empty, and no ladies. There was a baseball game on, drowning out the jukebox. I drank a beer and left. East a few blocks, or North a mile? I hadn't been to the bars east, but the nearest has a big "Nascar Sunday" sign out in front, and the rest probably have exclusive black patronage. And the only kind of music I like less than country-western is rap. So I walked north.

There was a bar I hadn't been in before, named "Dempsey's", so I walked in that direction. It was doing fair business with what looked like college aged folks to me, some 1970s rock was on the jukebox, they had Rolling Rock for a buck a bottle, and a band was setting up. I got a beer and wandered around, unsuccessfully trying to flirt with the pretty ladies. All the women in there were attractive, some looked like supermodels to me. There weren't many available chairs. There was a table with a couple of young women at it and I asked if I could use the chair. The lip-pierced woman said "sure" and when I sat down they proceeded to studiously ignore me. I saw a couple of open chairs by the bar, close to the band so I hung my coat on one and sat down.

It's been a while since I've heard any live music, except the music that comes from my own guitar. The bartender said they had live bands every Friday and Saturday. Live band, cheap beer, no cover. I think I've found my new favorite bar!

The band started playing. It was a Grateful Dead tribute band. I'm no deadhead, but I like their music OK. Strange – most deadheads are older than me. But these young folks were getting into it. And the ladies seemed to be flirting with me.

It was a magically weird night.

The old joke goes, what's the difference between a dog and a fox? About four beers. But the more I drank, the more ordinary these women looked. Indeed, one thin and fit looking young lady looked petulant. I told her to cheer up.

There was a woman on the other side of the curved bar

wearing glasses, who had a bit of a nerdy look to her. I think I fell in love... or in lust, anyway. Glasses on a woman turn me on as much as extra poundage on one turns me off. I'm a very thin man who can't ever seem to get enough to eat, and anorexic women give me wood. This lady had perhaps five extra pounds, which somehow made her that much more desirable. Weird. Normally that would turn me off. Beer is funny that way. Anyway, I stared and smiled. She smiled back.

People were dancing, and I was getting excited by the ladies dancing, and smiling – you would have thought I was a really good looking guy instead of a skinny nerd with chipped coke bottle glasses. The nerdy looking woman seemed to be by herself with nobody much noticing her except me. She grinned hugely every time she saw me watching.

The crowd stared changing, people leaving and people coming in. The dot-com looking yuppie types with the expensive glasses and hundred dollar designer jeans seemed to be disappearing, and more longhairs in Levis were coming in.

It struck me that I was back in the early 1970s again. There is a war on that seems as if it will have no end (Afghanistan, Iraq, probably Syria next...), a self-serving right wing conservative in the white house, sappy boo-hoo music on the radio, recession – and here I was listening to the Grateful Dead with a bunch of long haired youth!

And then I smelled something I haven't had in quite some time. And then I saw it – a small, blue ceramic pipe. I stared at the pipe, which a fat bearded fellow seemed to have produced. He had handed it to what was probably a very ordinary looking woman, but who looked pretty damned good to me.

Especially holding that pipe. I looked at her, the pipe, and her again. She handed it to me. I filled my lungs and held it.

A couple of guys walked past, and I knew without a doubt they were the Secret Police; or "plainclothes policemen" as the mainstream media euphemizes it, not wanting the docile populace to realize that they live in a police state. I have no idea why I thought they were cops, except perhaps the paranoia pot produces. I don't think I was the only one who noticed, as fat boy and his pipe were nowhere to be seen and everybody seemed to be giving the narco type fellows a wide berth.

A few minutes later the cop types were gone and I had the pipe again. I got an even better toke. The herb tasted wonderful – as I said, it has been quite a while. And this tasted like some grade-A bud.

And... the music changed. No, my ears changed. The dancing crowd became a surreal artwork, beautiful in its movement. I was in bliss. The girl who had first handed me the pipe kept looking my way and smiling. She seemed to be trying to avoid the fat fellow who owned the pipe, and the fat fellow kept giving me dirty looks.

The song says "even the losers get lucky sometimes", and this was obviously my lucky night. I was going to get some!

I made the decision to let fat boy have hippie chick. I felt I owed him. It was the first time in a long, long time I had gotten high, and those two tokes got me wasted. To take over the woman he was trying to pick up would have made me feel like a huge asshole.

And then – an overweight woman who looked older than my mother started hitting on me. Now I know how the twenty somethings feel when I try to strike up a conversation with them. And understand the looks of revulsion on some of their faces when they see me eyeing them hungrily.

A couple of gays tried hitting on me. My stomach got a bit queasy and I kept staring at the nerd girl, dancing by herself, and the hippie girl who obviously appreciated the pipe but oddly seemed to prefer skinny men to fat ones.

They ran out of Rolling Rock. I switched to water and left a tip on the bar. Then they had last call. And people started leaving. Hippie chick was in fat boy's arms. And damn – nerd girl was being hit on by some normal looking guy. I walked out, thanked the band for a great show.

The three gays were outside arguing with each other. I saw nerd girl crossing the street alone, and crossed it myself. I tied my shoe, and she was gone.

I know I've found my new favorite bar. I'll be back. I hope all the folks that were there will be, too. Especially hippie chick and nerd girl. Well, I won't mind if Granny and the Gayboys stay home...

Chapter 2: Sweet little Anorexia
Sun May 11, 2003 at 02:06:47 PM EST

The last diary entry was a belated post from 4/20, which I should have put in "diary" in the first place. This one is kind of a continuation.

I found out later that Dempsey's did charge a cover, but if you were in before the band started you were cool. And they didn't charge the regulars any cover. Still, it was only two bucks. But hey, two bucks is two bucks. That was two beers – ¾ of the way to a good buzz!

The bar changed hands (again). The bartender denied it, but it was just too obvious. First, and most troubling to me, they discontinued the dollar Rolling Rocks. Both bartenders, who were part owners, disappeared, and there was this goofy kid with his Cubs hat on backwards tending bar. They have another new bartender, too, a very attractive blonde.

But Friday... oh my, I fell in lust badly. Here is a sorry tale of the evils of drink, and how to not get laid.

And I'm thinking of starting a record company.

It was hot in my building at work Friday. And my brain wasn't functioning properly. I thought it was because I forgot to take my Paxil Thursday morning and didn't take it until lunch, but everybody else complained about their being scatterbrained, as well.

Evil-X never showed up to take Patty to school that morning.

At lunch, Married Lady gave me a ride to the bank, gave Patty a ride to school, and I bought Married Lady an ice cream at McDonalds. The tease, she always unbuttons her top button when she drops by my cube. Married lady was complaining about being scatterbrained even, and she's normally scatterbrained.

I took a two hour vacation and left work early. K5 was down, so I read some of my spam from loser.com (the dating site). Popped open a beer and drank it on the front porch, and watched the cars go by. Daughter was at the mall with her friends by then. I went for a walk after I finished the beer.

Right as I was crossing the railroad tracks it started sprinkling, so I walked into the Track Shack. Bought a beer to bide my time until it quit raining. There were a few ugly women there, and a bunch of construction worker type guys. I found out what it was with all the dollar bills thumbtacked to the ceiling.

There is a kind of game there – put the dollar on the ceiling. It's a high ceiling, twelve feet or higher. There are dollar bills thumbtacked all over it.

The game is, you get a thumbtack from the bartender, stick it through the dollar, put two quarters on the head of the thumbtack, and toss it to the ceiling as hard as you can. Some fat chick, just turned 21, stuck one on her second try!

But I digress. I finished my beer and the weather got worse, so I bought a bucket. The tornado sirens went off. I borrowed Jason's phone and called home – no answer. Called my cell, which my daughter had. Either it was shut off, she was in a basement and couldn't get a signal, or a tornado had snatched it out of her hand and smashed it. Worried sick, I finished the rest of the beers in the bucket. The weather passed, and I hurried home.

There were a whole bunch of messages on the answering machine, from my daughters. I was even more worried about my oldest daughter, since she had moved in with Evil-X, and Evil-X lives in a house trailer, y'all.

Oldest was worried that I get the cats in the basement, she was at the civic center basement in the town they live in, right outside Springfield. Youngest was in the mall basement worried about me.

Relieved, I decided to walk some more. I hate sitting home on Friday night. Decided to go down to Dempsey's and see if they had a band and if it was any good.

Now mind you, I'd already killed more than a six pack. I was already way over the amount I normally drink. I was way buzzed, but good.

There was a band playing, and I couldn't tell you what genre of music it was. I've never heard anything remotely like it. There was a jazz drummer, a rock guitarist, an electric banjo player, and a conga player. I kind of knew the conga player, if not his name. He had been in the bar before as a patron several times, you couldn't miss him. Really tall, skinny white guy with waist length blond hair done up in Jamaican dreadlocks.

He had been in the crowd on 4-20. A lot of the same crowd was there. Hippie Chick and Nerd Girl were there. They both seemed to have gained a bit of weight in the last month.

And I noticed I was sitting next to the thinnest girl I've ever seen.

Now, in my youth, I was really attracted to skinny girls. The X was mostly normal sized, except the times she got fat. Sometimes really fat, over 250 pounds at times. I thought I was over my love of the skinny chicks – but I found I was wrong.

This woman was wearing a top that was barely a top at all, a cloth tied in the back in two places, belly button showing. Not a bad face... of course, I was drunk, for all I know if I saw her sober she'd be a dog. Now, I've never been one to chase big boobs. It's not like E cups turn me off, it's just that I've always felt that tits were for babies. This lady's chest was underdeveloped even for my tastes, but I was in lust, nonetheless.

I caught her eye (Lord that was a loud banjo) and remembered something from one of the kiddie shows my children watched when they were little. I pointed to my eye, slapped my chest, and pointed at Anorexia. She laughed. Between songs she said "I'm with him" and pointed to the Conga player.

She was up and dancing, and with every sip of beer my lust grew. As with every little wiggle of Anorexia's fifteen inch waist and twenty inch hips.

The band took a break and walked outside. I walked out for some fresh air, away from the tobacco smoke.

I smelled another certain, peculiar, sweet smell. Eyes darting around I saw it: a big fattie. "Can I get a toke of that, man?" ...and became part of the circle, which was mostly made up of the band. Named, oddly but fittingly, the *Green Grass Pickers*.

"You guys have a CD?" Nope. Can't afford it. "Dude, all you need is a computer!"

"Can't afford one." Of course – musical equipment is expensive. Doesn't leave much cash for anything else. I offered to record them, and that made 'em really happy. Of course, I'm going to have to find some way to get hold of them before their next gig, because my van's busted.

After the doob had gone around a few times I was handed a big, but dead, roach. I lit it. "You don't smoke cigarettes?" someone asked.

"Nope. Quit 3 years ago" I replied.

"But you have a lighter?"

"Well, lighting a lady's butt is a way to break the ice."

"And you smoke pot?"

"Well, not very often. But yeah. When I get a chance."

I lit the roach, took a big toke, passed it around again. It was a little roach when it came back. Handed it to Dreaddude, "It's short and out." We all went in. They started playing again.

When Anorexia had told me she was with Dreaddude, I kept staring hungrily but left her alone, and hit on one or two other chicks who, as usual, weren't impressed. Now, Anorexia was all of a sudden interested in me. "I'm not really his girlfriend or anything, I just follow the band."

A groupie.

We chatted and talked and... Jesus please let me have this woman!

No such luck. The room started spinning. I walked out for some air. Staggered down the street so if I puked it would be in front of a different bar... sat down on the sidewalk, resting against the building... the whole town was spinning.

When a quart of foam spewed back out, I realized without a doubt that I was miserable and would likely be worse in the morning. I marshaled my Prana Yoga, gathered up my Zen and stood up. Slowly if a bit unsteadily, I walked the two miles home.

Without the skinniest girl I've ever seen. She'll probably be dead from malnutrition before I ever see her again. But I don't know if I've ever lusted after a woman so badly.

Damned beer!

Poll:
How much do you weigh?
I'm anorexic/bulemic 7%
over 100 0%
over 120 46%
over 150 38%
over 250 7%
over 350 0%
I'm an American, dammit 0%
When I sit around the house, I sit AROUND the house! 0%

Chapter 3: loser+.5
Wed May 14, 2003 at 06:23:31 PM EST

muchagecko told me that we at K5 have no lives. If so, I must be a loser among losers. Laugh at me, and raise your chin in superiority! "Ha!" you may now proclaim, "compared to mcgrew I'm not a loser! Look out world!"

Yes, I struck out again. This was the most spectacular strikeout yet. I met a biker chick, took her home... and didn't even get to first base.

The worst part is, it didn't even bother me!

Ladies, tell me how a skinny nerd could get in your undies if he met you in a bar. Guys, tell me what works for you. Read on for a sad tale of geeky losering.

Yesterday morning when the alarm clock went off I got out of bed, and fell down. I got up, and fell down again. The over the counter sinus pill plus Paxil combination had me so loaded I couldn't even walk. I doubt I ever got this stoned on purpose back in my addle-brained drug-soaked youth. I got off the floor a second time and banged on my daughter's door, and told her she had to get up NOW, because I was going back to bed. I would never have made it down the stairs alive.

Later on in the afternoon, coffeed up and not walking too unsteadily, the doorbell rang. 2:30? Probably a Jehovah's Witness, or a deputy serving a summons, or someone wanting to cut my grass or something. I was busy typing a thank you note to the K5 denizens anyway. Oh, I forgot to thank Ascii Art for the portrait. Looks just like me when I take off my glasses. And cut my hair. And he or she didn't put a mustache on me. Other than that it's "teh spitting image" of me.

The damned door opened. Daughter must have gotten off school early. "Anybody home?"

Damn. Evil-X. But she was here to offer me a ride to the store, and I was short of groceries. Of course there was a catch – she was broke and almost out of cigarettes and wanted five bucks for "gas money", even though insurance on the damned PT comes out of my paycheck. This was actually not the curse her arrival usually is, because I needed a ride, and she's the antidote to Paxil, being the most negative individual you will ever have the extreme fortune of never meeting. At least I got to see my older daughter, who's living with Evil-X now.

Later in the evening, after Dopey Smurfing K5; Not really dopey smurfing, that's when you keep hitting the "refresh" button trying to bring a server down with your 300 baud modem. This "dopey smurf" was typing into one person's diary while five more Mozilla tabs were loading. On dialup. I guess this is a Dopey Steve Smurf. The real Dopey Smurf's name is "Marko" and he was a med student when I knew him. He's a Canadian medical doctor now, I think.

Anyway, after reading all the K5 diaries and getting

bored, eating steak strips and potato chips, I decided to walk down to Duff's Pub and get one of their $3.00 pitchers of beer. Yeah, the place you saw in The Simpsons, this *is* Springfield. The real "one". Groening got a lot of stuff wrong, like, Duffy is fat, not skinny. And there is no "Capital City"; Springfield *is* the capital city. And only a few of the denizens are bug-eyed. And a lot of other, non-Groening cartoon characters live here, too. Olive Oyle, for example, only the real Olive is flatter chested than Popeye's Olive. Popeye lives here too, but as far as I know Olive isn't with Popeye, Bluto, OR Brutus, all of whom also live here. Betty Boop lives here, too, only the Springfield Betty's head is bigger.

Now you all think I'm full of shit. But I'm not. This is a weird place full of weird people.

But I digress. Again. Sorry.

I walked down to Duff's for a cheap pitcher, figuring I might as well be bored there as at home. I held no fantasies of picking up any women; there seldom are any women in there, and when there are they're mostly old and fat. The back door is closest to my house, and it looked like the bar was full. Almost.

There were two empty stools at the other end of the bar, next to a larger but curvaceous, nervous young woman with a pretty face in jeans and a T shirt, who was nursing a Budweiser. I sat down next to her. She was talking to the highly tattooed bartender, who was trying to tend bar without ignoring her. I asked for a three dollar pitcher of Busch. "Only two bucks tonight."

"Cool!" I exclaimed. The young chick looked at her $2.50 bottle, and the old guy to my left looked at his, both in amazement. Barkeep took my five and gave me three back, I put one on his side of the bar and started talking to the large but pretty woman.

Now, when I woke up this morning my bullshit detector was sounding. I'm not sure why it didn't go off last night. Maybe It had beer in it or something. Or maybe she wasn't full of shit. Or maybe I'm just a clueless loser.

Seems she's a biker chick, owns two Harleys, her dad was a Hell's Angel, and her mom's in the hospital in Springfield. She drove her old T-bird all the way up from Carbondale, almost 200 miles south of here (rent *Poor White Trash* to become acquainted with that part of Illinois, and the college there). She's supposed to get 72 year old Mom out of the hospital, and she's supposed to be spending the night with "Sam". Only, she's one digit short of Sam's full phone number. And she doesn't know his last name. And "man, I wish I had a big doobie," she says.

I'm badly in need of a haircut, by the way. Hasn't been cut in months.

"Save some beer money for a motel room," I suggest. "Not enough," she says. And she left her credit cards at home. Mom's got one but she's old and poor and besides, Gypsy (her biker name) couldn't afford to pay her back. I told her I'd let her stay with me except that my daughter would explode (and besides, since the X is a slut, Daughter needs somebody to give a better example, but I didn't tell Bikerchick that). And Gypsy sure wishes she had a doobie.

So she's wishing this, and wishing that, and I'm listening to her life story and we're talking motorcycles. Tells me about her last bar fight, shows me her tattoo, tells me about her Tough Guy Competition trophy. She wishes she could get on her computer because the phone number's on AOL. She's sitting next to the bar phone, I suggest that with 3 of the last 4 digits in her hand, there are only 10 possibilities. Try 'em all, and if that doesn't work we can walk down to my house and she can use my PC.

"Walk? I have my car!" But, it's only 4 houses. "Walk?" Hmm, I'm starting to figure out why heavy people are heavy. Her perfume is getting stronger and arouses parts of my brain, but oddly, not the part that controls blood flow. I should have had a woodie by then. "You know where we could get a joint?" she asked. "Yeah," I replied, "you want to drive all the way down to St. Louis and get one?"

So she tries all 10 combinations, I finish my little pitcher, and she finishes hers. We walk down to my house. She's 32 and has a 15 year old daughter. She had showed me the tattoo on her ankle, a guy's name. She remarks on what a BIG old house it is. "I love big old houses," she says. "Is that your busted van in the street?" Yeah, I'm hoping a bus hits it. And she sure wishes she had some pot.

So we go in, sit down in the kitchen, and she gets on AOL IM (which is only installed because of Daughter). I get out two beers. She can't find anybody online that could tell her "Sam's" number.

So we go back to the bar, I ask Barkeep for another pitcher, he brings it and two glasses. She keeps talking about how drunk she's getting, and oddly, I don't feel drunk at all. And she outweighs me by at least 50 pounds.

Pitcher finished, she leaves with an older woman.

I walk home, and when I get there I realize that I am drunk. And I sure wish I could have gotten Bikerchick high. Maybe that's the secret, buy some pot and get 'em stoned.

Gah!

Poll
I should have...
Put my arm around her 0%
Kissed her 0%
Grabbed her ass 25%
Offered her money 25%
Told her how big my dick was 0%
Asked "wanna fuck?" 12%
Nothing (what I actually did) 37%
Other 0%

Chapter 4: Different bar, same results
Sat May 17, 2003 at 11:59:05 AM EST

I'm a little bummed this morning, not sure why. I mean, my life... life? Hah, poor choice of words. Existence doesn't suck any worse than it's been sucking.

Oops, that whole paragraph was a poor choice of words... because now the British are all giggling. Ah, well, so what, the British suck fags.

Maybe I forgot to take my Paxil once last week. Or maybe it's the Evil-X, who is the cause of my need for Paxil in the first place, as well as the antidote to it.

Patty's on drugs too, since her mother has a worse effect on her than on me. Both daughters are on drugs. I mean, X is their mom. Poor Daughters. Younger's on two drugs, one she takes to "help her sleep" (that's what the doctor told her... it's an antidepressant).

Daughter was ready for school in plenty of time. I walked off to work.

Daughter calls me at work. She finally got hold of her mom, X isn't giving her a ride. X's boyfriend, who we will simply refer to as "Motherfucker," is giving her sister a ride. She's going to flunk band for missing too much class. She's really upset and takes her frustrations out on me. I tell her I'll call her mom, and get her mom's phone number.

OK, here's some more unbelievable stuff for you. This would never be a soap opera plot, because nobody would believe it. Here's a little background on Motherfucker.

The first month or two after X left, Leila, my oldest Daughter, the one in special ed, wouldn't even speak to X. And then Patty, my Youngest Daughter, discovered, when MF was showing pictures of his kids (none of whom he has custody of) that MF's son was OD's boyfriend! So, oldest daughter gets along with the guy that's fucking her mom now. That pisses off younger daughter, the gifted one, to exasperation.

I should probably call one daughter Yin, and the other one Yang. But then you would think I was oriental instead of a hazel eyed white man.

Anyway, I don't know why you guys hotlist me, I don't write well at all. I digress too much and my sentences are too long. But Patty is all pissed because Leila is getting a ride and she isn't. And bummed because she's not going to get in to college and "I might as well drop out of school."

AAAARRGH!!! So, after nearly being brought to tears by Patty's tale of woe, and then getting more pissed the more I think about it (Brits, over here "pissed" means angry, not drunk. So grin and light up a fag), I call up X like I promised. Answering machine answers. She's home, just not answering the phone.

I don't remember exactly what vitriol I left on it, but I do remember that it ended in "God Damn your evil soul to hell, bitch". After I hung up, I belatedly remembered what my religion was and felt bad about it. I could see Jesus putting a little mark by my name, "OK, one down on the list. He'll have to wait in the flames a bit longer."

The phone rings. It's Patty. I tell her no ride, has to take a bus. She's hoping she gets run over by a car on the way to the bus stop.

So, yesterday didn't feel much like Friday. I had a hard time concentrating on my job. That's not unusual lately, they're probably not going to give me a very good writeup next review time. Doesn't much matter, budget cuts mean nobody's getting raises anyway.

I had to walk to the other building, half a mile away and missed my morning visit with Married Lady. But the walk cheered me up a bit, and I forced myself to cheer up some, too. But I didn't wear the smile I usually do these days.

Married Lady's right, I need new glasses and a decent haircut. As she reminded me again as we were all in the parking lot after the fire alarm went off. I blamed the fire alarm on Tom's SAS program. Boss says no, it was the smoke coming from Tom's collar when he was working on it.

Married lady's off work early and gives me a ride home. Her husband's out of town gambling. I think if I was an evil bastard I could have had some pussy. But shit, I just couldn't do that. Integrity is a heavy burden for a horny man!

So, daughter is home, and she's going to some ska or punk show with her rudie friends, can she have a dollar? Sure.

I get on the computer, check my mail, check out the want ads at loser.com (the dating service), then log on to K5. Read diaries and get pissed at all the dumbasses who think I want to know what they thought of Matrux Relarded, especially Egg Troll. So I did a review of the reviewers (one word: TARDS).

And no, I can't explain the apparent conflict of language there, considering my "special" older daughter who I love very much. But If I'm not going to be PC about race, ethnicity, or sexual orientation I'd be pretty damned hypocritical to be annoyed at any other word usage. The word doesn't change the reality. "Sticks and stones". "Geek" and "nerd" used to be insults, and were hurled at me as a youth. No big deal.

I didn't want to repeat last week's mistake, and get shitfaced before I got around any women. So I stayed at K5 until about 9:30, then walked down to Dempsey's.

The band is setting up, I get a beer. No trouble finding a chair, not many people and all the women had matching men. A few men had matching men, too. The band starts playing; a jazz band. Technically good, but too slow and depressing. I finished my beer after the second song and slipped out the back. Walked down the alley through the sparkling broken glass, and wondered whether to just go home or what.

Said the Lord's Prayer and choked on the part about being delivered from evil and being led into temptation; I wanted some pussy. Stood on a corner trying to decide what I wanted to waste the rest of the evening on, pretending to wait for the light, and I notice that a very attractive, well kept blonde driving an expensive car is looking at me. I smile at her, and she smiles back really big. Then the light changed and she drove off.

So I walk up the street, and I notice a few blocks north a bunch of police cars blocking the street, and tents in the street. Must be where all the people were. So I walk that way. Whatever the tents were about is over. A dozen cops are standing around in front of a bar, and I hear what sounds like 80s rock. So I go in.

Somebody tugs at my jacket. "Three dollars."

"Oops, sorry." I give him a ten and get change.

The place is packed. Good band, playing hard rock from mostly the '80s. I notice that most of the women are pretty ugly. Not many people are smiling.

Hey, I recognize that guy, the devil worshiper from the movie *Little Nicky*. They must have let him up here for a while. Or kicked him out. I think they were torturing him in much the same way I was being tortured, as he was only about five feet tall, and squat, as if something heavy had been sitting on his head for a decade. And I noticed that all the old ugly women were looking at him longingly, and the beautiful ones were studiously ignoring him.

I felt better. Wonder what he did to piss off Nicky's dad? Hell, probably nothing. After all, why would he NEED to?

I recognized somebody else – a woman who had told me "fuck off" when I tried to hit on her at Dempsey's, standing alone with another woman, who all the guys who she was trying to hit on were hitting on.

The Paxil bottle says "Do not drink alcoholic beverages while taking this medicine". Hmm... when I first started taking it, two beers had me bouncing off the walls. I think it may be slightly... psychedelic with alcohol? That would explain why the cartoon characters all come out after a few beers too many...

At any rate, I started to see humor everywhere. I didn't even try to hit on any women. But I was grinning, and doing the rock yell after every song and the crowd, who seemed bored when I came in, was cheering up, too.

MMMMMMmmmmmm, beeeeer....

People were dancing on the bar...

I wound up sitting between two very beautiful women. And the band stopped playing and the lights came on and I was sitting by myself.

Good band, if you're a rocker and find yourself in Central Illinois this summer, look for The Lost Boys.

Poll
How many drinks before you'll dance on the bar?
20 33%
10 44%
5 11%
4 0%
3 0%
2 0%
1 0%
Drink? 11%

Chapter 5: It's Sunday again, fellow sinners
Sun May 18, 2003 at 04:17:44 PM EST

I started reading a little of the Koran yesterday. A hearty thanks to the Arab gentleman who gave me the link, whose name I can't remember. I'm sure I'll run across him here again.

Now, more than ever, I can't figure out WTF the Crusades were about. Except that the "Christians" were a bunch of total jerks and dumbasses. Because from what I've read so far, there is absolutely nothing in the Koran that contradicts the Christian Bible.

OK, that's enough church. Lets talk about music and women. I hope the cops don't close Dempsey's down.

I saw at *New Scientist* that they've cloned muchagecko.

Speaking of women and clones, I figured out why that chicken killing maria's lab is trying to clone chickens – they want a replacement in case the original GW Bush dies.

My grandma was a chicken killer, too. Only we ate the ones she killed. I don't think I'll ever forget the sight I saw as a small child, of the headless chicken running down the hill while its head lay there on the chopping block with its beak and eyes opening and closing... boy those were some good tasting chickens! Lots of work getting the feathers off, though, and those feathers were *hot*.

But none of that has the slightest bit of relevance to what I originally set out to write here. I had a link to the *New Scientist* article in notepad and my mind wandered a bit. I haven't had enough coffee to wake all the way up yet.

You K5 people made me get out the *Matrix* tape and watch it again. A lot of you are poseurs, you know that? That was a good flick, well filmed, art, and if you didn't catch the deeper meanings, the nuances, well, you're just thick. But yeah, I know, it's "kewl" to bash it now, just like it was "kewl" to slobber all over it when it first came out.

So anyway, after I watch the tape I walk on downtown to find some live music. About three blocks from home it starts sprinkling. Then harder. My glasses are wet. I pray for it to stop. It doesn't. I remember the mustard seed thing, and add "if it's your will."

The rain stops. I sure love God. Even though he does seem to want me to be horny, in debt, and on foot. The "thorn in the side" thing, I guess.

I walk down 5th street through the fog that lingered after the rain toward the bar I was in Friday night. As I cross Monroe, I hear music from the direction of Dempsey's. So I walk on down there.

The place is packed. There are three empty tables outside on the sidewalk, and chairs. A band is inside jammin'. Yep, this is the place tonight! Their ad poster is on the door,

"The Station". As I walk through the door they're singing...

Come on in, have a mighty fine time...
been walking for miles,
Sit yourself down...
Have a drink or three...
Just let that fog be...

I thread my way in, trying to find somewhere to squeeze in to get a beer. "Hey Steve!" I look up, there's a guy from the other building at work. Talk with him a little, finally catch the poor, busy as hell bartender's eye and get a beer and a water. It's hot in there, so I wind my way through the crowd again to sit outside, at one of the tables out there by the door.

As I'm walking out I see Holly, the beautiful Perkins waitress I had met at Dempseys a week or so earlier, the one who I spoke to for a while before she moved to the other side of the bar. *sigh*

She'd be perfect if she'd stop smoking those Camels. And if her "real" personality is as sweet as what I saw in the bar is. And if she didn't have those two little kids. Since she pretty obviously isn't interested in me anyway, I sit down outside and drink the glass of water, and start sipping the beer. I'm sipping, because the women are, all but a few, breathtakingly beautiful, and I don't want them turning into cartoons. Mind you, I'm a lonely guy...

A twenty foot long twelve door limo pulls up, and a half dozen or so more beautiful young ladies start getting out, one by one. One spies me and walks up. "Want a lay for a buck?"

"Huh???"

Oh, duh. I notice the leighs on her neck. "Uh, I guess." Beggars. They were there to sell leighs.

The limo driver gets out and asks can I do him a favor. Sure. He wants me to spot the absurdly enormous vehicle into three parking spots by the corner. It barely squeezes in.

I finish my beer and go in for another. I give the leigh to

an otherwise very attractive lady with an enormous nose. The beautiful Holly is still trying to get waited on.

I squeeze in between two big, muscle-bound guys at the bar, who probably think I'm gay, because they disappear in a hurry. Sometimes being a skinny nerd the women don't want is handy. Holly walks up and starts chatting! Cool. She could be a movie star. The word "Hollywood" takes on a whole new meaning.

She gets a beer and walks over to dance. A dozen ladies are dancing, the rest are standing around looking bored, as the guys all hit on them. One that had studiously ignored me a month ago when I was trying to hit on her is sitting by herself, frowning. Hah! She's not bad looking, except in comparison to the other ladies there. Nope, I'm not going to get rudely turned down twice by the same woman.

I get my beer and start to go back outside. The song ends and the singer says there's a stack of CDs on the table, to take one. I think I'm the only one that notices. I take one and stick it in my shirt pocket.

The limo is gone, and there are a bunch of college dudes sitting at the tables with one fat chick. I go back in and wander around, smiling at the bored ladies, who smile back and keep smiling. I'm starting to realize that most of them are here for the music. As I've given up on any chance of ever having sex again, so am I. Meanwhile every other guy in there is trying to get laid, and annoying and boring the beautiful ladies.

There's one girl at the bar with a very nerdy pair of glasses... maybe it isn't the glasses. She just looks so serious. Half a dozen guys are crowded around her. I push my way through, tell her to stop being so damned serious. She laughs, and I disappear.

The band finishes the set and goes out for a "fifteen minute" break. I get another beer and go out for some air.

I'm standing there talking to a young neohippie when a police car shows up with its lights flashing. Two burly uniformed cops brush past us and go in. I drink the rest of my beer and go in, and the dorky bartender goes outside, accompanied by the two cops. Wow, they're busting the bartender?

It wasn't quite so crowded now. A lot of the college type guys were gone, but most of the women were still there, standing around in front of where the band played, waiting to dance some more. The other bartender, the pretty one, looks pissed. Mad pissed, not drunk pissed. There is a thin blonde sitting by the sound mixer. "Are you with the band?" I ask. Yeah... "Well, thanks for the CD. You mind if I rip it and put it on the internet?" Hell NO she doesn't mind!

I get another beer. A couple of very attractive, young looking ladies are sitting next to me. There's a sparkle from the left hand. Oh well, it's not like I was going to get laid tonight anyway. "You're wearing that 'No Tresspassing' jewelry," I tell them. "Yeah," they say. "Sorry."

"Not as sorry as me! I'm jealous of your husbands." They liked that! Big smiles. "Thanks!"

The goofy bartender comes back in, a worried frown on his face. The band plays Muddy Waters' *Champagne and Reefer*, only they play it a lot faster than ol' Muddy.

I started outside once during the night, beer in hand, not sure exactly when. Goofy bartender won't let me out with the beer. "No patio license?" I ask. He shakes his head. "That what the cops were here about?"

"That and a whole lot of other things."

Shit.

Somehow I found myself in the dance area, dancing. I never dance! Exil-X would be PISSED, as she always wanted me to go dancing with her, and here I was dancing with the beautiful Holly. I probably looked really stupid, as like I said, I can't dance, but hell, so what...

I handed Holly one of the CDs. Explained the bit about the free CDs. She asks the thin blonde at the mixer, then sticks it in her tiny purse. Holly's starting to look a little unsteady on her feet. Beer, gotta love it!

She starts outside and I follow her. "You're not leaving already, are you?" I say.

"Yeah... I have to get home. See you next Saturday?"

"Well yeah, especially if you're going to be here!"

She gives me a big hug and walks down the street. I stand there with my jaw hanging open. Ooooohhh....

I walk back in, sit down next to the married ladies and wait for the bartender lady, and ask the two lovely things where their husbands are. They played golf this afternoon and were too tired. I tell them their husbands are fools. I sit there talking with them a while, and they ask me how old I am.

I hate admitting my lack of youth. "Ah, well, you're married. And you wouldn't be too young for me but I'm sure I'm too old for you."

"Well how old are you?"

Why is it OK for a woman to ask a man his age, but it's not OK to ask a woman hers? "OK, I'm fifty."

They look at each other in amazement. "how old do you think we are?"

"No more than thirty."

One was thirty six and the other was 43. They ask me to save their seats for them while they visit the ladies' room. I'm wondering if they really have husbands. Maybe they just didn't want to get hit on. Maybe they're lesbians. I had lesbians try to hit on me when I was married. Maybe... Oh hell, stop dreaming, dumbass!

While they're in the can, the band finishes and leaves. The married ladies come out of the pisser, I tell them I saved their seats but probably didn't need to as the show was over. I tell them good night and walk on home.

Sigh. God'll let me have women, he just won't let me have sex with them. I sure wish I could get to know Holly better.

Chapter 6: More music more music more music
Sat May 24, 2003 at 03:33:47 PM EST

Of course, I've been reading the K5 diaries. It's either do that, or chores. So the dishes and laundry and mowing the grass can be put off a while...

Since I'm sober today I'll expound a tad on last night's diary. And some other stuff relating to music.

I went down to Dempsey's a little early, about 9:00. The band usually starts at 10:00, but I saw no sign of any band. So I ask the bartender for a beer and if there is a band tonight.

No, but Perfunctory is playing tomorrow (meaning tonight). That's the Dead tribute band, and Holly is a deadhead. Which explains why she asked me if I was going to be there this week, probably hoping I'd say no...

So I drink the beer and wander around downtown. I find my way to Marley's, the place that had the kickass rock band last Friday night. HUGE bar, lots of room. Last Friday it was packed. Last night there weren't many people there. The band is playing some wimpy minor key song.

So, the guy that takes the cover says predictably, "three dollars". I say "I know, I was here last week and it rocked, but this band... well, is it all like that?"

He says he doesn't know, they just started and he's never heard them before. So wtf, it's only 3 bucks. I pay up, go in and buy a beer. As I walk by the band I yell "Zepplin! Major key!"

I have a deep, booming voice that carries. You wouldn't think it from my small frame, but I have a thick neck with a big head, and huge lungs from years of holding pot smoke in. My voice annoys some people.

The song ends. Nobody applauds.

Bands that kick ass usually like me in the audience, because I have that loud voice that helps get the rest of the audience in a cheering, applauding mood. Applause, like smiles and laughter, is contagious and gets the mood going.

So I boo them. And suck down most of the beer in one gulp. Maybe this music will sound like rock if I'm higher.

There are like, a bartender and a half for every patron. They obviously expected a big crowd like last week. I imagine most people were smarter than me, and saved their three bucks when they heard the sucky, boring music.

It wasn't badly played, the musicianship was good, but the music just sucked. Boring and whiney.

So again I yell "major key!" and rest my head in one hand.

Lady bartender comes by and asks if everything is alright. I answer, louder than necessary, "Yeah, but this music... if I wanted to be depressed I'd have stayed home by myself." I notice a few fellow patrons grinning about that.

So I get another beer and the band takes a break. Three songs and a break?

There's a baseball game on the TV. One of the lady bartenders is cheering the Cardinals. I get a third beer.

A guy bartender tells me I'm "going to have to keep it down." At a rock show? I reply "yeah, well this band sucks. I'm going to finish this beer and leave, I wasted my three bucks on the cover."

The band comes back on with more whiney, minor key shit music. I walk over and talk to the doorguy, then walk up to the other side of the bar.

The song over, the singer says something about "that guy with the blue jean jacket." Not sure what, I wasn't really (yawn) paying attention. I stand up, grin at him, nearly flip him the bird but raise my index and pinkie in the "heavy metal salute". The audience cheers and applauds me.

I down my beer and leave.

I should have gone to bread stretchers. The band there was good, but the crowd was way too young, mostly teens; bread stretchers is a sandwich shop.

Nobody's collecting a cover there so I go in and get a beer. The band is playing "tequila".

That was their last song. Damn.

So I finish THAT beer and walk down to Dempseys, and get another beer. Not sure why. But I drink it, tip the bartender and leave.

Sucky, boring night.

Poll:
Do you answer polls?
Yes 50%
Yes 0%
Si 0%
Yes 0%
Uh Huh 16%
No, I'm just here to troll and crapflood 33%

Chapter 7: Fun with offline trolls
Tue May 27, 2003 at 02:33:07 PM EST

I could have gotten laid last night if my car wasn't broke. Damned car!

It's hard to do anything when you can't see. So I was bored out of my mind yesterday, as my glasses broke Friday night. I discovered the reason the lens came out – the frame broke.

So I go out and sit on the front porch to watch the cars go by. That's no fun, as I can't even see the people in them. So I go inside and get a beer. I wish I knew where to buy pot and could afford it, I seem to vaguely remember that when there's nothing to do, pot makes doing nothing very enjoyable. But I couldn't afford it even if I knew where to buy it.

So I drink my beer by myself. Daughter's out at the mall gallivanting with her friends. I finish the beer, still bored. Decide to go for a walk. Slip my now "framed monocle" in my pocket so I can get across the street without getting run over. Maybe I can find a bar with people. At least I'll have somebody to talk to.

Walk past Duff's. One car in the parking lot. Walk past Track Shack, look in the window. Nobody there but the bartender. Shit, Dempsey's probably isn't even open. But there are a bunch of bars downtown, one surely is open.

I walk down third street, by the railroad tracks. Little black kids playing basketball in the street with a portable backboard and hoop in a driveway. A few blocks down a car pulls into a driveway, a white couple gets out and walks inside. Other than that the whole town seems lifeless.

I get to Monroe Street, and the door to Dempsey's is propped open with a chair, so they're open. At least I can talk to the pretty bartender.

And there are people inside! A bunch of guys, and a couple of women. I walk down to the first empty seat at the bar, next to a heavy guy that's in a gay mood. I mean gay in the old fashioned sense, like laughing and almost falling off of his stool gay, not gay as in "not that there's anything wrong with being gay" gay. There is a woman next to him, and she's frowning at him. I put my monocles on and close my unlensed eye. Pretty girl, wearing a loose heavy sweatshirt with a hood hanging down the back.

The bartender comes up. "Hi, Busch?" I tell her yeah, and a glass of water, please. She opens the beer and pours the water, and I walk over to the restroom.

I come out of the restroom and the pretty girl in the sweatshirt is beating the hell out of the heavy guy. "God damned fucking dickhead, you're embarrassing me!" she exclaims rather loudly as she punches him.

"Hey barkeep!" he yells.

"God DAMN it Jarry, STOP IT!!"

I sit back down. He turns to me and says "check out the torpedo titties on that bartender!"

"GOD DAMN IT JARRET! You're going to walk home!"

"Man," I say, "You're pissing off your wife."

"She ain't my wife, I just fuck her."

"YOU FUCKING BASTARD!" she yells.

"Girl friend then?"

"No, I just fuck her."

"GOD DAMN YOU COCKSUCKER!"

Now, I'm perplexed. I look at the girl. She says "He's just fucking drunk." And slaps him again. He gets up and walks back in to the restroom. The girl is talking to the guy on the other side of her. Apparently the three of them are together.

The bartender comes over and asks me if I'm OK. Yeah. Mandy's a good bartender, but this Jarret guy is obviously pissing her off, too.

Pretty little pissed off pottymouth looks my way. I'm thinking she's burning up in that sweatshirt, and I say so. It's not chilly outside, and decidedly warm inside. "I'm real thin," she says, "and I get cold easy."

I open my arms, "hey, I'm skinny too. But it's warm in here."

"All I have on under it is a T-shirt."

Um, that's what I have on.

Jarret comes back. "Man, I figured you would have took my chair to sit next to her."

"Jarry, BEHAVE!" she orders.

"OK. HEY BARKEEP!"

Thwap! "OW! What was that for?"

"Have some respect, damn it!"

Mandy comes over and fills my water, asks cute girl and the other guy if they're OK, and decidedly ignores Jarret. Jarret says "Hey barkeep, can I have another beer?"

Cute girls says "say please, asshole."

"Please?"

She gets him a beer. He goes back to the rest room, and I steal his chair. And drink half of his beer. Cute girl laughs. "I'm Steve," I say, and stick out my hand. "Gin" she says, and shakes it. The other guy had called her Jennifer.

So I'm talking to the two of them, who by now felt they had to explain themselves to me.

It seems they were from a town about thirty miles away, and had known each other all their lives. Jarret and the other guy were mid thirties, Jen was 22 and had just graduated from SIU in Carbondale.

The other guy was married. "So where's your wife?" I ask. He says "She didn't want to come."

I guessed she knew Jarry then, but didn't say so. It seems that the married guy had a few beers, too, because he's telling me he was fucking Jennie when she was 15. She looks decidedly embarrassed by this. So I make a shot in her behalf. "Oh, then you're a pedophile?"

He blushes. "Er, well, I was only 26."

"But still," I say. He looks uncomfortable, and Jennie laughs and starts talking to me. "Fuck him, his dick isn't big enough."

I was starting to get into the swing of this, trolling the trolls. "So how big is big enough?"

"Ten inches," she says. "Oh," I say, "then you like black guys?"

Her turn to blush. "Well, no..." she says. "Ah well," I say, "Mine's too small even if I weren't too old for you. The ex measured it at eight and a half." I added, "but I bet you could make it bigger."

She grins at that. "Seven's big enough. Six is average, you know." Er, no I didn't.

Jarret, who has been quiet, shuffles the money he had on the bar, yells "BARKEEP!" again. "Man," I tell him, "Gin's going to knock you on your ass again!"

"That's OK" he says. I point at his money and say "and I'm going to steal that dollar and feed the jukebox!"

"Play some Doors and some ACDC. HEY BARKEEP!"

I lean back. *THWAP!*

I go play the jukebox with Jarret's money. Gin is pummeling him again.

I sit down, Mandy comes over. "Hey," Jarret says, "Do you prefer 'barkeep' or 'bartender'?"

"Bartender." Ginny asks the bartender "What's your name?"

"Mandy."

Gin says "Her name's Mandy, asshole."

By this time I was on my second beer and having fun. Married guy, whose name I never did hear, has wandered off trying to hit on three young women who had come in later, and were at the other end of the bar. I talked with Ginny for a while.

She was a nice girl when Jarry wasn't provoking her.

Seems she's going to Europe for the summer before going to grad school to study law. I groaned. Another baby lawyer! I had run across one just last week at K5. "A lawyer?" I ask. "Why a lawyer? People HATE lawyers!"

"Well, there are other things you can do with a law degree" she says. "Like a judge or politician?" I ask. "Well, maybe, but there are other things."

I mention that it was at least better than my major, fine art. She mentions that she was in Europe before. I tell her I'm jealous, that I've always wanted to go to France and see the Louvre. She says she liked the Sistine Chapel better.

"HEY BARKEEP!" I lean back. THWAP! "OWW!" Jarry says.

Gin repeats, "Her name is MANDY, you fucking jerk!"

"Yeah, dude. Be cool, she's a good bartender," I tell him.

"Leave a big tip."

Gin makes him go outside. She goes out and has a long talk with him, while I chat with Mandy.

Married guy has bombed with the three chicks. I notice when I put my monocles on they aren't too bad but aren't exactly beauties, either.

Ginny comes back in, Jarry following. "He's going to be good, I had a long talk with him." It's getting to be about nine, she lets me use her cell phone to call my daughter. I'm of course wishing my car was working so Married Guy could take Jarry home and I could have Ginny.

I excuse myself to go to the rest room. As I'm going in I hear "Hey barkeep!"

When I come out, they're gone and some guy is sitting in my chair. He excuses himself and moves over another stool and orders a drink. Mandy asks him for I.D. and he shows it. She gives him the drink and he tries to give her money. "It's your birthday. Drinks are free."

"Wow" I say, "I'm coming here on my birthday!"

So I talk with the guy, who's having his first legal drink, about the world and women and so forth, and it seems that I must have my beer goggles on, because he's not impressed with any of the women. I notice it's getting later, and I'd better be going, so I finish my beer and leave.

But before I go I see that one of the three women at the other end of the bar, a blonde one with a nice body but a too small chin looks lonely and forlorn – her friends are talking with two guys, and she's alone.

So I walk up. "I love you," I tell her. "But I have to work tomorrow, I'll see you sometime" I say, and leave. As I look over my shoulder going out the door she's looking around in amazement, hand on her chest, too small chin dropped and smiling mouth hanging open.

Score several for the nice guy. Even if the nice guy can't score.

Chapter 8: Blindness, envy, and jail
Thu May 29, 2003 at 08:50:24 PM EST

Woohoo! Yeow! Yippie!

YEEEAAAAAAAHH!! No more glasses! Well, except to read or get on my computer at home. Now I'm going to have to get a new monitor.

Plus: tales of the Evil-X and her white trash family.

Tuesday I went to work with my monocles, and, well, it just wouldn't work. Fortunately we had a meeting, so I didn't need my eyes for that. The boss was informing us of some more bad news (Damned Bush and his handling of the economy), and the meeting took a good part of the morning. I had an email when I got in that the backup tape had run out at the other building, so there was something else I could do blindfolded. I had explained the situation with the boss lady, who told me I could take the afternoon off. They're real good about that, especially since a boatload of people retired last year and took a king's ransom in vacation pay with them. Now they like us using up our vacation.

So I walk over to the other building and change the tape and go on home. I eat lunch, and hope one of Daughter's friends can give me a ride to Walmart, where I should be able to get glasses pretty fast. And unexpectedly she walks in the door.

"What are you doing home?" I ask. She replies, "I called your work and you weren't there so I figured you were here. I came for lunch money. You forgot to give me any."

"You forgot to ask." So I give her lunch money and ask if her boyfriend can give me a ride? Nope, he works tonight. I suspect she's skipping school to be with her boyfriend, but a girl from school had given her a ride and they had to get back. Her boyfriend has Thursday off.

Damn. I can't go that long without glasses. I wonder if the bus goes to Walmart?

I had forgotten completely about the Mall, with two probably expensive eye doctors. The bus goes right there. So I call the bus company and yes, the bus goes to Walmart. Woo Hoo! I find out when it leaves downtown, walk to Duffy's to get change for bus fare and trudge on downtown, putting my monocles on to get across streets. Being blind sucks!

I get to Walmart and they're able to fit me in. It's been so long since I've had my eyes checked that I only recognized one piece of the equipment, which looked the same as they had when I was seven. Would I like to try contacts?

I had tried contacts 30 years ago, when they were made of glass. They felt like I had glass in my eyes. I had wasted about a hundred twenty bucks on them, back when you could see The Who or Led Zepplin for five dollars and a pair of glasses cost thirty. But the technology has really improved, and this was a free trial, so why not? Especially since I could get contacts right then and would have to wait two days for glasses.

They're disposables. They are really thin transparent rubber-like things. The girl shows me how to put them in, and I'm cringing, remembering the horrible torture of sticking glass in my eye, and I finally get it in – and I can't even feel it! At all! Wow! I'm looking around in amazement; I can see! And I only have one of them in. I get the other one in, and wow! This is great!

So I pay for the exam and some cheap reading glasses and go to buy a DVD. While I'm there I pick up a few groceries, and wait for the bus.

While riding the bus home, a truly blind lady with a white cane gets on. God has a way of making me count my blessings!

I show up at work yesterday, and boss lady sees me without glasses and looks crestfallen. "You couldn't get glasses?" I tell her about the contacts, and she's pleased. So I walk down to the library and do some research, and the research isn't easy – I need more powerful reading glasses. And it makes my eyes really tired. It looks like it's going to storm any time, so I go back to the office.

It starts raining a little, and wow! I love it! The first time I can remember that I could walk in the rain and see! Either you take your glasses off and not see, or they get wet and you can't see!

Married Lady had been urging me to ditch the nerd glasses for something stylish "or better yet, get contacts" so I could better attract members of the opposite sex. So I paid her a visit. She didn't even notice my lack of glasses. So I ask her, "how do you like my new glasses?"

Her jaw drops. "Wow!" It's nice having friends.

She's planning on going to the farmer's market at lunch and wonders if I want to go along. Sure, especially since I don't want to walk home in the rain. We can grab some dead cow at McBurger's.

So at lunch we walk downstairs, and it's pouring outside. She's not sure if she wants to go now, and doesn't even want to move the car, risking a parking ticket. I offer to get it and bring it around.

First time in my life I've driven a car without my glasses. Wow!

So last night Daughter's at church with her friends, and I walk up to Walgreens for some milk for my coffee, chat with her boyfriend, walk down to the liquor store for a six pack, and walk home. A little sticky from walking in the sun, I go upstairs to wash my face – and I can't see out of my right eye! Shit!

Shit Shit Shit Shit Shit!!!

Damned thing must have come out and gone down the drain. SHIT!!! What to do? The buses don't run in the evening. Maybe they have disposable contacts at Walgreens, so I walk back up there.

I'm thinking hell, I might as well get a white cane and a dog. Lots easier than this!

Walgreens doesn't have them, but can special order them... I don't see Patty's boyfriend, but Joe's in the pharmacy. He calls Walmart for me to see how late they're open. He's off at 8:00 and offers to give me a ride. Maybe Walmart will take some to the Customer Service desk or something.

The lensless eye is itching. As Joe's on the phone with Walmart, I rub my eye, and the lens comes out! It had been in there all along, back behind the eyeball!

This morning Daughter's slow, and Evil-X is a little early picking her up for school. X walks in the kitchen as I'm struggling to get the second lens in. She does a double take and her jaw drops, and she has a crestfallen look on her face.

"You got contacts!"

"Yeah."

"How can you afford contacts?" I explain that they're cheaper than glasses, that I would have had to wait for glasses. Daughter had told her about my broken specs, but hadn't mentioned the contacts. Good girl! This was certainly enjoyable. Yeah, I'm going to hell when I die...

"I wish I could get contacts!" She can't get contacts for her eye condition. "I can't even afford new glasses and I need new glasses!"

"Well, gee, I wish you could too..." Not really, that was a lie.

"My sister's going to jail."

"Huh? Sandy?"

I like her sister. Not like, *like* (shudder), Sandy's a horrid looking thing; fat, toothless, wrinkled, froward. But she and her husband Porky have been more than in-laws, they've been friends. I've been to visit them since X left. I've been promising to visit X's dad, too. I bought him a bottle of the cheap whiskey he loves drinking so much but the van broke before I could get it to him. It's still sealed, in the bag. Porky tells me X's dad is disappointed that "his old drinking buddy" couldn't come by.

"Yeah," X says, "the bank's pressing charges."

"Bank? What bank? She robbed a bank?"

"Well, I told you she stole some money from my dad."

"Yeah?"

"Well, she stole my dad's checkbook when he was out of town and cashed eighteen thousand dollars worth of checks. The bank made good on them to his account and now they're going after Sandy. She's probably going to go to jail."

Wow. That explains a few things. I thought I was just being paranoid, but I guess I really am being investigated.

I found evidence that the Windows side of my PC had been compromised, and figured it was a script kiddie. Nobody else would want in my computer. There are no important passwords, CC numbers or anything else that would let someone steal my identity, and I have my photos and MP3s backed up on CD, so a script kiddie couldn't do much more than annoy me if he tried to do mischief. I was amused by the "law13 dot something dot hotmail dot com" it was sending "important" info to. The most illegal thing I do any more is jaywalking.

When I had spoken with Richard there was clicking from the phone, and I joked that one of us must have had our phones tapped.

Now that I hear about Sandy, I think it really is tapped, and it's not a script kiddie in my PC. I used to get high with Porky all the time, and they probably think I still have pot. She probably gave them my name to stay out of jail.

This is rather amusing, as like I said, the most illegal thing I'm guilty of any more is jaywalking! But they follow trails from person to person.

So, the fellow posting at K5 as "the terrorists" should be afraid. Be VERY afraid!

Chapter 9: No music no music no music
Sat May 31, 2003 at 02:55:56 PM EST

Civic functions in Springfield suck, but I had fun last night anyway. By popular demand I shall attempt to turn an ordinary night in an ordinary life into something somebody might actually want to read. Besides, I promised a pretty lady I'd report on how I did with the opposite sex without my glasses.

Married Lady said yesterday that not having the glasses made me look younger, but I think the real reason I got carded last night – twice – had more to do with stubborn bureaucracy than my handsome, youthful face. I haven't been carded since before I was a dad, and I was a dad before a lot of K5ers' dads were dads.

I was happily cruising through K5 last night, and it occurred to me that maybe it was time to start walking. There wasn't supposed to be a band at Dempsey's, so I thought I'd try Marley's.

I locked the door to my house and started walking down the street, and stared in amazement at sheer beauty. Wondrous beauty. Eye popping beauty. Breathtaking beauty.

No, you fucking sex maniacs, I'm talking about the sunset. There were thunderheads in an infinite variety of reds and oranges, and grays and blues. It was an incredible sunset. I complimented God on His artistry. That's probably some kind of a sin, but I'm a sinning fool.

There were birds flying around in the beautiful sky. A flock of geese was heading north in their patented, copyrighted, and trademarked "V" shape, turned around, flew back toward me in a big "M" as if God were telling me this show was for me only (or that I was a Maniac with a few screws loose). The patterns of the geese flying became letters of some arcane foreign alphabet I didn't know and they went away back north.

I looked around at the people in their cars, and a few on foot with their heads down, all frowning, and not a single one of them noticed the show. What in the hell is wrong with people? They'll pay millions of dollars for a piece of cloth stapled or tacked to a wooden frame with some paint smeared on it, but they won't bother to look at beauty no human artist could ever dream of coming close to matching. I just don't understand.

So the sky's colors fade as I get to Marley's, and I see the dorky kid bartender from Dempsey's, only instead of the backwards hat, he's wearing a white shirt and tie, yelling into a cell phone and gesturing wildly, completely oblivious to his surroundings. "Listen goddamned it you fucking asshole, I'm going to have all your fucking teeth pulled out, you got me? Now get the goddamned shit straight and no more fuckups!"

There are some guys carrying musical equipment back

and forth across the street, cursing. "Damn it! God DAMN what a shitty day this is," one guy putting a case into a car exclaims.

"Dude, you're the band," I say. "That doesn't exactly put me in the best partying mood, you know?"

"Fucking shitty day job, ya know?"

"Yeah, did you see that fantastic sunset?" I ask.

"I ain't got time for no fucking sunsets, man! I gotta work!"

So I ask what kind of music they're playing, he says jazz. Yeah, the RIAA sure is doing this guy a service. Poor sap. I tell him I'll probably drop back to give it a listen.

I decide to go back to Dempseys for a glass of water.

More suits. Suits and ties everywhere. As I get a beer and a glass of water, Frank Sinatra is playing on the jukebox. Old farts. They're probably not much older than me, but I feel young. Only a couple of ladies, and they are with men, except for three tattooed ladies, one with an arm band tattooed on, one with a small tattoo on the small of her back, and another with a tattoo above one breast.

Tattoos on otherwise good looking women, wtf?? I see it more and more. It's like marking up one of the paintings in the Sistine Chapel with a crayon.

I finish my beer and walk down to Bread Stretchers. It's a sandwich shop, but they have beer and sometimes have a band. But there were only the two twentysomething guys working there, and no band. I get a Grand Moo and a beer.

Elton John is coming from the radio. As if reading my mind, one of the guys working there says something about the shitty music. I suggest they change the station. He says it's a CD, I tell him to hit "skip". A different shitty song comes on. He says "fuck! Fucking god damned shit" and must have hit CD skip, because some real music comes on. Phish, I think.

So I finish the giant sandwich and the beer, and amble back on down to Marleys. Nobody's taking covers. I go in and get a beer, the bartender says there's no band tonight. Shit. I finish my beer and leave.

The jazz band is playing next door, where there are a bunch of people wearing ties and dressed "nice". I don't go in.

Somebody must have some music, WTF?? It's Friday night!

A young woman is walking down the street and I smile. She says "hi." I say "hi." A guy comes around the corner. "Oh there you are," he says frowning. I ask them if they know where there's any music.

"The Underground."

"Huh?"

"Bottom of the Hilton."

The Hilton. A huge, round shaped building towering over every other building in town, five or ten times as tall as the next tallest. You can see it from Highway 55 heading north ten miles away, a temple of the green god known as Mammon. The Hilton is otherwise known as "the prick of the prairie".

So I walk down there, find my way in a door, and the place looks empty. I finally find some bellhop looking guy, who tells me how to get to The Underground. I start to go in, and another guy asks for my I.D. A guy coming out that looks older than me calls him a fucking moron. I tell him I'm flattered. He wants three dollars. But the band doesn't start until 10:30. I tell him I might be back, and leave out a different door.

And I hear music.

I follow my ears, and there's a band in the street behind a construction barrier. So I walk around the building. Two attractive women are getting into a car across the street. I smile at them. They hesitate, exchange words with each other, and leave.

I go around the corner and Washington street is blocked off by a dozen police cars and maybe fifty chopped Harleys. The music is loud. There is a line of people to get past a table at an opening in the construction barrier.

"Five dollars." It's the same band that was at Marley's last week for three, named K5. No, that's not right... F5. Not quite good enough for a "K" I guess.

They want to see some picture I.D. too. Gee, such flattery, probably to make up for the shitty way they're doing things. 21, you get an arm band. That means I can drink? Must be an all ages show, with the slutty looking girl singer who looks like she's had a few tokes of crack too many and a ruby in her navel, all these biker types... actually, there are all kinds. A few children.

I go buy beer tickets; it's a really stupid thing they do at these civic functions. Buyer be damned, who gives a fuck, bleed them and herd them and treat them like shit, the cows will still come. You can't buy a soda or a beer, you have to buy tickets and trade the damned tickets for your drink. It annoys the hell out of me. Tickets are a buck apiece, and a soda is one, a 12 oz draft is two, a sixteen oz bottle is three. And all they have is Miller Lite.

I hate Miller. But I get a bottle anyway. Fuck it, it's beer. Or an almost reasonable facsimile thereof.

I walk around, find a place to stand. A young chubby blonde walks up next to me and smiles. I say "hi," she smiles bigger and says "hi". She looks nervous. She looks 13, but she's got an arm band, a cigarette burning, and a beer. I feel like a pedophile. "Here by yourself?" I ask. "No," she says, and looks over at her two girlfriends who are laughing nervously.

I can't think of anything else to say. So I raise my beer for a toast, she clinks bottles with me and I walk off. She didn't even look as old as some of my teenaged daughter's friends.

When my beer is almost gone, I go stand in line for tickets. I get my beer tickets and think well, now's about time to piss.

There aren't near enough porta-potties. Long lines for them. I take the last drink of my beer and decide I'll leave to find a toilet or an alley or something, if they'll let me back in.

"Will this arm band get me back in?"

"No, we'll stamp your hand." Stupid fucking bureaucrats.

I walk back to the bar where the jazz is playing, and it's

packed with these people who were dressed "nice" before their ties got loose and their blouses and shirts started getting sloppily half tucked in to their trousers, and use the rest room. Too packed to get a beer, so I walk back down to the stupid city-sponsored thing. Nobody even bothers to check my hand stamp.

I wind my way back to where the beer is. I ask for a sixteen ounce. They're sold out. I sigh. OK, give me a draft. What am I supposed to do with this damned ticket? There's a harried looking woman searching her purse, "I knew I had another ticket..."

So I gave her the ticket. At least it didn't go to waste.

I walk back up close to the band, kind of almost dancing and drinking my beer, and somebody grabs my ass! I turn around, and there is a group of laughing, drunken women. But I couldn't tell which one grabbed my ass, or I would have pinched her tittie. So I turn back around and watch the band, and this fat chick sneaks up behind some other guy and grabs *his* ass. The poor guy jumped four feet in the air, fat chick scurries away laughing. Poor guy whirls around, fists ready, anger on his face. I could read his mind... I mean, "not that there's anything wrong with that..."

I finish my beer and get the hell out of that madhouse. Joe's band, Subaudible, is playing at Dempsey's tonight. Joe's good, but I haven't heard his band.

I'll be there.

Chapter 10: Good time last night
Sun Jun 01, 2003 at 05:46:44 PM EST

Joe's band kicked ass. I drank some whiskey, and didn't even hit on any women. This morning I'm wondering why not – Daughter spent the night at a friend's house, so I could have brought a woman home last night if I'd found a suitable one.

I'd met Joe at Dempsey's last Thursday and promised to see has band last night.

So I walk on down the street at sunset, and the sunset was pretty, but not nearly as spectacular as Friday night. I'm a bit drowsy, so decide to drop by Bread Stretchers for a cup of coffee first.

As I'm about to get there, a fat woman gets out of a car and I smile at her, she smiles back. She follows me into Bread Stretchers. There's only one person behind the counter, a thin, attractive woman. I walk around to order some coffee and the fat blonde is standing there as if she doesn't know why she walked in.

The lady behind the counter says she's not sure if there's any coffee left, it's been there since morning... so I decide to go down to Emilio's for some coffee.

Emilio's, right down the street from Bread Stretcher's, is a Mexican restaurant. It's a real Mexican restaurant with real Mexicans, not one of these Corporo-Amerishit Taco Bell places. The people working there speak Spanish to each other, and the waitresses don't speak English all that well.

The first time I'd been in Emilios I had been downtown and hungry (I seem to always be hungry any more since I started taking the Paxils) and it was the only place close to where I was that had breakfast. The sign said burritos were four dollars and I thought, "damn that's high." But I was hungrier than I was broke and ordered a breakfast burrito. I expected something like a grocery store burrito.

Damned thing was as big as a football! Delicious, too. I ate the whole thing.

I think I'm starting to gain a little weight, what with all the walking and eating. And muscle spasms in my sleep the Paxil wakes me up with.

But I digress. I walked up to the counter and ask for "a cup of coffee to go." She rings it up. $2.15.

I'm thinking damn, lotta cash for a cup of coffee. But I'll be paying more for a beer later, so I don't say anything.

She pours two cups of coffee. Misunderstanding – she interpreted "to go" as "two cups". I smiled said "*discúlpeme, uno cafe por vayo por favor."* She laughed, gave me a buck back and said *"gracias."*

I walk down to Dempsey's, and the place is deserted. The only one there is Mandy, the pretty bartender, watching *Armageddon*. I just get a glass of water, to go with my coffee. She tells me she's bored, hopes it's not a slow night, because the time goes slow on slow nights.

I finish the coffee and ask for a Busch. She says they're out, that they told her somebody bought bucket after bucket the night before and drank them dry of Busch.

Shit. If I hadn't promised Joe I'd be there I'd probably gone and checked out Marley's. Probably would have gotten laid, too. I'm trying to think of another inexpensive beer I can stomach, and I can't think of one. So I go with a Carona. I guess the Spanish at Emilios rubbed off on me or I would have chosen Heineken. And I decide to drink slow, because they're three bucks apiece.

Joe and his band "Subaudible" come in and set up their equipment. Joe gives me his business card and a sticker, and they go off saying they'll be back in 45 minutes. Nobody else comes in for quite a while.

Two middle aged women come in, one with a real short lesbian looking haircut. They ask Mandy where Joe is. They get on their cell phones, then move to a table in the back.

The band comes back, and puts playlists on all the tables. It's a pretty good gimmick; they ask for requests after each song, and everybody knows what to ask for because they have the playlist!

I tell Joe all he needs now is an audience. He seems nervous, afraid nobody will show up to hear him play. I tell him I owe his friend at least a shot for getting me high on Thursday but I'll buy him one instead.

"A shot of what?"

Seagrams, I tell him. So I buy two shots and I toast his music. A few more people came in and they started playing.

Good band, party music band. Their covers are actually

more interpretations than covers.

More people come in. It's actually getting crowded in the back.

I had staked out my stool with my water, beer, and jacket hanging over the back. There are two young guys and a young lady standing by me, and she's holding a cigarette and asking them for a light, and they don't have one. I whip out my lighter and light it for her.

A minute later her cigarette has gone out, she asks me to light it again. The men she came in with are kind of ignoring her, So I chat with her some, and light her cigarettes.

A few lady friends of hers come in and sit at the table close to my bar stool, and she goes over and sits with them. She takes out another cigarette and looks at me. There are no more chairs at the table.

This game is getting old. Not very fun. So I got a book of matches from the glassfull next to me on the bar and hand them to her. She smiles sheepishly and lights her cigarette.

Ray from the other building at work comes in and says hi, introduces me to his wife. She sits down next to me and Ray stands, we talk a little. I pull the stool on the other side of me around and give it to him so he can sit by his wife.
I think he sat there for maybe ten minutes before he was around the other side of the bar. His wife sat there quite a while before she disappeared.

I'm drinking expensive imported beer and running out of money. So I tipped Mandy before I ran out completely. I'm thinking, I'm going to run out of money before the music runs out, so I ask her what kind of cheap domestic beer she has that isn't Miller. She says they have Coors Light for a buck and a quarter. Damn, I could have gone home with half my money left instead of two dollars. So I get a beer and go to the rest room.

When I get back there is a crowd around my chair, all trying to get served. Poor Mandy is working her ass off, she got her wish. I stand there for a while and push my way back to my chair. There's a kid standing in front of it. I reach for my beer, and he seems embarrassed and apologizes. I tell him "no problem, we're all here to party and have a good time" and raise my beer for a toast. He offers to buy me a shot of Southern Comfort. "I'll puke," I tell him. "I can't handle that sweet St. Louis whiskey, but I'll drink a Seagrams with you."

He orders a Seagrams and a Southern Comfort. Mandy asks him for I.D., looks at it, and tells him it's his birthday that he should be getting free drinks. He says he's been getting free drinks all day and wants to buy one for somebody else for a change.

I toast his birthday.

I got pretty toasted last night. I was going to post a link to Joe's email from his business card, but I can't find the card, the sticker, or the playlist. I probably left them on the bar.

They're playing down in Edwardsville next week, I may ride down there with him. I haven't been to Edwardsville since college.

Poll
Best reason to go to Dempsy's
Frankie is an asshole 14%
Dempsey's has live music 0%
Dempsey's has Coors Light for $1.25 0%
Dempseys has more and better looking women 14%
No rednecks at Dempseys 28%
The bartender at Dempseys is a nice girl 28%
Other 14%

Chapter 11: Fuck Frankie
Tue Jun 03, 2003 at 09:51:55 PM EST

    I posted a Diary for Mariahkillschickens tailored to her specifications, and I don't think she even read it.

    I don't think she likes me. Probably doesn't like guys who aren't as smart as her. She's a chicken killing mad scientist who's going to be a neurosurgeon, and I'm just a computer geek.

    But I digress. In the diary I wrote tailored specifically to mariahkillschickens, HideTheHamster noted that "It has been two days since you've written a proper diary entry!" I answered "per your request, I shall trudge the two miles on down to Oscos Supermarket so I can cash a twenty and get some rolls for breakfast tomorrow, and drink a beer or two at Frankie's."

    I like Frankie's bar, but in the immortal words of Marilyn Manson from the *Smells like children* CD, "Fuck Frankie!"

    So I look outside, and the rain has finally stopped. No excuse. So I go on outside and start walking.

Evil-X had come by yesterday morning, blaring her horn in the driveway like the white trash redneck bitch she is. "I think that horn's for you," I tell my daughter. "Well, she can knock on the door like she has some manners," Patty answers.

"You're going to be late."

"Huh uh, I don't have band today."

Ding dong. Patty goes to answer the door. "I risked a speeding ticket to get here on time, you're not ready?"

"Leila didn't tell you? I called last night and told her I didn't have band!"

So X starts bitching at Leila. "God damn it Leila, you dragged your ass all morning and I risked a ticket to get here on time, why didn't you tell me?"

Leila answers "You don't have to fucking yell at me damn it!"

I calmly interject, "Er, you let her talk like that?" I've never heard Patty as much as say "damn," although she does call her mom a slut and a whore. Patty doesn't like her mom's boyfriend.

So X screams at Leila "No computer for you tonight! I'm taking it with me!"

Since moving in with X, Leila pretty much does anything she wants. Patty says "If I talked like that Dad would ground me for a month!"

I go out the door, the yelling is loud and annoying. "Her medicine isn't working," X screams at me. If I don't walk fast I'm going to be late. All three are screaming at each other.

Patty called me at work today and said X never showed up to pick her up from school at all. Leila told Patty later over the phone that X went straight to her boyfriend's house after work. I guess Leila didn't go to school today.

Patty calls X's boyfriend "Faggot". Nice family, eh? And you wonder why I'm drinking and taking Paxil!

I've noticed that not only have I added a pound or two, my belly seems to be getting a bit larger. That's not exactly where I want to gain weight; the ladies usually don't go ga ga for beer guts. So I've been cutting back a little, stayed away from the bars the last day or two. Well, I did have one beer at the Track Shack last night.

Anyway, Oscos. The walk down there is pleasant, but thoroughly boring. Except maybe for the unmarked black Secret Police car hoping to catch somebody doing something wrong, or at least illegal, parked on the side of the road. I think he was reading the paper. Lots of crime in the paper, I guess.

A redhead gets out of her red van with a ten year old redheaded boy. The sky is gray, no sunset tonight. Cars go by. I walk.

You're still reading?

So I get to Osco's and get some pastry stuff for breakfast and cash a check. There was some light banter with the probably underaged cashiers, and I walked over to Frankie's.

I had stopped going there completely late last fall when Frankie had said something rude to me. I don't remember exactly what it was, but I do remember that he's a stupid fat fuck and if he doesn't need my business any more than that, fuck him. I didn't go back until after the van broke. After a two mile walk in the hot sun, you want a beer.

There are almost always good looking waitresses and bartenders, and the jukebox almost always blasted stuff I have on my PC. I noticed that there wasn't much business any more. Frankie probably pissed everybody off.

So tonight I walk in, and there's that commercial shit that tries real hard to be rap without actually succeeding. The place is full of redneck men, and maybe four ugly middle aged women scattered around the room, and five big black men at a table in the middle.

Frankie's behind the bar. "How ya doin'?" he asks. "Pretty good," I say as he walks off. "Can I get a Busch?" What a shit bartender! He waits on 3 or 4 other people and comes back with a Busch. I hadn't had time to ask for the glass of water so I add, "thanks, can I get a glass of water too?"

He pours the water. "Three dollars." I should have just

told him to fuck himself and left, but I didn't. I hand him three dollars. "For a fucking Busch?"

"It's two bucks but I'm taking three."

It's going to be quite some time before he gets my business again. He can treat those rednecks like that if he wants, but this town is infested with bars.

Fuck Frankie. And the horse he rode in on.

Chapter 12: Real Poetry from a Real Poet
Fri Jun 06, 2003 at 08:07:35 PM EST

The Pool Players
Seven at the Golden Shovel

We real cool. We
Left school, We

Lurk late, We
Strike straight. We

Sing sin. We
Thin gin. We

Jazz June. We
Die soon.

-Gwendolyn Brooks, *The Bean Eaters*
Harper, New York, 1960 ISB#9781258269692

The boss lady comes into my cube this morning, looks at what I'm typing. "Oh! An email! Good! I was hoping you weren't entering that data, the clerical can do that. Why don't you go on down to the library, I'd like to get this done before the boss guy gets back."

Boss Guy is the second in command, and this is his baby. "Boss Man, PhD" is head of a national organization this year that is very loosely related to my employer's business, and it needs cash to fund travel for an annual conference that we are hosting.

My job, should I decide to accept it, and even if I shouldn't, is to find people willing to part with huge sums of cash so we can ferry folks from all over the US, every single state, to this shindig that they do every year, and this year Illinois is in charge.

So Boss Lady says "you should start now before it starts raining." Indeed. I pull up the Weather Channel's radar on my PC and it looks like the rain is at the Missouri-Illinois border.

So I fold up a few sheets of paper and start walking to the Illinois State Library, who has this fatassed book with ten thousand funding organizations in it. Four inches thick.

It's going faster since Boss Man says to limit them to orgs with assets over fifty million.

I call home, just to make sure daughter Patty hasn't left with my cell phone, and she has. So I call the cell and tell her to bring it.

It's raining.

So I go see Coworker Guy, who Boss Lady told me had volunteered to give me a ride. He grimaces. He didn't actually volunteer per se... but he'll give me a ride anyway.

As we're on our way out, an attractive woman says to him, "Hi, Trouble!"

"Trouble?" I ask. He tells me a story of golf clubs, shots of alcohol, and whipped cream. Seems this lady used to work at a mental health center and was good friends with the inmates...

But I'm not going there. It's all heresay to me.

He remarks as we pass the Capitol, across second street from the Library, that the lazy cops haven't removed the "no parking" bags from the meters; Congress was in session yesterday. Every one of the "no parking" bags has a car parked there.

I thank Co-worker Guy and walk up to sign in. Fearing "Teh Terrorists," they've locked all the doors except the one across the street not from the Capitol, but across Monroe from the bars.

Your tax dollars at work.

They have an unarmed guard at the only unlocked door to keep the terrorists out. You have to show ID and sign in.

Only today, the guard doesn't seem to care if anybody signs in. And there are state cops, none of whom have their guns. Instead, they have flags. And a whole lot of chairs lined up. I walk past the cops, long hair flopping, and take the elevator up to the second floor where the Big Fucking Book lives.

As I take the forty pound book off the shelf I ask the librarian what's up. They're renaming the Library.

As I'm doing my research, a gillion people come in noisily. Among this gillion people are the Illinois Secretary of State, most of its Congress, and its state Senators.

And the children and grandchildren and great grandchildren of Gwendolyn Brooks, Illinois' Poet Laureate from 1968 until her death in 2000.

As I'm doing research, people give speeches. The late Ms. Brooks' daughter gives a speech about what it was like to have your mom as the state's Poet Laureate. A preacher gives a sermon and makes a prayer. A gospel choir sings, including a very, very excellent and soulful rendition of *Amazing Grace.*

The Illinois State Library is heretofore to be known as the Gwendolyn Brooks Illinois State Library. A plaque now graces the (locked) front entrance across from the Capitol.

So I'm thinking, they're not even asking anyone for ID

today, nobody's armed, most of the state's legislators and its #3 in the death chain is here (he's Governor if the Governor and Vice Governor do a murder-suicide), it would be a lovely day for Al Kaida and his Arab friends to show up... or Timmie McVeigh's friends. One good sized bomb would have taken out half of Illinois' government, and all of its last Poet Laureate's family. Not to mention Illinois' most valuable resource, as far as I'm concerned. Me, I mean. I was glad Al and Timmie's friends stayed away.

But it's OK to inconvenience airline passengers, just don't piss of any rich people. No matter how absurdly stupid the situation becomes.

Fucking shindig must have cost a few million dollars.

Did I mention that Illinois has severe budget problems, is laying off workers and cutting services to the poor and other residents?

But it's Friday!! YAY! I'm going back downtown in about ten minutes and find some music...

Chapter 13: Vielie's Planet: Bummer
Sun Jun 08, 2003 at 02:09:54 PM EST

I spent too much money Friday night.

The words aren't coming out of my fingers as easy today. And I've had a touch of the blues since Thursday morning, and I can't really figure out why. Maybe I need to cut back on the beer or something. Maybe writing this little missive for my friends at K5 will help me figure it out.

I hired a lawyer Wednesday.

I had the appointment with the lawyer right after work. Her office is almost halfway between my house and my work, so I walked straight there after work.

I had tried to hire another lawyer several months ago, and that guy wanted two thousand dollars for a retainer, and was clear that he really couldn't do much for me, that I was better off continuing the mediation.

The mediation had come to an abrupt end earlier. Evil-X wouldn't cooperate. I had already spent nearly a grand on mediation, and still owe the mediator another thousand bucks. Now this guy wanted another two grand.

But I wanted this divorce to be done. I want that evil bitch out of my life. She's been gone since September, and her name is still on my car and house, and mine is still on her car. She calls and bitches at me to catch up on my gas bill so she can get her gas turned on. And I'm paying her insurance. And it would be nice to get a little child support for my younger daughter. The Two Grand Lawyer said X didn't make enough money to ask for child support and besides, the eldest, 18, is living with her.

The new lawyer was different. For one thing, she was a very attractive woman. I was hoping she would be fat, old, and ugly. I don't need the distraction, you know? And I don't want to hit on my own lawyer...

She had a big ruby on the wedding finger.

It was a strange meeting. Of course, I have little experience with lawyers, but this lady was extremely personable. I told my story, and she told me that when I had to take the kids to their mom's work on Christmas just so they could see their mom on Christmas, and then we had no phone number or address for her and she never as much as called for three weeks I should have seen her right then.

"How did she meet this guy? Who is he?"

I told her that he worked at my (then) mechanic's shop. "Gee," she said, "why doesn't anything like that ever happen to me?"

I looked at the ruby on her finger again. A lot of the conversation had absolutely nothing to do with my case. I really enjoyed talking with her.

This lady seems to take pleasure in helping me stick it to Evil-X. And she only wants an eight hundred dollar retainer. That's almost my whole paycheck, and it's going to have to be the money I was going to use on catching up on my mortgage, but hell, that's life.

Maybe that's why I woke up blue Thursday. Because I'm broke and in debt and my house is a mess and my car is broke and two of my three toilets don't work and I'm so lonely and that lawyer was so attractive and pleasant...

But I was going to write about the Friday night bar adventures. A bummer.

A black one. I wasn't halfway downtown when he walked up and asked for seventy five cents.

"Sorry," I told him, "The only change I have is a buffalo."

"Well gimme a dollah, man!"

"I need all these dollars. I want to hear some music, and they want covers. And the beer's expensive. And I have to work for these dollars, dude, nobody gives 'em to me."

He walked the biggest part of the way there with me, trying to talk me out of a "dollah". For once I was glad these places charged covers.

A woman in business attire was standing in the doorway of an office building, lighting a cigarette. Bummer stops, "Hey, can I buy a cigarette from you?"

I went around the corner and did the disappearing act I learned in Thailand.

I had checked the *Illinois Times* this week for Friday music, and the two best prospects were Marley's, and Veilie's Planet. I'd never been to Vielie's, although my daughter has been there several times for the "all ages" shows.

Marley's was billed as having an Irish rock band. They wanted a four dollar cover. I figured, well, maybe it's an expensive band, all the way from Europe and all.

    I went in and got a draft. The band wasn't playing, just messing around with their instruments and so forth. After standing there for maybe five or ten minutes, the singer introduced a song, and he sure didn't sound Irish to me. So they sang the song, and the song sounded Irish. At least, it had a mandolin and an accordion.

    And then they took a break. So I decided to check out Vielie's.

    As I'm walking down the street, here comes Bummer.

    "Hey, man, gimme a dollah!"

    I'm thinking, gee, I've seen an awful lot of cans on the street lately, these fucking bums aren't doing their jobs. "I told you, man, I have to work for this shit."

    He sees another "client" and runs across the street. "Hey man, you got a dollah?" I walk on to Vielie's.

    I get there, and there are a half dozen rough looking guys standing around a van. "You the band?" I ask.

    "Yeah."

    "What kind of music do you play?"

    "Rock. Kind of metal."

    "Cool," I say. I look at the signboard – "Vielie's Planet Friday Pound for Pound." I point at the sign and ask when they're starting.

    "That ain't us, they suck. We came here all the way from New York. We go on in about an hour."

    I tell them I'll come back later, and walk back to Marleys.

    Bummer is pissing on the railroad track. "Hey man, gimme a... oh, fuck it."

    At Marley's I show the doorman the green "M" stamped on my hand. All the bars in this town seem to want to be Irish pubs, even if and despite the fact that they have little or no food. They all have shamrocks on the walls, or "pub" in the bar's name. Even "Duffy's Pub", the redneck bar down the street from my house.

I get another draft and sit at the last empty stool at the huge circular bar, between two attractive women. The one on my left seems to be with some guy, and the one on my right is especially good looking, with an average looking woman next to her and a dog next to her. There are few men, and I seem to be the only one here without a woman. Except for the few couples, the audience seems to be composed of groups of three women, all of whom seem to be here solely for the music. None are interested in me, of course.

The band stands there and doesn't play. I strike up a conversation with the three women on my right, just to relieve the boredom of the band that cost an extra dollar cover and won't play.

They finally play another Irish sounding song, and then don't play some more. I get another beer. By the time I've finished the beer they still haven't played another song, and I drink slow.

So I decide to go back to Vielie's, and leave.

Bummer is standing next to the railroad track, counting a stack of ones.

At Vielie's I give the doorman my four bucks and show my ID, even though any twenty year old that looked like me would surely be close to death. I hear metal sounding music. I go to the bar and order a draft. They want more for a draft than the other bars want for a bottle!

The place has character – It's a dump. Windowless sagging dirty brick walls, concrete floor and black ceiling. "Through the Discipline," the New York band, is on stage playing what my daughter calls "hardcore".

They're playing their asses off, to an almost empty place. Five guys in the other room by the bar, and maybe five more in the room with the stage. Two or three young looking, not very attractive women, all wearing platform shoes.

One better looking dog pulls out a cigarette and stands there. I light it for her. She frowns, and I walk away.

I finish the beer and walk into the other room and get

another overpriced draft, and drink it. I get another, and walk back into the room next to the room with the band, where tables are set up with CDs for sale.

Cigarette woman is standing there smoking. I walk up to buy a CD and she lights into me. "Fucking asshole, leave me alone, I'm not interested in you, fuckhead!"

I give her a funny look. "I don't know what your problem is, bitch, I came over here to buy a CD. Go fuck yourself."

I buy two CDs for eight bucks, and the guy gives me a third. I walk back to get another draft, and rankle at the price. Cigarette bitch has me in a bad mood. I drink the beer and leave.

Back to Marley's? No, fuck it. I walk home.

Dempseys Saturday was much better. But that's another story, and I'll save it for tomorrow.

Chapter 14: Two bands at Dempsey's!
Mon Jun 09, 2003 at 01:49:12 PM EST

Married Lady has been pressuring me to get my locks shorn, so considering my total and utter lack of anything remotely resembling sex, I decided to take her advice. Maybe that's what I needed; someone at K5 said that old guys with long hair look "creepy."

So, since my transmission has not magically repaired itself, and the money necessary to repair my finances has not magically appeared in my banking account, I walked on down to Married Lady's hairdresser, the "Magic Comb". $5 haircuts, the sign says. If they screw it up I'll just shave my damned head.

The sun was hot as I walked down there. I passed a big Catholic church, where bells were ringing and scores of young people dressed in suits and tuxedos were milling around outside. Ah, June: the month where the moon rhymes and young women dream of fairy tales, and young men dream of young women who will magically stay beautiful and fuck their brains out forever.

I tried to stay in the shade, as it was damned warm. Not too easy.

There is an old woman slowly walking in front of me. I go to walk around her, and she turns to walk straight into me. After nearly falling while trying to avoid knocking the senile old biddy down, I do my impersonation of a gentleman and say "excuse me". She looks around as if she didn't see me, and continues walking in the direction she turned.

I go into the hairdresser's, and it has the awful organic chemical smell that ladies' hairdresser shops always have. The barber is probably forty but looks much older, a homely, ungainly woman.

There was a woman in one chair who looked like she was on the other side of a hundred, curlers in her head. A young man with curly black hair was in another chair. A too plump, matronly looking thirty something woman waiting, with a little girl that looked about eight or so. I sat down.

She told the little girl to sit in the middle chair and asked how she wanted it cut. The old woman I had almost collided with came in.

"There are two or three ahead of you," the hairdresser told the old woman. She punched a button on a stereo, and modern country music came out. "I should have been a cowboy" the radio crooned, with incredibly stupid lyrics.

She finished the young man's haircut, and he left. She cut the little girl's hair in about two minutes, and they left. I sat in the chair as she worked on the relic some more, and she asked me how I wanted it.

I told her short, I wanted it out of my eyes. I added, "I'm

recently single, make it so the ladies will like it."

The old women seemed to get a kick out of that, especially the centenarian. We talked about teenagers and how they know everything, the barber talking about how she takes off work to take her son to his baseball game and gives him money while he cusses her.

Somehow the conversation turned to how the world is going to hell in a handbasket, with the hundred year old woman talking baseball and how terrible it was that Sammy Sosa got caught with a corked bat.

I pointed out that there have always been liars and thieves and scoundrels, and reminded her of Shoeless Joe Jackson. I said goodbye and left, with the three women still talking about how horrible those kids are today.

I had five bucks left in my pocket and nothing for Sunday breakfast, so decided to walk down to Oscos, where I could buy groceries with a check and get cash back.

It's a lot farther from McArthur than home. And it was getting even hotter. I started sweating a lot. By the time I got to Osco's, I was sweating profusely, weak, and was shaking. I'd been walking in the sun too long.

I went into Frankie's. After all, in a bar they're used to people passing out.

Thankfully, Frankie wasn't there. There was an attractive young woman behind the bar instead. I asked for a beer, some water, and chips. I drank the water down before the chips came, she refilled it, and I gave her a tip.

The jukebox was playing. "I should have been a cow, boy..."

By the time I finished the beer and chips, I felt almost human. She asked was I doing OK, and I told her I was going to finish my beer and go next door to the store but would probably be back for another beer. I wasn't ready for more walking yet.

"I'll put one in the cooler for you and get it really cold."

We like our beer cold here in the midwest, unlike

Europe and everywhere else in the world. The first beer was almost frozen, and tasted like heaven. There's nothing like an ice cold beer when you're about to pass out from heat stroke.

I got some pastries and some almost food you can cook in the microwave, and went back to Frankie's for another beer. The cow boys were gone, and some Rolling Stones were playing.

A blonde haired boy maybe ten or twelve ran in the back door, sweat streaming down his face. There were about three women there, all of whose maternal instincts took hold. It seems some other kids were chasing the boy. The other kids must have been terrorists, because this boy was terrified. By the time I left, they had called the police to take the boy home.

I went home and my daughter, of course, wanted money. So I gave her a five, and she wanted more. I thought of the old ladies in the beauty shop. She then said she was going to Walgreens for some "girl stuff" and then going with her friends. Sigh. Why couldn't I have had boys?

I nuked the almost food, and ate it with another beer. Man, cold beer sure tastes good when it's hot. I took a bath, and decided to walk on down to Dempsey's.

Before I got as far as Walgreen's, my daughter came walking down the street toward me. "I thought you were going with your friends?" I asked.

"They weren't there, I'm going home and IM them." She didn't have her key with her. So I walked back with her. Before I left, she had gotten hold of her friend, who was going to come pick her up. So I stuck around, sitting on the front porch, and when her friend showed up I asked her for a ride to Monroe Street.

Patty was mad that I had asked her friend for a ride. They dropped me off at the Capitol building, across the street from the newly named Gwendolyn Brooks Illinois State Library that "teh terrorists" had thankfully for me failed to bomb Friday. I could hear music coming from Dempsey's. They were starting early – it wasn't even 8:30 yet, and the music usually didn't start until 10:00.

I walked in and waved at the band, whose only audience so far was the bartender, Mandy. Mandy walked up with a big grin. "You got your hair cut! It looks good!"

I thanked her, and she got me a beer. I sat down next to her at the bar. I told her that my daughter had taken part of the twenty I usually spent there, could they cash a check for me? She said they wouldn't let her, but if things picked up later and her tips were good she'd cash one for me.

The band was rocking. Everyone but Mandy and I were missing a good show. I asked why they were starting so early. "Somebody fucked up," she said, and they were double booked. This band was from Columbia, Missouri. They'd played down in St. Louis Friday night.

Mandy had just broken up with her boyfriend. Again, she said. We compared tales of exes. I thought she was drinking water, but she said it was vodka. "But it's only my third one." It was a six ounce glass.

Joe Frew, the singer from Subaudible, a Springfield band, came in and grinned. He ran his hand over his crew cutted head and said "looks good. The women will probably like it better." I told him that was the main reason I had gotten it cut.

He started playing a videogame on the bar, and I went back to talking to Mandy. As it started getting dark outside, people started coming in. "Write me that check now before it gets too busy," she said. I wrote it and she cashed it for me.

It was a much better night than Friday. I had fun, listened to good music, talked with folks. I didn't get laid, but you can't have everything!

Poll
Should I go after Mandy?
No, hitting on a woman while she's working is harassment 0%
No, hitting on a woman while she's working is sleazy 12%
No, hitting on a woman while she's working is insulting her 0%
No, she'll turn you down, loser 25%
No, you'll spoil a budding friendship 12%
Yes 12%
Hell yes!!! 25%
Are you fucking CRAZY, dude???? Go for it!!!!!!! 12%

Chapter 15: Heather and Ann
Fri Jun 13, 2003 at 01:01:52 AM EST

It seemed too good to be true.
It was.

Saturday's overheating had me sick all day Sunday. Normally I walk to the church down the street for their Sunday night services, but I didn't go. I went to bed very early.

Monday morning I got up and fell down. I got up again, and somehow made my way down the stairs, and called in sick to work. I went back to bed, and slept until well in the afternoon. I got up, gorged myself, drank some coffee, logged in to K5 and probably made really stupid remarks, watched some TV and went back to bed.

Tuesday I got up, still not feeling well, but had a mostly normal morning, aside from feeling that half my brain was missing and all of my joints and muscles were on fire. I think I had a slight fever.

I went to go to work, and just couldn't get off the porch. My muscles hurt too much. I went back upstairs and went back to bed.

I got up at two or so, and felt a little better. Daughter Patty was in the kitchen when I went down. "What are you doing home?" she demanded.

"Well," I answered, "seeing's how I slept all day what do you think?"

She snarled and went back to the computer. "Everybody's in such a bad mood," she snarled again. "What's wrong with people?"

"Hmm," I answered, "Is it that time of the month?"

"I need some money," she demanded. "For female stuff."

She's just starting a job down at Rally's, and went to work at six. By then I was feeling pretty good. I watched the first fifteen minutes of a movie and shut off the TV, and remembering that beer was two bucks a pitcher at Duffy's, I walked down there.

By eight, pitcher drunk, I decided to walk up to Rally's and give Patty some company home. As I got there, she was coming out of the parking lot in a car with some young fellow. "What are you doing?" she demanded. I told her I came to walk her home. "I'm a big girl," she said, glaring. "Hey," she said, light bulb going off in one of those little cartoon thought balloons over her head... I could almost see the bulb. "If we give you a ride to Dempsey's could I stay out until 10:30?"

Why not? It's sure to be slow, being a Tuesday night, I'll talk with Mandy for a while. I was bored. They dropped me off, and as I walked across the railroad track I smelled burning hemp.

I went into Dempsey's, and Mandy was off. The kid with the backward hat was there behind the bar, with some new girl. The place was surprisingly busy for a Tuesday. I sat down at an empty seat, asked the new girl for a beer, and looked around the room at the sparse crowd. Mostly men, a few women scattered around. There was a blonde to my right, turned away from me, talking with a guy who looked to me to be around my age, face looking like it had been weathered by years of being soaked in rum. He looked happy, as if he had showed up at happy hour and kept setting the clock back. He and the woman with the beautiful long, hippie style blonde hair were waving unlit cigarettes around, as if they were doing some kind of animal mating ritual. The guy lit his smoke and laid the lighter on the bar in front of the girl. I pulled out my lighter and lit it.

She turned around, and she wasn't bad looking. No, not at all, way better than the rum bum sitting next to her deserved. She looked a well kept 40, thin frame hid in the back by that long, thick hair. Nice little bosoms. Not big, but well shaped. Her too-pointy nose somehow made her more attractive. "I know you!" she said, and picked up the lighter and lit her cigarette, and took a sip of her wine. Rum bum was frowning. He'd obviously been hitting on her.

"I hope so," I said. "Probably here, I come here a lot, but not usually on Tuesdays; I come for the music."

She had just come into town, she said. She was originally from Alton, had been in Springfield in the mid 90s before going out to Colorado.

She was hitting on me! Wow! I loved this. Meanwhile, when "happy guy" went to the john, I discovered that his name was John, he was a drunk, and Heather, my new friend, hated drunks. She had been a bartender at one time.

John came back, and Heather asked me if there was any old blues on the jukebox. I walked to the jukebox with her, and we picked out some songs. She was 32, and couldn't believe I was 50. The mirror says I'm 10 years younger than John, who was 40 but looked 55.

As Heather told me her life story, at least her life after adulthood, I could see why she looked more like 40 than 30. She had been a needle coke junkie, and had given it up about four years earlier.

She didn't seem like a coke addict. Coke addicts are assholes. She was nice. For some reason, every time she touched my arm I would start to get an erection.

She was a glass blower, with a masters degree. In what, she didn't say. I really liked this woman.

John staggered back and started hitting on some twenty somethings at the table closest, sitting down between two of them.

I talked with Heather, having a hell of a good time, and there was a loud thump. John was on his back, still in the chair which was on its back. Heather, I, and a young lady at the table helped the drunken sod up. The young girl was a Dempsey's regular.

John staggered off and disappeared. Heather and I sat back down at the bar talking. I felt like I had known her for years. There seemed to be some magic, some chemistry. She handed me a cigarette and I lit it, and handed it to her. She lit another with it and handed it back. I took a puff, and told her I had quit three years ago.

"You quit smoking?"

"I quit tobacco," and took another puff. And laid it back on the ashtray. She started talking about what she blew – glass smoking pipes. She had been shipping them to Penny Lane from Colorado, and when Penny Lane got busted in Ashcroft's paraphernalia bust a month or so ago, that's when she decided to come back to Illinois. Hmmm.

She excused herself to use the rest room. I stood up, doing my best imitation of a gentleman. The young regular who I had helped get John off the floor walked up, and *she* started hitting on me! Holy shit, that *was* a magic comb! This young lady, Ann, was only 22, and cute as a button. I told her my daughter forbade me from dating anyone under 30, and she grinned slyly.

We were talking, and Heather walked back. "Hey, slut, leave him alone!"

Ann's jaw dropped; I started wondering what kind of psycho I had gotten mixed up with, when Heather started laughing and put her hand on Ann's shoulder. Ann started laughing too.

My first beer empty, I figured it was time I visited the small room. I passed a fellow I'd met a few weeks earlier, a musician. He smelled like burning hemp.

When I got back, Ann and Heather were standing there talking about breasts. They looked like sisters, one older and one younger – or mother and daughter. They were bemoaning the sizes of their own, and speculating whether the new bartender's were real.

I told them their tits were fine, tits are for babies anyway.

I sat back down with Heather. God, I liked this woman! We talked as I finished the second beer.

I had to work the next day; no longer sick, I couldn't call in hung over. Especially after being out the two previous days. It was 10:00, and I was supposed to call Patty so she and her friend could give me a ride home.

I grabbed a matchbook and wrote my phone number, cell number, and email address down. She grabbed another and wrote her number and made me promise to call her, and we traded matches. She said something about the number and repeated it, in case I couldn't read it. I went and called Patty, who had my cell, from the bar's phone.

Heather started getting self-conscious, she thought her nose was too pointy. I grinned, touched her nose, and told her I thought it was a cute nose. She gave me a hug and a kiss, and walked off. I walked toward the door, at least an inch or two above the floor, as Patty was walking in.

"You sure look happy," she said. I told her I'd met someone, and told her about Heather. "How old is this woman?" she demanded. I replied "Within your specifications, she's 32." I told her we had exchanged numbers, that I was supposed to call her after 2:00 the next day, etc.

I got in the back of her friend's car. As we crossed the tracks, I smelled hemp again. "I've been smelling pot all night," I said. Patty frowned. She doesn't like anything that people smoke, and she doesn't like people when they're high.

"You smoke pot?" her friend asked. I told him it had been quite some time since I'd gotten high. "How long?" he asked. "I don't know, maybe a month or two. I can't afford the stuff," I told him. He said, "If I brought some by your house would you get high with me?"

I asked him how old he was, knowing some of Patty's friends were older than others. She's said that some of her friends went to Dempsey's sometimes. He said he was 21. Well, OK. Sure, I'll drink a beer with you.

Patty and I got out at home, and she was livid. Here she was trying to get the friends she had that got high to stop, and here I was encouraging it!

Wednesday I couldn't keep my mind on my job. My mind kept wandering back to Heather, the fat book in the library open but little looked at. I had to force myself to work. Would 2:00 never arrive so I could call her? I had the matches in my pocket.

At two, I walked down to Bread Stretchers for a cup of coffee, and sat down with my reading glasses, matches, and phone, and the last digit was messed up, but looked like a 5.

It was a wrong number. Nobody named Heather there.

I dialed it again, and dialed 6. "The number you have called..." and something about the number's being checked, or tested, or something.

Same thing all day long. She could call me; I had given her both my landline number, cell number, and full name, and told her where I lived. But no call.

I got home in a funk, and Patty had been busy – the kitchen had been cleaned up, living room straightened. I turned on the air conditioner and took a shower.

Her friend showed up, as promised. Patty had work at 6:00. I got out two beers. "So," he said, "you still want to get high?" Sure. I got out some papers, and a pipe was produced. Patty went to work, making us promise she'd be gone before anything was set on fire.

I got wasted. Zombiefied. He was pretty loaded, too, and was in awe of the number of MP3s on my computer.

He pulls out a teeny, tiny little bag of white something. Meth. Talk with him, I can see he's got a problem. It's not a trivial problem, and if he doesn't solve it now it will be a life-altering problem.

I'm thinking, damn, I'm all loaded, I want to go back to Dempsey's and look for women. In the corner of my mind I'm thinking Heather, but somehow have the idea that she's vanished for good. I'd seen Ann at Dempsey's before, but never Heather. I'm thinking, the last digit was ruined on purpose. She doesn't want me.

I moved the two man pot party out of the kitchen and into the living room, and put on *Fritz the Cat*. It was storming outside.

Movie over, and he says "wow, that was the strangest flick I've ever seen." I grin and say, "Fucking nasty weather. I'd walk down to Dempseys but it's raining its ass off out there."

He offers to give me a ride to Dempsey's, and does so. But, he doesn't want to go inside, he's only 17.

Fucking shit. I'm going to start demanding ID from Patty's friends.

Dempsey's is full of men. I drink a beer, and walk on back home.

Patty is on the computer. I tell her she needs to help her friend, that he has a serious problem. She says she doesn't see him very often.

I slept without the hassle of those damned Paxil dreams waking me up every hour or two. But I spent today thinking about Heather.

Chapter 16: Amy and the Teeniebobbers
Sat Jun 14, 2003 at 01:25:39 PM EST

Yesterday there was supposed to be a birthday party after work for a woman turning 50. I didn't go. It was hot, threatening to rain, and the party was at Chantilly Lace, a couple of miles away.

I took a shower, opened a beer, and drank it on the porch before walking downtown in search of music.

The sunset was pretty, although not spectacular. The big Catholic church on 6th Street was letting out, and the sidewalk was crowded with people milling around.

There wasn't any music scheduled at Dempsey's, but I thought I'd go by there just to make sure. Sometimes they get their bookings confused.

As I walked past Bread Stretchers, a band was setting up inside, and it was packed with people, most of whom looked like teenagers. A young fellow was collecting a three dollar cover at the door. I asked him who was playing. "Three New York bands, and a local band." I told him I might drop back later.

Dempsey's had no band. I used the restroom, and asked the bartender if there was a band "scheduled tomorrow." He looked in the book, and said no, but there were two bands next week. I decided to try Marley's.

The doorman wasn't set up yet, but a band was lugging equipment in. I sat down and got a draft and a glass of water. Two plump young ladies walked in. A fat, geeky looking fellow a couple stools down said "I got dibs on the brunette."

The ladies sat down around the other side of Marley's roundish bar, and the bartender brought the fat guy a big plate of food. The plump blonde laid down a pack of cigarettes. I talked with the fat fellow for a while about women, smoking, and woman smokers and decided to go back and check out Bread Stretchers.

As I left Marley's, the doorman asked "coming back?" I said yes, and he stamped the green "M" on my hand. No cover for me tonight, I got there early enough, and stayed late enough.

I had promised myself not to go chasing women tonight, and here the fat guy had my mind on women.

The band at Bread Stretchers was rocking, so I gave the door guy three bucks and squeezed in. I squished through the way too full sandwich shop to the counter, and got a beer. I squeezed back through, looking for a nonexistent chair. There were none, so I sat on a big drum case.

This was truly an "all ages" show. There was one boy dancing who couldn't have been over ten years old. A few older folks, and mostly what looked like teenagers.

I had forgotten to take my Paxil Thursday morning, and took it after work. Yesterday, Friday, I remembered in the morning. So my dosage was off. I had only drank two beers and sipped out of a third, and the people started turning into cartoons, although only slightly.

A very young woman, probably a teenager I figured, sat down on the drum case next to me, almost falling down in the process. "It has wheels," I remarked intelligently. She laughed. "Yeah, I found out."

She was a caricature of a very pretty woman. Very cartoonish.

I chatted a while with this pretty girl who was obviously way too young for me, and with her friends who were sitting on the other side of her. One pulled out a camera and laughed and pointed at me. The girl smiled and got closer to me, so I put my arm around her and smiled at the camera, which then flashed.

They were seventeen and eighteen year olds; legal, yet still too young. Two had just graduated from high school. Catholic girls; that was probably what the shindig on 6th Street was about.

I told them I wished I could get a copy of the picture to make my ex jealous. They promised to bring one to Bread Stretchers next Friday at 8:00.

I finished my beer, the band finished their set, and the young girl and I got up so the drummer could have his box back. I told the girls I would see them next week, and left, getting my hand marked so I could come back without a second cover charge.

I walked back to Marley's in search of less youthful

female company. Fat boy was gone, but the women he was ogling were still there. I sat down next to the smoking blonde and ordered a beer.

The chubby blonde cartoon studiously ignored me, the band played, I drank my beer and continued watching the live version of *Cool World* at Marley's.

Did I mention that I like Paxil?

My empty beer bottle glared at me angrily, the band took a break, the blonde cartoon's cartoon smoke danced and smiled and winked, and I decided to see what the next band at Bread Stretchers sounded like.

As I walked past *Jake and Elwood's*, something told me to go inside.

Annie was in there, standing by herself. "Annie!" I exclaimed. "It's Amy," she said. "Amy?" I asked. "I thought you said your name was Ann?" No, Amy. Oops, sorry.

I asked her about Heather. Tuesday was the first time she'd ever seen Heather.

I chatted with Amy about her brother, who had just committed suicide. She had mentioned her brother's death at Dempsey's Tuesday. I told her I was going to get a glass of water. "Get me one, too," she said. So I walked up to the bar and got a couple of glasses of water. I gave hers to her and we walked outside, where people were milling around.

Somehow a lit joint wound up in my hand. I hadn't even smelled it. I hit it, and as I inhaled its green smoke it whispered "give me to Amy, she's cute."

I offered it to Amy, and she declined and went back inside. Heather would have hit it. Ah, shit.

I walked on home.

Chapter 17: Ginger and the Mickey
Sun Jun 15, 2003 at 02:30:08 PM EST

  I've read about so-called "date rape" drugs. What I hadn't read was that there are other criminal uses for them. This is a cautionary tale for everyone – women aren't the only victims of the purveyors of these substances.
  Last night is a bit hazy in my mind this morning.

My daughter's stoner friend came by looking for Patty, who was at work. So I asked him for a ride downtown, and didn't have to walk. I was very early for music, so I went by Dempseys, thinking I'd pass some time talking to Mandy.

Mandy wasn't tending bar, the dorky kid was bartender. I got a beer and watched "Cops" or some other equally inane government propaganda. I sipped the beer slowly, and gulped water.

Boring. I was the only patron in the bar. I finished the beer and walked next door to the next bar, and ordered a coffee. They sold me a very small coffee for a dollar. I felt cheated.

I walked down to Marley's. At least there was a small crowd there, and music was playing. It played so softly it was hard to hear over the din of the bar; it was some ancient crooner, maybe Frank Sinatra.

I sipped another beer and drank more water. The music and the buzz of the crowd were making me drowsy, not to mention I was getting damned bored. They had no coffee at Marley's, so I walked down to Bread Stretchers for more coffee, and brought it back to Marleys.

Coffee, water, and beer.

The band started setting up, and I bought a CD from them for ten bucks, the "Oohs."

They played, and they were good. I started having a pretty good time, even if I was alone. Another beer or two and the restroom called. I walked back to answer my bladder.

There was a cute, thin young black woman sitting by herself at a table way back in the back of the bar. I smiled at her. I smile at everybody. It's one of the nicer effects of Paxil.

She smiled hugely and got starry eyed. She stood up, and her nipples popped out, seeming to try to rip their way through her sweater. She put her arm around my neck and whispered, "wanna fuck?"

I sat down and grinned. "You're a policewoman trying to bust me on a prostitution sting, aren't you?"

She laughed hugely. "No, baby, I ain't gonna charge you no damned money. You can buy me a beer though." I laughed. I was looking for blondes, and here was the polar opposite. Ginger was her name.

I went to the rest room, then got her a beer and a new one for me. The Paxil cartoon started – she became a crow from *Fritz the Cat*, only for a few seconds. I asked the bartender for more water.

And then I was outside, walking down the street with her, and didn't remember leaving the bar. And then she was gone and I was home, and I don't know how that happened, either. As I sat at the kitchen table trying to figure it out, it occurred to me that how I felt wasn't like booze normally made me feel.

And my money and CD were gone.

poll
Most violent race
Blacks 15%
Whites 15%
Asians 0%
American Indians 0%
Hispanics 15%
Irish 7%
Nascar 46%

Chapter 18: Family
Fri Jun 20, 2003 at 06:11:16 PM EST

Monday night I stopped by the gas station in search of Rolling Rock, which is only fifty cents more a six pack than Busch but tastes almost like Heineken. They were out of it.
Damn.

I got home, and daughter Patty was sitting on the porch swing with some blond kid. "You're three minutes late," she demands. "So ground me," I reply.

Patty introduces me to Mike, who's driving a little Honda. Patty's cats need food, so I persuaded her friend to give me a ride to get Patty's cats some food. While I'm at the grocery I get some soda (on sale) and a 12 pack of Rolling Rock.

We get back, and Stoner is in the swing. Patty has to go to work at 5:00, I borrow some Anti Flag CDs from Stoner, and start ripping to wav.

Patty says she doesn't know when she's off work.

About 10:30 I walk down to Rally's where she works, and the place is closed. Some fat guy in a Rally's hat tears out of the parking lot.

She's in trouble.

I walk on home and check, maybe I passed her. Nope. So I leave a note and walk down to Duffy's for a beer.

Before I take two drinks, Patty comes in. The place had been closed, she had been in the back cleaning and just got off, the boss gave her a ride home.

She's off the hook.

Tuesday she goes to work at 4:00. Stoner comes by for his CDs, I talk with him for a while while we listen to some Black Sabbath and Budgie, who Metallica roadied for and covered in their *Garage, Inc* CD. Stoner had never heard Budgie, and couldn't believe the singer's not a girl.

I stubbed my toe. It felt broken. I probably impressed Stoner with my knowledge of vulgar, obscene language, as I cursed for a full ten minutes without repetition or redundancy.

I have Stoner drop me by Dempsey's, it'll be dead there but I can chat with Mandy.

Mandy has Tuesday off. The airheaded chick is working. She has some diamond thing hanging from her belly button. If she had a veil I'd think she was a belly dancer. I compliment her on the jewelry.

I walk around downtown for a while. I walk by Marley's

– Rock House is playing at Marley's Saturday. They're friends that I haven't seen in a couple of years. Eddie McCann, the singer, used to live down the street from me when I lived on Reservoir; we've both moved. His house was right next door to the crack house that the gangsters who couldn't shoot straight lived in.

Oh, you haven't heard about that... well, ten years ago when it happened, it wasn't the nicest of neighborhoods. Like I said, the house next to Ed was a crack house with Crips living there. Early one evening I hear what sounds like a string of firecrackers going off down the street.

Then I hear sirens. I walk outside to see what's going on, and all the neighbors are outside, also looking around to see what's going on. A police car races down the street doing maybe 90 miles per hour, becoming airborne as it crosses the railroad tracks at 13th street..

There had been a gunfight, with a dozen Crips and a dozen Bloods shooting at each other, outside, in public, in the light of day. A white man who lived across the street from Ed was shot in the back, trying to rush his two small daughters inside. He lived, but it cost him his job, his health, and much more.

Everybody who lived in the crack house was arrested. It mysteriously burned down a few days later. I read in the paper a few months afterward that the shooter who almost killed the innocent bystander was sentenced to two years. If he'd been caught with drugs instead of shooting at people he would have been in the pen for ten.

There's something seriously wrong with the laws in this country!

Anyway, Eddie is playing at Marley's Saturday. Rock House Rocks, I'm looking forward to it.

I go back to Dempsey's, and Mandy shows up, but not to work. Talk about committed to one's job! Especially a second job... a beer or two later and it's time to go home. I'd hoped that Heather would show up, but I don't know why I thought she would. I'll probably never see her again.

The next day my foot hurt like hell. I limped in to work, but I stayed home that evening.

Thursday morning there was a note on the table from Patty: "Please wake me up before you go to work." Seems her mother is going to take her to get her driver's license.

In the middle of the afternoon, my phone rings. It's my daughter, outside calling from the cell phone, wanting some money. I tell her I don't have any, she says "write Mom a check."

So I go outside to face the Evil-X. It's been a few weeks since I've had the displeasure.

The white PT is out there, Patty driving, X in the passenger seat. And oh my GOD! X has gained at least 40 pounds since I saw her last. JESUS the woman has gotten fat!

"Hi," I say. "I see you've put on a little weight..."

Sometimes life is good!

Chapter 19: Revelations
Sat Jun 21, 2003 at 09:10:20 PM EST

I walked downtown last night earlier than usual. Last week the teenyboppers told me they were going to meet me at Bread Stretchers and give me a copy of the picture they took of one of them and me. I really didn't expect them to show, but went down there, just on the odd chance they might.

I got to Bread Stretchers about 7:30 and walked up to the register, and asked for a Rolling Rock. He opened it and asked for $2.75.

"What?" I said. It was a buck too much. "Imports are $2.75," he said

"Then give me a Busch," I said. "Besides, Rolling Rock is brewed in Pennsylvania," I told him, pointing to the label, where it was clearly marked "Latrobe, PA".

"Well, since I already opened it..." he said. I gave him a buck and three quarters.

I sat down and watched a baseball game between two teams I had no interest in at all, while the kid played pinball behind me.

I couldn't remember if the girls had said 8:00 or 8:30. I finished the beer about quarter after eight, and walked over to the register. "If I get another Rolling Rock are you going to charge me two seventy five?" I asked. He blushed.

"I can never get it straight... the microbrews like Sam Adams are priced like imported."

I got another beer, and drank it. As expected, the teens had forgotten all about my old ass. Before it was finished, the dorky kid from Dempsy's came in, said something about an interview, and left.

Then came back, and said to me, "Uh, man, if you go down there tonight, don't say anything about the interview, OK?"

After I finished the beer, I walked down to Marley's. Couples everywhere, except for close to the stage, where a few girls were taking pictures of the band setting up.

I walked over to the stage, and talked to the band. They were a "hard rock" group. Well, they weren't that hard, I found out later, but weren't bad. They didn't have a CD "but we're gonna make one sometime this summer."

"Just set up a computer and a couple of mics," I told them.

The door guy was setting up, so I got my hand stamped

and walked down to Dempsey's, where they're starting "acoustic night" on Fridays. Last night was the first one. Joe Frew was around the other end of the bar with his girlfriend, so I walked over and talked to them for a while before wandering off.

As expected for an acoustic show, it was mostly women. Most of them looked rather lesbianish, which doesn't bother me... at least, not if they go both ways.

As I came out of the rest room, a pretty lady at a table of lesbianish looking women smiled at me. So I walked over and lit her cigarette. I chatted with them, and lit all their cigarettes for them (which is about all I carry a lighter for, as I gave up tobacco a few years ago).

One especially lesbianish looking woman with real short hair and a four hundred pound frame was a disk jockey at one of the college stations in town – and it turned out that I have my car radio preset to it. Like most college stations, they play an eclectic mix, from old jazz to country to ska to punk to about everything. Her show is at 8:00 Sundays, I asked her what kind of music she played. "Female rap."

I don't think I ever heard of female rap.

One of them took me aside later and asked politely if I would leave them alone. My feelings were hurt. The Paxil stopped working. I walked to a table by the door and sat there by myself, finishing my beer. Sad and lonely, I needed company and could find none.

I finished my beer and walked down the street, dejected.

Mandy walked up behind me, with another woman. "Hey, Steve, you OK?" she asked. I guess my face belied my mood.

"Yeah, just kinda lonesome, ya know?"

It was her friend's birthday, and they were making the rounds. In Springfield, the bars all give you free drinks on your birthday.

We chatted a bit and I cheered up a little, and I turned

to go to Marley's and they went straight.

Couples. Everywhere I looked, couples holding hands, walking with their arms around each other. I'm not even feeling horny, just lonely. Shit. I sit down and get a beer and some water.

As I was leaving, I saw Mandy and her friend again and chatted, then went on home.

The bar thing isn't doing it. What's worse, I can't afford it; they shut off my gas a couple of days ago. Fucking shower is freezing cold. I need to catch up on my bills, and I'm getting a beer gut, and this is just no damned good. I'm not meeting any women, and listening to music isn't as fun as it was.

By the time I got home, I decided that there would be one more trip downtown. My old friend Ed McCann is playing at Marley's tonight. I haven't seen him and Judd in a couple of years.

This morning there was an email from one of the dating services – a woman was interested in me. She left her email, and I wrote back. She seems like a dream; short, thin, likes video games, and in fact she says she's addicted to them.

I'm going to ride a train down to St. Louis for the July 4th weekend, and see some old friends about getting some wheels. I'll probably leave after work on the 3rd. Ironically, July 3 is my wedding anniversary. I may meet this new lady in the flesh then!

So, I'm off to Marley's to see Rock House. I plan to make it the last regular trip; like I said, I just can't afford it.

But I'll still be writing diaries. They'll just change a bit, like my life.

Chapter 20: Am I too picky?
Sun Jun 22, 2003 at 01:53:42 PM EST

The thought occurred to me that I can't find any decent women because my standards are too high. The ones I want don't want me, and the ones that want me I don't want.

I saw this in one of the computer dating services' ads for some brown haired, "average" body type (fat) woman: "I want to be treated as an equal. I am looking for someone who [sic] still old fashioned and opens car doors."

This sounds like The Evil-X. There are way too many women like this. They want to have their cake and eat mine, too.

Ladies, if you want to be treated as an equal, ask me out, drive, and pay my way. I'll be glad to open your damned door!

Last night daughter Patty walks in the kitchen and, in usual teenager fashion, asks for money.

I tell her OK, but I'll have to walk down to Osco's to cash a check.

"But Rachel's going to be here in a half an hour!"

"OK," I say, "just have Rachel give me a ride down there."

"NO! I'm not going to ask my friends to give you rides! Why don't you get the car fixed or get another one?"

Yeah, right now. Teenagers are so reasonable, rational, and logical... as are females generally. Probably why I was so drawn to muchagecko at first, she seemed more rational than most women. Of course, then I found out she's tall and likes 69... besides being a thousand miles away... see? I'm too damned picky.

Go for it, Jay!

So I get a beer and sit on the front porch and drink it. Presently Patty's friend pulls in the driveway, and I ask her for a ride to Osco's.

"Sure."

I let her in the house as Patty's coming out. She tells Patty "I told your dad we'd give him a ride to Osco's."

Patty's furious.

Kids. Girls. Sigh...

I cash a check and get some bread and breakfast, and Patty says she wants ten dollars. I give her five and she argues about it.

If you have teenagers you're snickering now. If you are one, just wait...

They drop me off at home and leave.

I walk on downtown to Marley's. Rock House is starting to set up, I see. There is sound equipment piled everywhere. I get a beer and a glass of water, and leave the bartender a tip.

Not many people there yet. Mostly couples.

I see Eddie, so walk over and say "Hi." Ed's the singer and bandleader, and he used to live down the street from me.

We've both since moved.

He says Judd, his old guitar player, isn't with the band any more. Judd had moved to Memphis for a while, and when he got back Ed had already replaced him. I told him I guessed he might not be with Rock House any more, since I'd seen him last winter running the sound board for Ray Lytle's Itchy Pickles Band, but I hadn't had a chance to talk to him. Ed says the new guy is even better than Judd.

He was right. Judd's good, but this guy kicked ass. Joe Satriani, Van Halen (Eruption, no less!), Aerosmith... the new Rock House is even better than the old one was.

I tell Ed I'm divorced now, he says he's sorry to hear it. "I'm not," I replied. I told him how fat and ugly(er) Evil-X had gotten.

I went back to sip my beer and drink my water while the band finished setting up. My stomach feels empty. I'm always hungry anymore, it seems. So I had the bartender stick my beer and water in the cooler, and walked down to Bread Stretcher's for a Heiffer and a Rolling Rock.

A Heiffer is a bigassed huge sub sandwich. There were two very attractive ladies at the next table, one with the round tattoo on her lower back you see so much these days. I can't understand it, it's like putting a mustache on the Mona Lisa with a crayon.

I smile at them, and they sneer, put their noses in the air and leave.

I finished my sandwich and went back to Marley's. Rock House is rocking. I get my beer and water back, finish the beer and go to the rest room.

There aren't many attractive ladies there, but no matter, I went there to hear Rock House. I didn't expect to pick up any women.

After a while I walked outside for some fresh air.

Ginger walks up.

"Steve! Hi! Buy me a beer?"

I looked at her in amazement. Nervy for sure. But I

guess a whore needs nerve.

She laughs. "Boy, you sure were fucked up last time I saw you, how much did you drink? Hey, give me ten bucks and you can fuck me."

I laughed. "You got my money last time, but we never fucked. Do you still have my CD?" The look on her face said she would have blushed if black girls could blush. "Yeah, I'm gonna give it back to you, honest. Buy me a beer?"

I tell her sure, but "let's go somewhere without a cover as my cash is running low." I'm thinking Bread Stretcher's, with cheaper beer – in bottles, where it will be harder for her to slip me a mickey.

"Oh, I already been inside here."

So we walk back in Marley's and I get two drafts. She's sitting on my left, I keep my beer in my right hand, and one eye on it. She keeps trying to sell me some pussy.

After she finishes her beer she slips away. I'm relieved. I get another glass of water and drink the whole thing down, still sipping my beer.

I went to the rest room, and took my beer with me. I learned my lesson last week!

When I got back someone was in my stool, so I walked around. I smiled at a plain looking fat girl and lied that she was cute. I lit an ugly old hag's cigarette for her. I was having fun, I wanted everybody else to, too.

I wound up back in my original stool, trespasser gone.

People are getting drunk. Including the bartenders. The good looking ones must have gotten better jobs, or have been drinking too much beer, because the ladies behind the bar are all sort of heavy tonight.

Except one, who is standing on the bar, walking around pouring something red at people's upturned mouths. Mostly missing, as she's standing on the bar with the bottle held high and the people she's pouring it at are standing on the floor. It's an entertaining spectacle; I'd seen them do it before. I held my empty beer glass up, and she poured some, mostly missing but leaving two fingers at the bottom of the glass.

It was fruit juice. But these drunks would never know!

Ginger walks back in, carrying my CD! She's written on the cover, "Happy Father's Day Steve Love Ginger".

Nervy, crazy chick. I buy her another beer. I see her drop something in mine, as she looks outside exclaiming "wonder what the cops are doing out there?"

I switched beers with her. Not tonight, honey!

She downs "her" beer, and presently staggers off with a blank look on her face.

I leave the rest of "mine" in case it's a double switch and walk outside for air, and there are three police cars outside. It seems that someone took exception to the girl pouring the juice and attacked her.

I went in for one last beer, and the band did one last song.

I sure wish I could afford to keep doing this every week!

Poll:
Where the hell was I ???
Heaven 0%
Hell 0%
Some bar 0%
Nowhere, man 66%
The wrong place at the wrong time 33%

Chapter 21: Is Ted Turner gay?
Thu Jun 26, 2003 at 06:36:23 PM EST

When I went downstairs yesterday there was a note on the table under my contact lenses: "Wake me up before 7:00." My daughter had found a ride down to "Warped Tour", a collection of 20 or 30 bands playing in St. Louis. All of her friends were going, and she got a seat in another carload of teenagers.

Heaven help anyone driving on I-55 yesterday.

I took a shower. Damn, I'll be glad when I get the gas turned back on! I should be able to pay them tonight. I got dressed for work and woke Patty up, and as I was drinking my coffee she, of course, asked for money. I'd already told her she could borrow ten for the Warped Tour. She had, of course, argued about it, saying admission, refreshments, and CDs wasn't enough.

She wanted shirts and stickers and the whole kit and kaboodle. I had told her ten was all I was giving her. I pulled out my wallet, and all that was in it was a twenty and four ones. She got the twenty, promising to repay me when she got her paycheck. She's a good kid. She has a job, goes to church with her friends, mostly makes good grades.

Walking to work was a little warmer than it had been. My van is broken, but I'd walk anyway. It's real close, and there's no parking.

By lunch it was downright hot, and humid like it gets here in the midwest. I decided rather than walk home and spend the afternoon sweaty, I'd eat in the cafeteria. I spent the four dollars. Including sixty cents the hungry soda machine stole.

When I got off work at 4:00 it was damned hot. My thermometer on the front porch said it was well over 90. Summer, it seems, has arrived.

And I needed to go get something for breakfast. Damn. Osco's is a mile and a half or farther.

My other daughter Leila, 18, who is living with her mother, has a thing about the weather.

She's always been afraid of storms, and before she hit puberty she could predict rain or snow 100% of the time, and tell you when it would rain, accurate to within twenty minutes. Now she watches the Weather Channel.

So she called to warn me that it was going to storm.

I looked outside. It was indeed clouded over. Maybe the heat had subsided.

I put on my shoes and went outside. The thermometer

said 90, and the humidity was worse. I sighed, locked up the house, and started walking.

The walk wasn't really all that bad. The wind started blowing a little, cooling me off. I heard rumbling in the distance.

I got to the store, and got coffee filters and pastry. As I'd gone in, I had noticed that Frankie's had burgers for a dollar and Budweiser for a buck fifty. As I came out of the store I could smell the rain. Maybe I could eat dinner, and the rain would pass.

I expected Frankie's to be empty, being Wednesday and all. I was wrong.

The place was packed. Not a single empty stool at the bar, and people standing up milling around. There was one empty table, so I sat down and plunked my groceries on it.

An old man with shoulder length gray frizzy hair was tuning a Stratocaster on the green "stage" platform. There was a black acoustic on a stand next to him. No drums, it must be a solo guitarist.

The waitress came and took my order. Very pretty young girl, with light blonde hair and a very low cut blouse. Mmmmmm..... cleavage....

Most of the female patrons were between fat and obese, with a few thinner tattooed women. A half dozen men and a lone woman were sitting at the table next to me.

The fellow at that table closest to the stage area was a dead ringer for Ted Turner. For all I know, it could have been Ted Turner, come to see Lincoln's tomb or some other sightseeing shit.

The cleavage... er, excuse me, the "waitress" brought my beer, and I asked her for a glass of water, which she brought fairly quickly.

Another, younger fellow got on stage and started tuning the black guitar. "Ted" was sloppily eating a burger. A young fat woman and an older fat man and an incredibly obese woman were sitting across the room. A guy that looked like the raftman from *The Outlaw Josie Wales*, only younger, nastier looking, with a bald dome and long brown hair, stood drunkenly by the bar, leering evilly at everyone.

Frankie's is almost kinda sorta divided in two, with a three foot long wall behind the table I was sitting at and the bar area behind it. All but my and the two other tables had moved back into the bar area as the musicians started their sound check, and a few people left. The bar area was still pretty full, and pretty badly lit.

The waitress brought my burger. She had the nicest smile, and pretty blue eyes... a stark contrast to the patrons, who were fat and/or tattooed. The one at the table with Ted would have been pretty nice looking were it not for the nasty ink markings on her back, and the tattooed slave anklet. The things folks think are sexy or attractive these days... I just don't get it. A permanent magic marker mustache on the mona lisa. "Grandma, why is there a black ring around your ankle?"

The old guy with the stratocaster was singing a Neil Young song, with the younger fellow playing rhythm. The burger was a half pound or more of ground cow, with lettuce and tomato and onion. I left the onion off. It was a very good burger. They normally charge five bucks for them, but Wednesdays they're only a dollar. The song ended, I had to put the burger down to applaud. Another song started.

I couldn't tell if the nasty looking "raftman" was leering at the women or the men. Presently I figured out that this was just how the poor fellow looked. He held his beer as a man holding a pole that is holding him up on a storm-tossed boat.

It was raining harder outside. Shit! My burger finished, I got a second beer.

I noticed the tattooed lady holding an unlit cigarette. Before I could get my lighter out of my pocket another attractive woman with an odd look on her face swooped over and lit it for her, and sat down next to her. The men at the table seemed to be ignoring both of them.

I looked around the wall. Still crowded, but not as

much. One or two attractive women, with ugly men. Maybe that's the secret, I'm not ugly enough. Should I practice my sneer or my leer? Ah, hell...

Over the music and buzz of conversation I hear a female voice exclaiming "I love you!" I turn and see the woman who had lit the tattooed woman's smoke reach out and hug her. It looked like more than a hug, almost a grope. The tattooed woman looked embarrassed, the hugging woman looked drunk.

I had left the waitress a two dollar tip on a $4.30 meal, and she kept coming by to see if I was OK. Mmmmm... Cleavage... God, I need to get laid...

The two man band played on. "I'm a joker, I'm a smoker, I'm a midnight toker..."

The rain was a torrent, coming down in bucketfuls, lightning flashing and thunder booming. These guys didn't need a drummer tonight, God was playing drums. They took a break, while God did a drum solo.

I overhear tattooed lady telling one of the men at Ted's table "I'm going to take her home." They went toward the back door.

BOOM!

They came back. One of the men asked the drunken lesbian if she was OK.

The old hippie guitar player was talking to Ted, the two women were talking to each other, and the rest of the men at the table were talking among themselves. I got a third beer.

Ted exclaims loudly and angrily to the guitarist "I'm not gay!!" Jesus, these people were loud.

BOOM rumble...

The rain didn't seem to be coming down as hard. The drunken lesbian and her friend left.

The band started back up. I looked around the short wall, and it was quite a bit less full, with a big gap in the bar. I moved to the bar, and got a fourth beer. I'd been drinking them slowly, but still felt toasted.

Number four almost gone, I grabbed my grocery bag and walked back to the back door and peered out. The rain wasn't going to quit. I was going to get wet.

I walked back toward the bar, bag in one hand and almost empty beer in the other, trying to decide whether to get another beer or get wet. It was probably late, I had to get up in the morning...

A woman who should have been attractive but somehow wasn't, turned around and glared at me. "What do *you* want?" she sneered,

"I want the rain to stop so I can go home without getting soaked."

She lightened up a bit. "It's supposed to rain all night."

"Yeah," I agreed, "I imagine it will. I guess I'll finish my beer and go home. I should have left two beers ago."

She turned back around toward the bar. I finished my beer and walked out into the rainy night.

Chapter 22: Mr. Opporknockity
Sun Jun 29, 2003 at 01:12:51 PM EST

I woke up with a sinus headache Saturday (yesterday), took a sinus pill, which combined with the Paxil put me right back to sleep.

I didn't even finish this until this morning, Sunday. So only one diary this weekend, but I did combine the two.

My thanks to the fellow who prayed for me to not commit adultery – Married Lady's husband took a day off work to spend with her, and it appears she realized she still loved him.

She still went for a walk with me on afternoon break. But at least it appears she's not going to seduce me. Until, I suppose, he leaves for a week's gambling again. I keep telling her that if that's his only fault and he doesn't gamble them into Chapter 7 she's lucky.

Friday I woke up with a bit of a sinus headache, and aspirin fixed it pretty quickly. Something's in the air, as a woman at work complained of a bad headache, too.

I wasn't going to go out Friday night. But I wanted some company.

Daughter Patty and her friend gave me a ride downtown, and I walked down to Dempsey's. There was only one woman in the place, the bartender, Mandy.

Usually a musclebound guy is there on Saturdays, making me look extra puny, so I usually go to Marley's. Dempsey's has acoustic night on Saturdays anyway, and one of the bigger local bands was at Marley's.

"Bush?" Mandy asks. "uh, depends," I say. "If you'll sell me a Rolling Rock for two bucks like Chris does I'll have one of them." Chris is the dorky looking kid with the backwards hat.

"Chris don't work here any more," she says. I feign surprise, remembering his request that I not mention his interview last week. "He got another job. Probably wanted out before he got fired."

So I got a Busch and a glass of water, per my usual. I walked around the bar where Mandy sits, and she was talking to a fat, effeminate fellow wearing earrings. I think he was trying to hit on Mandy, although somehow I got the idea that he was going to hit on me. He was giving me that look I give beautiful women.

"So how ya doin'?" Mandy asks. "You seem in a better mood than last week."

Heh, I took an extra half Paxil. "I don't know why I was so down," I said. "Probably because I can't get a girlfriend." Fat fellow spent all of two seconds looking crestfallen. I don't know for sure he was gay, I've known effeminate straight men before.

Mandy pulled out a cigarette, and I lit it for her. "Well first," she said, "that pink lighter has got to go." She traded me for a black one.

The gayish guy was pleasant enough to chat with, especially with Mandy between us. PC? No, but I don't like hurting people's feelings. Sometimes it's necessary, but I really don't like to. As long as he wasn't going to shove any "gay pride" in my face...

Talk somehow got to cute kid stories, Mandy talking about a niece that was learning to read. I wish I could remember the story, but I slept since then. Twice.

Anyway, I recounted something that happened to me when I was 6 or 7 years old.

We had company, some kind of family party with Aunts and Uncles and cousins, and my mother sent me to the store for napkins.

I came back with the *sanitary* napkins – Kotex brand.

Mandy cracked up at this and laughed for a full five minutes. The effeminate guy seemed embarrassed by the story, but laughed too. I think Mandy was half drunk; her water isn't always water.

She'd be really good looking if it wasn't for that nose.

Anyway, I finished my beer and went to Marleys to get in before they started to collect covers. They start at 9:00, Dempsey's starts the Acoustic Night at ten.

Too late. I'd spent too much time talking to Mandy and the effeminate guy. Three bucks.

I went in, and they were selling hats, T-shirts, and CDs. "How much for a CD?" I asked. "Ten bucks." I frowned. New price for indie records, I guess. "But if you buy one we'll give you another one free!"

Well, that sounded like a good deal – two CDs for the price of two. I bought the CDs and had the band sign one, and talked to the band members.

"So," I said, "I sure hope you guys don't suck!"

They laughed, and one said "me, too!"

We talked about P2P and the RIAA. The RIAA and its labels seem to be universally hated by anyone who doesn't have a contract with them, and quite a few who do have contracts.

Mr. Opporknockity, like most sane independent artists, not only doesn't mind P2P, they rely on it. They don't, however, like folks burning copies of their CDs. I personally think this is self defeating, as there is no legal way to prevent it under the Home Recording Act, and a bootleg CD may lead to a sale, but I generally try to respect the artists' wishes.

I walked around and got a draft. The place was pretty crowded, with little miniparties. I felt alone. By the time I finished my beer, I decided to walk back to Dempsey's and have Mandy hang on to my CDs for me.

As I was talking with Mandy, a familiar face walked in. "Hey, I know you," I exclaimed. "You're Joe's girlfriend." Joe had a gig somewhere else tonight, according to the *Illinois Typo*; er, excuse me, *Illinois Times*. "Why aren't you with Joe?"

"He's in the restroom," Mandy said. Joe's gig was an early one.

I got a beer and Mandy got busy. Last week it was mostly women on Friday, this week was definitely lacking in the fairer sex. And the fellow playing couldn't seem to keep his guitar in tune. In fact, he seemed to spend more time tuning than playing.

I walked outside, and a portly fellow I'd talked to before, a keyboard player, was holding a hitter. "Damned thing's clogged," he said.

I decided to stick around. I really should buy some pot. I'm starting to feel like a bum.

He got his hitter cleared and offered me a hit. I lit it and handed it back. "It's just one hit, go ahead."

Mandy walked out. "Hey, guys, you're gonna get me in trouble. Go back in the alley!" I wandered down closer to the next bar and lit it again.

This was one big "one hit," that was for sure. I kept hitting the pipe, got wasted, and handed the pipe back and wandered back inside. He told me where his band was playing next and I promised to be there.

The guitar player got two whole songs out before somehow getting it out of tune again. After he spent ten minutes trying to tune it, Joe walked up and tuned it for him and handed it back. The guy played another song and took a break. I walked back down to Marley's.

I got a draft, "Mr. O" played two more songs and it was closing time. I hadn't realized how late it was; must have been the pot, the night had zoomed by.

I walked back to Dempsey's. It was dark and locked. The night was over.

The next morning I woke up with a clogged nose and a splitting headache. And no coffee made.

I used to have a Bunn. Those are great, they brew a pot of great tasting coffee in five minutes. When we moved here, Evil-X threw my Bunn away and bought a Black and Decker, and it's a total piece of shit. One of the most poorly misengineered crap laden kludges I have ever had the displeasure of wasting my money on.

It has a timer, so you can set the coffee up the night before to make itself. Good thing, too, because it takes half an hour to make a pot. But coffee on a timer doesn't taste as good as straight out of the can.

It has a "sneak a cup" feature that stops the coffee flow if you remove the pot while it's perking, again, necessary because it takes two eternities (at least, when you really really want a cup of coffee) to make. The rubber stopper that allows this feature to work lasted maybe two months.

The pot itself has straight sides, so when it's full you

can't pour it without spilling it. There is an opening in the back by the handle, so steam comes out and burns your hand when you pour it.

I miss my Bunn. But damn, those things are expensive these days.

I tried starting to write this, but without coffee it was hopeless. I finally got the coffee done, and drank it on the front porch. I fell asleep sitting there. I woke up, took out my contacts, and went back to bed.

I woke back up about 3:30. Daughter Patty was in the kitchen on the computer, complaining about a killer sinus headache. She was supposed to work at 4:00, but had called in sick.

By 6:00 she was feeling better, and one of her friends was giving her a ride to some Karate thing at the mall.

I took a shower, worked on the hopeless diary some more, and walked downtown. I stopped at Bread Stretcher's and ate a heifer and drank a bottle of Rolling Rock.

"Cops" or some Fox shit like it was on the TV. A young cop came in and got dinner. I finished mine, walked outside, past the police car and down to Dempsey's.

Box Spring Station (I think that's the band's name, I should have stolen a flyer) was setting up. Pretty good for a local band, which is really a compliment. There are better local bands in Springfield than I have heard anywhere.

Don't tell the RIAA, Reel Big Fish (not a Springfield band) kicked ass until they signed with Britney Spears' label. Their label CD sounds like they were bored recording it; it's lost all the life their previous CDs had.

I talked a while with Mandy, who was worried that they wouldn't be busy. By the time the band started playing she was working her ass off. "You want your CDs now?" she asked. I told her I'd get them when I left.

Joe and his girlfriend came in. The Dempsey's regular preppie barfly that looked like a petulant Barbie Doll came in. A woman with a flashing red light on her left breast, and a wedding train on her head came in, followed by a dozen women, half of whom had butterfly wings on their backs.

This was going to be an entertaining night.

I went to the restroom, and when I came out my seat was taken by a butterfly girl. I said "excuse me" and got my beer and water, which were sitting in front of her.

"Oh, I'm sorry," she said.

"That's perfectly OK," I answered "What's with the wings?"

"My friend's getting married tomorrow," she replied. "This is her bachelorette party."

I chatted with the young butterfly girl some more, politely neglecting to ask if she was a worm when she was small, then walked through the crowd to Joe's table. By then, Joe was sitting in with the band, playing his harmonica. Joe plays a mean harmonica.

I said "hi" to Joe's girlfriend. The song ended, Joe came back and I chatted with him about my inability to get a girlfriend. "I'm a fucking loser," I told him. He laughed heartily.

"Dude," he said, "these girls are all half your age!"

"Yeah, but the ones my age are all ugly!" I exclaimed. He laughed again. "Besides," I said, "They're all married and at home with their husbands. Where else are they?"

"Down at the lake," he said. That was why Mandy was worried about it not being busy; there had been some shindig going on at Lake Springfield with ten bands.

"I've been there all day," he said. "Lots of women your age."

I lamented that my goddamned piece of shit car was still expensively broken.

A couple of songs later, Joe went up and sat in again, this time on a conga drum. I walked outside for some air.

A couple of young fellows walked up. "You own this place?" he asked. I laughed. "I wish!" One particularly short fellow with a pierced eyebrow looked familiar. I don't know where I've seen him.

He started telling me about his band, Hed Krush, hyping themselves up shamelessly. "These guys are amateurs. We kick ass!"

I told them I could introduce them to the guy at Dempseys who did booking, which was Joe. "Naw," the tall one said, "We have gigs."

"Well," I asked, "you have a CD?"

"We're working on one, should be done the end of the year."

"A web site?"

"It'll be up in a few weeks," he answered.

We'll see. These guys could suck like a Hoover, or be the new Beatles. They walked on down the street, and I went back inside.

By now, girls were dancing. I noticed Hippie Chick was there. I hadn't seen her since Rolling Rock was a buck. I walked over and "danced" (if you can call it that) by her. The song ended and she walked over to the rest room. The next I saw her she was sitting in some young guy's lap.

I drank more water than beer, and aside from the butterflies there were no cartoons. The night was winding down, and I took what would likely be my last beer to the restroom, put it on the back of the toilet and pissed in the urinal.

Joe walked in as I was zipping my pants back up and threw my beer away!

"Dude!" I said, "You threw my beer away!"

Joe was apologetic, I told him not to worry about it; the band was done playing and I was about to leave anyway. He promised to buy me two beers the next time I came.

Maybe he'll have some good bud. Maybe I'll find out where I can buy some. I think if I'd had some reefer last night, I could have taken Hippie Chick home.

Oh, the poll (p148): I spent twenty bucks Friday, and eight Saturday. Not bad, eh?

Chapter 23: Hey, Q!
Tue Jul 01, 2003 at 06:30:09 PM EST

I won't be taking the train to St. Louis, I found a ride. Email me with your phone number and I'll try to make it across the river for that beer when I get down there, assuming I can get Mike or somebody to ferry me over.

I'm riding down with three lovely young ladies. Yesterday was an interesting day!

One of our printers at work was giving people fits. Half the PCs had the wrong driver for it installed.

One of my unit's other tech guys had discovered this when a user's machine printed certain elements of documents strangely. So he had put the right driver on it. I was tasked with making sure everyone else's machine in the office had the right driver.

No sooner than I was finished than the first machine, the one that had me checking drivers, wouldn't print duplex. So I was supposed to download the newest driver and upgrade everyone. I tested it on my machine, and there was a paper jam. I cleared all the paper and it was still jammed. Thinking there was a sensor broken, I called it in to the hardware people.

They sent a gorgeous woman up, who knew this printer inside and out. She showed me the hidden place where the paper was stuck, and showed me what the real problem with the driver was. We, of course, have no FM to R.

God, but I hated the big diamond on her left hand! Such a pretty smile and beautiful eyes...

When I got home, Patty, my daughter, had left a page about Asperger's Syndrome on the computer. Her, or me, I wondered? Maybe her sister? No, probably me, her dateless old dad.

She went swimming with her friends yesterday, and Stoner came by looking for her. So I copped a ride to Dempsey's with Stoner to take advantage of the two dollar Heinikens there.

Joe was sitting at a table with the owners, and Mandy was training a new girl. The slim new girl is cute as a button, a very attractive young lady. Mandy introduced me to her, and trolled "If you get him drunk enough he'll leave a tip." She laughed out loud when I protested that I always tipped before I got drunk, and Mandy confessed to the new girl, Kate, that I tipped first before I ran out of money. I noted the ring on her finger and said nothing.

They were stocking the bar, Joe was talking business with the owners, so I decided to see if anything was happening anywhere else.

The bars were all empty.

Except for The Alamo, where a guy was doing something with a bass drum. "Putting them up or taking them down?" I asked. "Putting them up, we start in about half an hour."

I drank a beer, and decided to walk down to Bread Stretcher's for a sandwich. When I got back to the Alamo the band had started. I didn't catch their name, but they were a very good blues band, playing all the old classic blues songs. They mentioned that they would be at the State Fair in one of the beer tents.

The place was fairly busy, with a few couples and quite a few ladies of all ages, not many of them very attractive. There were oldsters that made me look young by comparison making time with young, attractive women. I couldn't even pick up an ugly old hag my own age. I left, dejected, and decided to walk back to Dempseys for one last Heineken before walking home. God, I felt like such a loser. Ass burgers.

I was bummed out badly as I walked back in to Dempsey's. The blues music had fit the night perfectly.

Five minutes of talking with Mandy and the new girl, Kate, who it seems was an old friend of Mandy's, and their other friend who had come from out of town on a visit had me cheered up and laughing. I told her friend Kate that I wished I was younger and she was single. Mandy's friend Samantha laughed and said "you're only as old as you feel." Kate gave me a puzzled look; "I'm not married!"

"But you have that ring," I said. "Oh," she laughed. "I just like jewelry." It turns out that she's even younger than Mandy, and just turned 21 a week or two ago. She doesn't even have a boyfriend.

The jukebox was playing loudly "...she's too cute to be a minute over seventeen..."

Talk got to the July 4th weekend, and it seems the three of them were driving to the Ozarks Thursday night. I wrangled a ride to St. Louis with them, and after they said "sure, no problem" I offered to pay for gas.

I stayed at Dempsey's way too long. The night got away from me, and I had no idea how the time flew by so quickly. Must have been the ladies.

I walked home in a damn good mood. It seems I have a traveling date with three lovely young ladies Thursday! Now watch, Mandy will have to work Saturday and I'll wind up on the damned train anyway...

Chapter 24: Secrets of the Q revealed
Sun Jul 06, 2003 at 10:32:28 PM EST

...to me. Unfortunately, I was sworn to secrecy so I'm afraid I can't reveal them to you.

Thursday was interesting, to say the least. Actually the whole weekend was very short of normalcy. As I type this, I haven't logged in to K5, and am only retrieving my mail and microwaving some pseudo-food. All that mail is having a hard time coming in through the old 33.6.

This will probably have to be in chapters. It may not get posted all at once. We may not get to Q tonight. Who, by the way, bought my beer, gave me a very interesting ride (more later) and I had a good time. I left him in the deepest darkest ghetto. I hope he made it home alive...

Wednesday

All week I was walking on clouds – provided nothing went wrong, I was riding down to St. Louis the next day with three attractive young ladies, maybe one of which I could get to know better...

I was supposed to go to Dempsey's Tuesday or Wednesday to make sure the trip Thursday was still on. Mandy was supposed to work those nights, and would let me know. I was looking forward to it, since Wednesday was "Open Mic Night" and I didn't have to work Thursday.

Mandy wasn't there. Joe, the musclebound part-owner, was tending bar. Joe Frew was there too. I talked to Joe Frew; I don't know the owner Joe. At least, not the owner Joe at Dempsey's. I know the owner, Joe, at Track Shack. But that's a different Joe, Joe.

Joe started the open mics; Not Bartender/part-owner Joe. I don't think he plays anything except clang irons. I mean Joe Frew, the musician, who will soon be Joe the Bartender and Joe the manager.

Boy, bars sure are confusing. So I decided to go looking for Mandy and her friends.

All the bars were empty. I wound up at the Alamo, where I still couldn't pick up a woman. So I finished my water, tossed the ice in the trash can, poured the bottle into the glass and tossed the bottle in the bin, and walked out the back door, across the parking lot, and down the street.

A cop passed me going the opposite way. The cop stopped, and then backed up. I took a big swallow.

"Hey!"

"Huh?"

"What's in the glass?"

"Uh, its, er," I looked in the glass, took a drink... "it's um..." I finished it. "It's er, um, empty!" I turned the glass upside down.

"Oh, a smart guy, huh?" He turned the blue bubblegums

on and the two of them got out. "Let's see some I.D."

I gave them my driver's license, and asked innocently, "what's the problem?" he answered my question with a question. "Where do you live?"

Well duh, it's on the license, asshole. But I didn't say that, I just told him where I lived. "I just walked down here for a beer, you know man?"

The other cop says "drugs?" The first cop shook his head. "Where'd you get the beer?"

"Huh?" I said.

"Look," the cop said, "it's against the law to walk down the street with an open container."

"What???" I asked, incredulously. "That's stupid!"

"Look," he said, giving me the evil eye, "we don't make the laws. We just enforce them."

"I know, I know," I told him. "Nothing against you guys, not your fault. It's just a really stupid law."

"So who sold you the beer?"

"Look," I said, "I don't want to get anybody into trouble."

"If we arrest you it's a $500 fine."

"It's from The Alamo. Uh, where can I find a trash can to throw this away?"

"Down the alley there I see a dumpster."

He handed my license back. "Look, you can't walk around with an open container, OK?"

"I'm sorry," I said, and walked down the street to the dumpster.

I went to Dempsey's for a third beer and walked home dejected. It looked like I was taking the train.

Patty was waiting up. "Where were you? I went into Dempsey's looking for you! That guy playing guitar was really good!"

"Fat guy with real short hair, needs a shave, wears glasses?"

"Yeah"
"That's Joe."
"Oh yeah, I saw him on a sticker..."
I drank a beer and went to bed.

Thursday

I woke up Thursday in a bad mood. Blue. Angry. I felt like Mandy was just having a few laughs at the fool's expense. Well, I'm a fool, so fucking what? I'd see Mandy again and we'd see what went on.

I felt better after I took my happy pill. But I still wanted pussy. But I couldn't worry about pussy for a couple of days, I have to get a car.

For those of you who tuned in to the show late, my incredibly nice Grand Voyager's transmission went kerflooey and they want a shitload of money to fix it. And I'm still making payments. And I'm not related to Bill Gates. An old friend who lives in a slum south of East St. Louis has one he can't keep on his property he's willing to give me, because another old friend is tired of the damned thing sitting on *his* property. So I'm getting a free car. All that's wrong with it is it's a twenty year old piece of shit that sat in a driveway for ten years without being started.

So daughter Patty says she wants to steal her mother's PT Cruiser, the one I bought her mother two fucking months before she moved out to have more time with her adulterous boyfriend. "If I can, I'll give you a ride to the train station."

"I don't want to see the goddamned parasitic whore," I said. "Especially not today of all days."

Thursday was my wedding anniversary. It would have been #27 if the fucking whore hadn't moved out last September. Funny, when you finally rid yourself of an albatross that's been hanging around your neck for 27 years, you miss the God damned albatross! ...at least for a while.

"Don't worry," Patty promises, "I won't let her in."

Patty's nickname for Evil-X's boyfriend is "Faggot". Patty seems to especially like that name since it pisses her mom off. Particularly since I told Patty about the other guy who Evil-X moved in with another time long before either daughter was born, who liked to stick it in her back door. A *real* back door man.

My guess is that X still likes guys with small enough dicks to go in through the back door, and my suspicions are heightened by the distaste that X finds with Patty's nickname for "Faggot".

I call him "Motherfucker".

Oh, they turned the gas back on Thursday. Yay! Hot water!

Later I'm sitting on the front porch drinking coffee and I see the white PT coming down 7th. I go inside and upstairs and get in the shower. I dry off, get dressed, come downstairs... and there's X sitting on my couch, on our wedding anniversary.

"What the FUCK are you doing here TODAY of all the fucking days you could have come???" I demanded. And added "...fucking asshole."

"I wanted to see my daughter, do you mind?"

"YES I mind, you heartless fucking cunt. You haven't seen her or even talked to her for three fucking weeks and you show up today of all days. I swear, I have known some pure evil, heartless, worthless fucking bastards in my time but you know, the worst doesn't come close to you. Don't you even realize the significance of today, bitch?"

"I know what day it is."

"Then why come here TODAY of ALL DAYS! Heartless fucking asshole cunt, God damned whore..."

Patty walked in, so I shut up and went in the kitchen.

A little while later Patty came in. I gave her the evil eye. "You said you weren't going to let her in."

"Well,... I'm sorry. It's just, you know?"

"Well, get rid of the God damned slut. I mean, er, sorry, get rid of her."

"She said I could take you to the train station in her car."

So my daughter took me to the train station while my adulterous ex-wife sat in my living room.

I bought a ticket. The next train didn't leave until 6:45. I called home, and Satan answered. No, Patty's not home and I'll have her call.

I walked across the street from the train station to a bar I hadn't been in before. A bunch of hippies and/or rednecks and/or bikers were shooting pool, drinking, and playing Virtual Bowling. I bought a beer. The phone rang.

"Yeah?"

"Mom said you called."

"Come back, the train doesn't leave until 6:45."

She took me home, and left with her evil mother.

Shortly after 5:00 I started walking, and thought I'd get a beer at Dempsey's while I waited for the train.

Joe Frew was tending bar. I shot the shit with Joe, who was waiting for a new girl, Amy.

Hmm, Amy? I wondered if it were the same Amy, the one whose brother had just killed himself.

About 6:00 a blonde figure flashed past the window. "Is that her?" Joe asked.

Mandy walked in. Sam was sick, Mandy was working and Kate had yet another birthday party. That's about 14 in two weeks. And here I spent my 21st birthday on the other side of the world where nobody gives a shit!

OK... Mandy eased my mind a bit. I got another beer, and drank it. At 6:30 I walked to the train station.

Next: The ride; a girl with an onion; St. Louis, and Q!

Chapter 25: The Q – continue, um...
Wed Jul 09, 2003 at 06:25:53 PM EST

For those of you waiting with baited breath, and those waiting with bated breath, well, blame Rusty. I needed to look up a link and the perl server was dead. So I'm going to go tinker with the junker and get a beer.

Where was I? Oh yeah, Thursday evening down at Dempsey's talking to Joe and Joe and Mandy. Mandy had to work, Kate had yet another birthday party, and Samantha was ill. I finished my second beer and walked down to the train station.

Someone asked after the last installment where my job fit into the picture. It didn't. I took a vacation day Thursday.

Daughter Patty had given me a ride to the train station earlier in the day, where I was grossly overcharged for a ticket. I had called two weeks prior, and was told the price for a round trip ticket was twenty to sixty dollars, depending on "seat availability".

So the way it works is, you can have your choice of window or aisle, and stow your gear on the one you don't want to sit in, and be assured of never standing in line for the restroom, or choose to pay three times as much for a crowd.

No wonder they're going bankrupt. Yeah, people buy train tickets based on price, sure...

The train came in very shortly after its scheduled 6:45 PM and I got on. Passengers going to St. Louis were seated in the very last car.

Beer was in the very first car.

I found the last double seat and sat down. Two more passengers got on, a woman and her young son. I gave up the seat and walked up a few seats and sat next to a young lady who was reading *The Onion* and listening to ear buds.

After the train started, I put my bag on the overhead and began the journey to the car with the snack bar, in the very front of the long train. Bud was $3.50. I got a Carona for $3.75, and trudged back to my seat.

It was so far away I almost got lost.

I finally found my seat and sat down. The young lady next to me was chuckling at *The Onion*. I watched the trees go by.

Some time after I disposed of my bottle she took off the ear buds and put the paper down. I offered that I was going to the snack car for another beer, would she like anything?

Sure, she'd like some chips or something salty, and started digging in her purse. I waved her off. "don't worry about it," I told her gallantly, and trudged on up the long journey to the snack car.

It was closed. The dining car was open. "Is there anywhere I can get a beer and a bag of chips?"

"The snack car, downstairs," the waiter said. "It's closed," I answered.

"Oh," the waiter said, "he's eating".

The snack car was to be closed the entire $32 two hour journey. They sold me another Carona for $4.50.

After trudging back I sadly informed the young lady that alas, the snack car was closed. She thanked me and turned to look out the window.

Presently someone passed a small bag of potato chips up to her. She offered me some, I politely declined. We were in the St. Louis area by then; I could see the arch. I pulled out my phone and called Mike. No answer.

So I called Q.

Presently the train pulled into the St. Louis Amtrak station; I had told Q it was Union Station. Wrong!

I called Q again and told him Amtrak, not Union Station. He'd be there in 20 minutes.

Half an hour later I tried calling Mike again. "We were wondering if you made it in," he said. "We just got home." I told him I was having a beer with a guy I knew and would meet him somewhere on the east side; Mike refused to cross the river. I later found out why, the hard way.

Fifteen minutes later I was starting to wonder where Q was, so called him again. "Man, it's crazy," he said. "I'm three blocks away and I can't get there! All the streets are blocked. You could probably walk faster."

He gave me his description, which was rather fortunate as he didn't look much like the picture I'd seen. Of course, I don't look a lot like my picture, either.

Maybe twenty minutes later he pulled up. I opened the door. "Am I getting in the right car?"

"Yeah, you are if you're mcgrew."

I can't recount much of the conversation on the way to the bar, partly because it's been since last Thursday and I've slept since then, but mostly because he told secret tales of K5 and its denizens. I felt honored – I know secrets even at least one long time K5er doesn't, and it pertains to this person personally. And no, I can't divulge who this person is.

There is a microbrewery down there that Q said was the informal K5 St. Louis Headquarters, which he unfortunately couldn't find. St. Louis was crazy; or at least, its political leaders were.

For you non-USians, the whole damned country went crazy since 9-11. Well, maybe not the whole country, just the politicians. Everyone else knows that if something bad happens to them, it will probably be cancer or a drunk driver. Our leaders, however, have been terrorized by terrorists, in utter, desperate agonizing fear of something bad happening that would cost them an election.

So there was no way in hell to cross the river, save going through the deepest blackest most poverty stricken part of East Saint Louis, across the Martin Luther King Bridge.

At any rate, after driving around for half an hour, he finally just pulled in to some random tavern.

Mike had told me not to be too late, so I told Q we could only have a beer or two. We went in and drank one, and I said fuck it I'll have another and pulled out my wallet. Q wouldn't let me pay.

I called Mike again, and he was gone again. Damn. I'd have Q drop me at Jeff's.

We had a hell of a time trying to cross the river. Every way we turned there was a blocked off street. If annoyance is the aim of terrorism, they've succeeded.

"I'm driving a Fibonacci sequence," Q joked.

We finally got across the river, and I knew where I was. Well, thirty years ago I would have. I didn't have a clue last Thursday.

We drove around more, and finally I saw a sign to interstate 64. We got on.

A few miles down the road I could see that we were

going the wrong way. We turned around. "But we're going back to St. Louis!" Q said. But I knew where I was now. We were going to Cahokia, the once nice town where the oldest church and the oldest court house in or west of the Mississippi Valley is that was now a crackhead and gangster infested slum.

I directed him toward the proper ramp, and we headed down highway 3, down 157, and on to Jeff's house.

Thankfully, Jeff was still awake. "Who's there!" he barked. "Hey, it's Steve," I answered.

I said goodbye to Q and went in. Jeff was ready to go to sleep. Before I sacked out on his recliner, Mike called. "Hey, we just got home. Did you make it to East St. Louis?"

I wondered if Q would make it out of the ghetto all right.

Poll
$32 for a hundred mile ride is
A little steep 42%
high 0%
damned high 28%
outrageous 14%
WTF?? 14%
other (post) 0%

Chapter 26: Independence Day
Sun Jul 13, 2003 at 04:11:11 PM EST

"You want some breakfast?" Jeff asked. "Sure." Dumb question, I'm always hungry anymore.

He turned on the TV, flipped through all the cable channels and settled on one that was no less boring than the rest and went in the kitchen. "Steak and eggs OK?" he asked.

Hell yes, I usually have donuts or something.

Jeff's black attack house cat was sitting on his chair giving me an evil look. At least it wasn't growling and hissing at me today.

Some badly censored movie was on one of the cable channels; I wasn't paying attention. Jeff's giant foot long goldfish that he had inherited from his late brother was more interesting. The fish, like usual, was watching TV. Or at least it had positioned itself so it looked like it was watching TV.

Jeff came in the living room with the food. The cat was rubbing against my shoes and socks, next to my chair. Strange, the only time that cat acted like that was when it was in heat. Normally it hated my shoes.

"Want a beer?" he joked.

About the time we finished eating, the door knocked. It was Mike. "Got a beer?" He was serious.

Mike had a little pot and a hitter. I talked Jeff into turning some music on, we weren't paying attention to the TV anyway.

Jeff's friend Bob came by trying to sell some seedy pot. Nobody was buying. Bob rolled a good sized joint.

Jeff's cat doesn't like anybody, but it especially detests Bob. "WROWRR!! HISS!!! SPIT!"

"He come to see you!" Jeff told Dog, the cat. Yes, his cat is named Dog. That particular phrase, "come to see you," sends the cat even more insane than usual. "WROWR!!!" Ears back, fangs barred, angry frown on its face.

I put on my shoes and socks, which the cat had been loving up to earlier.

The cat didn't like that one bit.

Jeff got out the welding glove so Bob could play with Dog, the cat.

Presently I left with Mike to go work on the car. Jeff followed us out. We stopped at the Shell station on the way, where I bought a six pack and Mike got a few cases.

Mike likes beer.

When we got to Mike's, "Hoss" was there waiting for us.

The hitter seems to have impeded my memory somewhat. Mike pulled it out and we hit it again; couldn't leave Hoss without a buzz.

It was a scorcher on the 4th. Before the afternoon was over it probably hit a hundred degrees. My shirt was soaked with sweat, and I took it off. "Wow," Jeff said, "You're getting fat."

Well, not compared to Jeff, who is about six five and weighs at least two fifty, maybe three hundred. But compared to me the last time he saw me I am getting fat. Which is still nowhere near "fat". Except for developing a slight pot belly from the beer and constant eating, I'm not quite as underweight as I was. I'm nowhere near needing to go on a diet, although a few situps wouldn't hurt.

I walked back up the hill to Mike's house to get some sort of heavy tool. Of course, since it was my car I was doing the gruntwork. When I got back they had already blown the lines clear and had it running. I gathered the air tank and the battery pack and all the other crap and loaded it all in the back of Mike's pickup, and drove the old car up the hill to his driveway. Mike followed in his truck.

Mike's house was full of teenaged boys. His youngest was camping, and his oldest was there with four or five of his friends who were there for a little July 4th incendiary munitions.

Mike's lucky those kids didn't burn his house down, or kill or even injure anybody severely. I felt sorry for Mike's wife, who had to keep an eye on a bunch of boys and their explosives, and men full of beer.

Mike remarked how it was strange, when he was a teenager he hid his pot smoking from his parents, and now he was a parent he hid his pot smoking from his teenagers.

We drank beer and shot pool since Mike has a pool table in his basement and bullshitted and occasionally hit the hitter and had a good old time. The boys were outside trying to set the house and surrounding woods on fire. That was entertaining, as well. Mike's wife cooked an excellent meal; I think Mike cooked the meat.

I'm not sure when I've had a better time on July 4th.

Jeff and Hoss went home, and Mike and I sat on the porch with his wife and watched the fireworks.

Mike went inside and passed out. Presently I went inside and went to sleep to the sound of fireworks, which went off all night long.

"God damn it stop shooting that shit at the house!!!"

Mike was awake, and it seemed the kids were still shooting off fireworks outside. I got up and went in the kitchen.

"Want some coffee?" Well, yeah. I don't think I even drank any coffee Friday, first time in years. We drank coffee, and Mike made steak and eggs for breakfast. What are these guys, astronauts? I didn't complain, though! Mike's eggs were better, as he has his own chickens (as well as turkeys and pigs).

I asked about his son's friends. "Are those boys' moms married?"

"Just one," he said. Of course, I replied "I want to meet the other boys' moms!"

"No you don't," he said, "they're sluts".

"Damn it Mike," I replied, "I don't want to marry 'em, I just want to fuck 'em."

"No, you'll probably catch something." Then he started talking about how good looking the married one was. I gave up.

After breakfast we drove to the Walmart in Cahokia for oil and antifreeze and all the other nasty stuff that automobiles require to brake and not break. We went from the private gravel bumpy one lane road to the twisty little back road and finally to the two lane, 55 mph highway that led to the interstate. If Q had dropped me off at Mike's instead of Jeff's he would have gotten lost for sure, unless he has an excellent sense of direction.

"God damned bicycles," Mike said. Stupid yuppies bring their bicycles to this road to ride on, and I do mean stupid. Little to no shoulder, two lanes, and 55 mph speed limit. You would have to be a total moron to ride a bicycle on that road.

"Stupid dumbasses," he continued. "One just got killed a couple of months ago."

"Yeah?"

"Yeah, some woman got in this guy's way and he followed her to a bar and they had a big argument, and when she left, he followed her down and ran over her ass!"

"So," I said, "I take it the guy's in prison now?"

"No," Mike said. "He's a rich fucking farmer, didn't even get arrested."

I think of OJ Simpson. Race doesn't matter in the US, except as a tool of the rich to take peoples' minds off of classism. The only way for a rich man, white or black, to get in trouble in this plutocracy is to piss off a richer man or woman.

Murder is legal, provided you have enough ready cash.

We went to change the oil, and I ruined one of his ramps. I owe Mike a set of ramps. Flushed the radiator, filled the fluids, etc. Started it up a bunch of times, it ran a bunch of times. Jeff showed up, then Hoss showed up with his two boys, maybe 10 or 11. I shut the car down and we went inside to drink some beer. It was early afternoon, and as I planned on going home Saturday I wasn't going to drink but one or maybe two.

The teenagers left, to go camping. We went in the basement and Mike pulled out his hitter. Hoss pulled out a big joint. Mike kept trying to convince me to party now and go home the next day instead. After about four beers I agreed. It's not like I get to smoke very often, or visit my old friends lately (although that shall now change).

Sunday morning we drank some coffee, ate some breakfast, hit the hitter a few times, and I put my bag in the car and turned the key.

It wouldn't start. It had run fine all day the day before.

The automatic choke is broken on it, and we had held it open with a piece of stiff gas line. I opened the hood and closed the choke. Still nothing.

Mike looked in the carburetor while I turned the key.

"It's not getting any gas."

We determined that the gas line must have plugged up again. I went in his basement, hooked the air tank into Mike's big compressor and filled it and lugged it back up to the car.

Mike stood behind the car as I blew it out. "God damn it!" he exclaimed. "What?" I said. "It's out of fucking gas. Fuck!"

Air, but no bubbles. We put a five gallon gas can, a two gallon can, and a gallon can in the back of his truck and went to get some gas for it. I bought a 12 pack of beer as well, Mike's brand.

We went back, and Hoss was there with his kids. I put the gas in and tried to start it. Still no dice. "Must not be enough to go through the lines," Mike said. "But," I argued, "if this thing's got a twenty gallon tank it has to be way over a quarter full, maybe half full."

"Well, it ain't starting!" he said. I couldn't argue with that. I took his truck back to get more gas while he and Hoss drank some beer.

Back, and put that gas in. I took the air tank back down to the basement and filled it again, and we went back outside, disconnected the gas line from the little electric fuel pump again and I shot some air in. "Stop! Stop!" Mike yelled. "I did!" I said.

"Shit, damn it, stop! Gas is shooting out all over the place!"

"The hose isn't even in it, put the cap on!" I said.

I tried pouring a little gas directly in the carburetor. It tried to start, then burst into flames. "Wow, cool!" Hoss' kid exclaimed.

Mike sort of freaked out. I yanked the air filter out and put the lid on.

Presently we finally figured out what was needed was to pour some gas into the gas lines from the fuel pump, both ways.

This did the trick. It started.

We went inside, and I opened a beer. Hoss lit a joint. I drank a second beer, and drove home.

Monday I got license plates. So I'm no longer without wheels. I now have a 1980 Malibu, which will be my daughter's as soon as I get the van fixed.

Poll
How much should a concert, 2 CDs, a pipeful and a six pack cost?
twenty bucks 20%
fifty bucks   50%
seventy five   0%
a hundred   0%
one fifty   0%
ONE HUNDRED ENGLISH POUNDS   20%
other 10%

Chapter 27: Fifty Cents (Believe it or not)
Tue Jul 15, 2003 at 03:57:07 PM EST

The sign on Duffy's had read "FRI LIVE BLUEGRASS" all week. I planned Friday around it.

I walked the half block to Duffy's around 8:00 and went in. Duffy was doing good business; they usually do on Fridays, when all the country folk and country wannabe city slickers and drug store cowboys show up for redneck kareoke.

I usually stay away from Duffy's on Fridays. I'm no fan of modern "country" music. Like Mojo Nixon sang in *Lets Go Burn Ol' Nashville Down*, "Country ain't got no flutes!"

There were two homely girls tending bar. I asked one when the band started. "9:00." So I walked home for a much cheaper beer and listened to a little Zepplin.

My daughter had the new old car, which I wasn't going to need anyway. I walked back to Duffy's a few minutes after 9:00 and ordered a mini pitcher. The band was already playing.

Three ancient, white haired fellows were playing and singing. One played guitar, one a banjo, and the third played washtub. I don't believe I've ever seen anyone playing that quaint old instrument before.

For those of you younger than my father, and those older than him from the city, this particular stringed instrument is made from an old fashioned galvanized steel washtub, a broomstick, and a piece of thin clothesline, aircraft cable, or something else to make the string from.

They played for half an hour or so, and sounded pretty good. They took a break, so I walked over to their table and made a request.

"You fellows know an old song called *Rollin' In My Sweet Baby's Arms?*"

They were just plum tickled that somebody had asked. "Well, yeah, we know that'n." They hopped up and grabbed the microphone. "Hey, folks we got a request!"

They played it, and went for another twenty minutes or so and took another break. After a fifteen minute break, the guitar player and banjo player packed up their instruments and left.

The kareoke DJ started up. I finished my pitcher and left, and walked on downtown to Dempsey's for acoustic night.

I had drank the pitcher pretty fast, and was a bit tipsy.

Dempsey's was completely uneventful. I didn't meet any characters, or women. I was actually pretty bored with the normal Dempsey cartoon characters, which had come out with that one last beer at Dempsey's. I decided to walk home and watch the trails from the cars' taillights, maybe sit on my porch and listen to the noise of the night. I'd about given up looking for sex.

A little more than halfway home, Holly Wood from the movie *Cool World* stepped out of the shadows. Not as shapely, not as pretty, darker complected and darker hair, but Holly Wood nonetheless. "Hey baby," she offered in a voice much more cartoonish than the movie, "want your dick sucked?"

"Uh, I'd love to honey, but I spent all my money at the bar." Actually, I probably had ten or twenty bucks but forgot I'd left early. Usually I don't have any money left when I go home.

"No money at all?"

"I might have some change..."

"How much you got?"

I dug in my pocket. "Maybe fifty cents."

"OK, that'll do!"

Nobody but a cartoon character from Springfield would be that cheap, I'm sure.

No, I don't blame you for thinking I made it up. I barely believe it myself.

Poll
LOL what?
- 16%
- 0%
- 33%
- 0%
- 50%
- 0%

Chapter 28: Saturday, written as Science Fiction from the early 1960s
Mon Jul 21, 2003 at 08:40:23 PM EST

But it's still not fiction, nor very scientific.

Patty's friend lost her grandmother, and she was staying the night Friday with her friend to keep her company. Patty's friend's grandmother had raised her friend.

Patty's a good kid. She promised to be home by 9:00 AM so I could go visit friends in St. Louis.

I woke up about nine, and wanted to sleep some more, but I didn't want to waste a perfectly good Saturday that I had planned travel on, so I got up.

I stuck some science fiction 21st century optical devices on my eyeballs and drank some coffee. The devices are great, they're nothing at all like sticking pieces of glass in your eyes, as you had to do back in the 1970s. This new, science fiction technology is usually completely invisible to the user.

Patty wasn't answering the voice communicator.

About quarter to ten she transmitted her coordinates via the aforementioned device, and said she overslept. Was it aliens? No, I believe her friend was born in the US. In fact, she doesn't have a foreign name. Now, if she had been named Gordo Burro, that would have perhaps been an interesting alien.

But this was just a blonde American kid.

I flipped a switch, and the computing device stirred to life, causing a pot of coffee to appear in its receptacle. I removed an antiseptic wrapping from a pastry and installed it in the radiation chamber for fifteen seconds. With butter.

I removed it from the chamber, and ate it. Not the chamber, I mean. I ate the pastry. I turned on my personal computer, and moved a cursor manipulator to the proper coordinates and clicked its button. After some whirring noises and blinking lights, my mail appeared on the computer's screen.

Damn, mostly junk mail. All but one or two went instantly into the trash, as junk electronic mail does here in the 21st century.

I love technology. Back in the past we had to talk to someone on the phone, tied down with a cord as if you were some trained, captive animal. Now we have these wireless science fiction communicators.

I backed the ancient machine down the driveway. The passenger compartment, as usual, reeked of exhaust fumes. The clear plastic window over the instruments in this old vehicle had a jagged hole in it, and there were a few dents and rust.

Bits of the antique foam rubber rained down on my head as I looked out the back window.

I filled up the ultra clean 21st century gasoline on the way, and got a carbonated beverage and a six pack. The old radio unprogrammed itself every time the car was shut off, obviously miswired. I tuned the old radio again, and made sure the 21st century communication device was handy. I called Mike's house on it before leaving. Somebody named "Ed," who wanted to know which Mike, answered. I told him "Old Mike," as this kid was obviously one of Mike Jr.'s friends. Ed said he was at Jeff's house.

Jeff has no outgoing communications, and limited broadcast receiving capabilities. His was an older model computer. So I decided to just drive over there.

By the time I got to the end of the hundred mile trip I was staggering from the carbon monoxide and other inhalants belching from the exhaust pipe. Mike was at Jeff's, as was Chris and his 25 year old son, Josh. I was starting to get a monoxide headache.

Josh had a little pot. His dad was drunk, as usual. But only a little drunk.

Chris hasn't had a driver's license for some time now.

Josh rolled a big joint and filled Jeff's pipe as we watched... uh, some movie. I remember seeing monkeys and a space ship or something.

When the movie was finished, they left. We followed them out.

The last time I'd seen Josh he had a new Kia. Now he was driving an old piece of shit with mud dauber nests under the hood. I asked him what happened.

"Had to let them repo it."

They drove off, and I remembered one of the excuses... er, "reasons" for coming down – to find out what kind of engine was in the Malibu. Mike had told me that Jeff had changed the engine with something else. Knowing what kind of engine was in it would certainly simplify buying the parts I needed for it.

Jeff told me the particulars, and said "that motor was in a high speed police chase."

One of his friends in California had owned a Pontiac Sunbird with a V-6, and it was stolen. The thieves used the stolen Sunbird to rob a bank, and a high speed chase ensued. The robbers were caught, after the Sunbird's frame was bent and it was pretty well otherwise trashed.

The car sat in the impound lot for months before Jeff's friend got it back. When his friend came to Illinois, he had the car transported on a flatbed truck. He gave it to Jeff, and Jeff put the motor in his Mom's old Malibu and junked the Sunbird.

We partied a little more, and I set off to make the hundred mile trip back to the 21st century. I wanted to see a local band, The Station, who was playing at Dempsey's at 10:00.

I got home, reeking of exhaust, and took a shower. Patty wanted money, like teenagers always do. "Can I have five dollars to get in the show?"

"No. All I have is a twenty and a ten."

"Well, give me the ten."

"No."

"I don't have anywhere to cash a check, and they'll charge me three dollars to use my card.

"Your bank sucks."

"Can I..."

"No!"

"How about I give you a ride to Dempsey's and you can give me a five? I'll be right down the street at Bread Stretchers."

"No, I just took a shower and I've had way too much carbon monoxide today. I'm walking!" I was starting to get a headache. I told her to get her friend, who she was giving a ride to, to cash a check for her, and I started to walk to Dempsey's.

"Dude, you're late."

Damn. I had to pay the two dollar cover. Mandy was tending bar, and was working hard; the place was pretty crowded. I got a Rolling Rock and a glass of water and sat at the bar and listened to the music.

There were quite a few rock and roll regulars – the Barbie doll, Hippie Chick (who I think is going to become a police woman, if I didn't confuse her with someone else a week earlier). A whole lot of young ladies who I wasn't even going to try to pick up.

A fat woman in her twenties was holding a cigarette as if she was waiting for someone to light it. I reached in my pocket and grabbed my lighter – and saw the wedding ring.

Nope, ain't gonna waste my butane. She kept giving me the sweet eye while her good looking girl friend ignored me.

Here's a hint, ladies – if you want to pick up an asshole, wear a ring on your wedding ring finger. Because those of us with sense and morals wouldn't fuck you with your husband's dick. If you want a decent guy, leave the jewelry off of that finger.

My headache was getting worse. After my second beer I walked back to the restroom. I saw Joe Frew's girl friend in the back. Good, I was looking forward to Joe sitting in with The Station to sing *Champagne and Reefer*.

As I walked out of the can I saw Joe behind the back bar. There was Levi in front of the back bar. "Hey, Steve!"

I sauntered over. The band took a break.

After talking with Joe and Levi for a while I decided to go out the back door and get a little fresh air and walk around. I walked out, and there were some guys standing and sitting around in the alley's dark shadows. I smelled tobacco – and reefer.

Joe and Levi followed me out. I was starting to walk down the alley. "Hey, man, where you going?"

I walked back. "I just came out for a little fresh air, I

have a headache from all that damned exhaust smoke."

Somebody said "Here, I got some fresh air for you," and handed me a pipe. The fellows standing around the alley were the band.

The pot helped my headache. The guys in *The Station* were happy for an extended break; there was another band sitting in.

One mentioned they were selling CDs for five bucks. I answered that last time I saw them they were giving them away.

"Yeah, our publicist found out about that and freaked out, man. But these are professionally done."

I mentioned yeah, I had heard the bad spot in the middle of the freebee, but didn't mention that I'll fix it when I make a copy.

Eventually we all walked back in and the band started playing again. I was talking with Levi, who always complained about not getting any girls, and Betty Boop walked in.

I like beer. Especially with Paxil.

"Hey, Levi!"

"Hey, Leslie!"

Leslie's friend was pretty good looking. Leslie said "Hi" to me and they both proceeded to ignore me and talk to Levi. I wandered back and got another beer from Joe, who was trying vainly to sell beer from the back bar while Mandy was working her ass off at the front bar.

Way too soon the lights came up and the music stopped. I bought a $5 CD and staggered on home.

I hadn't hit on a single woman! Does that mean I'm getting better, or was it just the monoxide?

Chapter 29: Friday night at home (and other dull stories)
Thu Jul 31, 2003 at 05:39:25 PM EST

This diary is so short and dull that I put off even reading it, let alone writing it.

Gee, I gave away the ending in the title... but these things always end the same, don't they?

This is a hard one, absolutely nothing happened this week worth penning, yet here I am typing. What a challenge!

Isn't "challenged" a euphemism for "retarded"?

I found some unopened mail in the living room last Sunday. One piece was a check from the mortgage company – they won't take less than the full amount. So I could have saved the interest charges on the expensive loan I took out to cover the even more expensive daily bank fees they were charging my daughter... at any rate, I had some cash.

I went to bed early Sunday night, and had trouble getting up Monday morning. The Paxil had me sleepy and queasy. It passed by the time I got to work.

As I was making changes to about 300 web pages, Married lady bounded in.

Married Lady has beady little eyes and curly hair, like a poodle. In fact, one of the bosses mentioned to me that Married Lady reminded her of a poodle, with her wild hair and doglike over-affection. I remarked that I preferred "too friendly" to surly.

Monday afternoon she wanted me to walk around the building with her on a break. So I did. She kept bumping my arm with her tittie.

Wednesday I got a $600 gas bill. I'd just paid the gas bill!

So I went to the gas company to find out what was up, and the check had bounced. Fuck. I'm going to stop writing checks. This is expensive!

The bank said I had $400 of the grand I had deposited. But at least I wasn't overdrawn. I hope they don't shut off my gas again.

Daughter Patty came home from work, got in the car and it wouldn't start. The battery was completely drained, without a hint of electricity in anything. So I checked the water, and it was low. Real low. I filled it up and stuck the charger on it.

The battery never woke back up. I'm walking again until I can get it to a battery shop.

Friday morning Married Lady blew me a kiss, and Friday afternoon she said I was cute.

Shit. The only woman in the whole damned world that

wants it from me is married.

Shit shit shit shit shit!

I went to bed early Friday night, without even going out. I've been kind of lethargic lately, not sure if it's the drug or symptoms peeking past the drug's mask. I think the latter.

I forgot to drug myself when I woke up. I've been doing that more and more often lately. Laid around the house all day without doing anything constructive, and walked down to Dempsey's for some music.

The music sucked. There was one guy with an acoustic guitar singing Locomotive Breath. And he stretched it out to about fifteen minutes.

Two ladies sat down at the bar next to me, one fumbling around for a lighter. Crap, I forgot my lighter.

Then I noticed they were both wearing wedding rings. In fact, I think every single woman in the place was married.

I went home early. At least I saved a little beer money.

Epilogue

I wrote this thing on Sunday or Monday and couldn't get into K5. Since then, I got the gas bill paid and bought a battery for the junker. And the mortgage company sent me a letter saying they are starting foreclosure proceedings.

Shit!

Poll:
How boring is this diary?
Who stole mcgrew's account?	4%
B O R I N G	4%
I went to sleep	0%
My spouse read it, and is now in the hospital in a coma	8%
I don't know, I never made it past the header	17%
More boring than watching a car rust	4%
I haven't been this bored since I was seven	13%
I don't know, I only visit K5 for the pictures	50%

Chapter 30: Duffy's "Pub"
Fri Aug 08, 2003 at 05:53:56 PM EST

K5... oh K5! Where are you, K5???

I haven't been able to get into the site all week, I think I'll email Q and a few other folks to find if anybody knows what's going on. Oh, there it is. Well hell, I'm emailing Q anyway.

In the meantime, I was amused to laughter last night. I actually met someone more trashy and redneck than Evil-X!

And Ted Nugent plays at the fair Monday the 11th.

I've been a bit ill all week, missed work Monday.

I was in a shitty mood yesterday. I called up my insurance company Wednesday and told them to drop the PT cruiser and add the junker. The PT is costing me $633 a year, and Evil-X has it. And my van is still broken. And my daughter has the junker more often than I do.

So I had been pretty happy that the insurance company seemed OK with dropping the Cruiser. They called me first thing yesterday, and told me that Evil-X had called and vetoed the cancellation. Damn!

Then Married Lady told me, again, how cute I was.

Then Evil-X called. "Where's Patty?" she demanded. "I don't know," I lied, "probably sleeping." Actually she had spent the night at her friend's house, but I'm so sick of X it's a pleasure to make the parasite worry.

She had, of course, dug it in a little farther a few days ago, telling me how she and her boyfriend got along so well, never fighting. Of course they get along, he's not supporting her parasitic ass (although he's paying for her cable TV), they're going out together all the time, unlike us when we were married and most of all, she's not telling him where his furniture has to go, what he can and can't eat (and when), that he has to be quiet and not watch TV or listen to the radio, what he can't and has to spend his money on...

I get in a bad mood talking to the fatassed ugly bitch. I'm glad she's gone. I wish she were gone completely, especially out of my car insurance.

I had told Patty that she had to be home and take care of her animals before lunch. No sign of her, and the cell phone didn't seem to be working. I had plans on grounding her.

She called at work while I was at a meeting, and left a voice mail message saying only "where are you?"

Well DUH, I'm at work.

When I finally started walking home (my house is only a few blocks from work), I stopped by the cell phone company to pay the bill, and it was huge. Did I go over my minutes?

No, the last check had bounced. Which was why the phone had stopped working.

I found a check for four hundred bucks from Uncle Sam in my mailbox – tax cut. OK, that's nice, but it isn't enough to buy my vote, George. But thanks, I can use the Goober Mint money.

I tried calling the cell again, and this time it rang. Patty answered. "Where are you?" I asked. "I'm at Faggot's waiting for Mom. Gasoline was spraying all over under the hood and I was afraid to drive it home."

And I had so looked forward to grounding her... she was off the hook, and came home about 45 minutes later. I was going to drive down to Dempsey's for a beer, but I let her talk me out of the car.

Like I said, I haven't felt very well all week, and wasn't going to walk to Dempsey's. So I decided to go to Duffy's.

It has been a fairly pleasant summer, except for the July 4th weekend. It seems our normal hellishly hot summer weather has been on vacation in Europe. I got hot yesterday, though, since the air conditioning at work was shut off or something; it was hotter inside than outside. I took a shower and walked to Duffy's.

I got a minipitcher and sat down by the north window and watched the sun set. Nice one last night, big orange and pink thunderheads in the distance. By the time the sun finished setting, there were a few empty stools at the bar, so I moved back over to a bar stool.

A couple walked in, a fat bald man who looked forty or fifty, and a redneck looking woman maybe twenty five, or even younger. "Looks like we get the last two stools," bald guy says. They sat down, she next to me and he next to her.

Somehow, I got involved in their conversation. I had finished most of my pitcher, as well as two or three beers before walking over. I had gotten into a jovial mood; these two were hilarious. She was trying to talk herself into a waitress job at his restaurant, and he was... well, it didn't take a mind reader to figure out what he was after.

I noticed a wedding ring, a very thin gold (or brass) one, no diamonds. "So," I said, "you're married? Where's your husband?"

"Oh, that asshole is at home. God damned dickhead, I hate his fucking guts."

"So, uh, if you hate him why don't you divorce him?"

"He doesn't want a divorce, and I can't afford one. I need a job."

Apparently the poor schmuck she was married to was supporting this woman, who was at least as evil as X.

"How long have you been married?" I asked conversationally. After all, if all I wanted was beer, I could drink it a lot cheaper at home. I was there to converse with and laugh at the rednecks.

"Almost a year."

"And you hate him?"

"Well, I only knew him for ten days before we were married."

"Ten days?"

"Yeah, I thought if I got married they'd let me have my four year old back."

"Huh?"

"Yeah, my Mom tricked me into signing him over for adoption."

"How did she do that?"

"I can't read. She told me it had to do with getting my dad out of prison."

"You can't read?"

"Well, not much. I'm dyslexic."

Her friend says "have you heard about the D.A.M.?"

"What's that?" I asked.

"Mothers Against Dyslexia!"

He had a million of 'em. He looked around to make sure there were only blue eyed rednecks around, and lowered his voice and asked, "what's the three things you can't give somebody from 15th street?"

"I don't know," I said.

"A black eye, a fat lip, or a job!"

She laughed uproariously. I'd heard it before. "I have to tell my dad that one!" she says.

"So," I asked, "What's he in prison for?"

"Armed robbery. At least he didn't kill anybody."

I was kind of at a loss for words.

"My mom's brother's in prison, too. Second degree murder, but he didn't really kill anybody..."

"Huh??" I asked, perplexed.

"He punched a pregnant woman in the stomach and she had a miscarriage."

Oh, there was a lot more. I wish I could remember it all... her stepdad was her uncle, because when her dad went to prison, her mom married his brother, who then went to prison himself. The whole thing was surreal, and I enjoyed it like a Cheech and Chong movie. I stayed longer than I usually do at Duffy's, just for the entertainment.

Poll:
WTF???

Beats me 10%
I don't know 20%
Huh? 20%
How should I know? 0%
I'm clueless 10%
Whatever you say 40%

Chapter 31: Brothers
Tue Aug 12, 2003 at 07:51:19 PM EST

I drove down to St. Louis over the weekend, and walked my legs off at the fair Sunday.

Ordinarily it's blistering hot this time of the year in central Illinois. My gratitude goes out to the UKians and other EUians who took it on themselves to trade weather with us so the fair would be so enjoyable.

Friday

I drove down to Dempsey's Friday night, and little was going on. Ro was tending bar, and Joe and Levi were supposed to play, but were late. As I couldn't sleep all morning Saturday, I missed the music.

Levi had been at the fair to see Hank Williams Jr. I drank a beer with him and Joe, and left before they picked up their guitars. Levi said ol' Hank is playing rock and roll these days, even covering ZZ Top.

Saturday

Saturday morning the alarm clock went off at 8:00. I finally rolled out of bed a half hour or so later, stumbled down the stairs and made a pot of coffee.

Illinois legislators have an annoying habit of taking a germ of a good idea, or at least what sounds like one, and implementing it in a fashion that, if anything, usually makes the problem it is supposed to solve worse. Witness, for instance, my inability to get the parasite and her God damned PT Cruiser off of my insurance.

Their "Children First" initiative is no exception. At least the only harm to come of it is the taxpayer loses a few bucks and a couple of hours.

The problem it was supposed to solve was that divorced couples kept showing back up in court, suing each other over custody, child support, and other nasty things that divorce causes. They decided to solve it by hiring some two bit hack to produce a series of videos about things that make the children of divorced parents lives a living hell.

You have to pay on a sliding scale. It cost me sixty one bucks.

Rather than wasting one morning and two hours, they break it into two sessions so you have to waste two mornings. Saturday was my second session.

Even though I had taken my kids to a real psychologist for family counseling (there were a lot of tears and shouting after Evil-X left us) I still had to go see the stupid videos.

And stupid they were. The actors were more amateurish than the worse skin flick's, and made William Shatner's portrayal of JT Kirk seem subtle and underplayed. The characters in the videos were psychopaths, all of whom needed strong psychiatric drugs, if not straitjackets, and none of whom would have been helped by the videos. One of the characters, for instance, had the kids spending the night at his house. The scene was in the morning, with the kids whining for breakfast and the dad drinking and snorting coke with his girlfriend in the bedroom. Another had a clinically depressed woman telling her little girl that if she chose to live with her dad "and that hussy, I'll die!"

In each and every one of the six videos, dad had a girlfriend while mom shared loneliness with the kids. I pointed this out to the presenter (who I presume was a psychologist, but I never saw any credentials), who told me that in nine years of showing the videos nobody had mentioned it.

I found this rather hard to believe. And if these videos were nine years old, then why were we given a "satisfaction survey" at the end? Perhaps it was for the satisfaction of flaming them mercilessly on paper, in order to keep us from burning the building down?

I had the ruined car battery to take down to Mike, so I tossed it in the trunk and dove down, dropping by Jeff's house in the Cahokia slum first.

I rode out to Mike's with Jeff, where we sat on his porch and drank beer and watched the clouds. Mike was already drunk when we got there, and was close to passing out when we left. I drank slowly, as I had another hundred miles to drive.

As we got back to Jeff's house, a woman friend of his showed up with a bag of pot, and rolled up a couple of big joints. It was almost dark by the time I left.

Sunday

I spent half of Sunday sleeping, and the afternoon doing chores. Tonight was Nazareth at the Fair. Daughter Patty was going to the fair with her friends, and wanted three bucks to get in. All I had was a twenty, so she went down to Walgreens and broke it, leaving me with seventeen.

I was on the internet and lost track of time; Nazareth was supposed to start at 8:00, and here it was seven already, and I hadn't even showered. Shit! I scraped a razor across my face, took a shower, and started walking.

Maybe I could catch part of the show.

The fair is weird, like everything else in Springfield. It only costs $3 to get in to the fair, but parking is $7. A bus ride is only seventy five cents, and I'm a cheapass.

I'm also stupid. I'm thinking that 9th street is only two blocks away, and the bus terminal another two blocks up, but forgetting that the bus starts downtown, not at the bus terminal. So I walk the mile down to Capitol street, making a little prayer that maybe I can catch the show, or at least part of it.

As I crossed Capitol, a bus was stopping at the light. I hurried down the street to the bus stop, just as the bus got there.

The bus driver was complaining about all the overtime he was putting in and how he only had four hours between shifts, so only four hours sleep.

When visiting Springfield, beware of the buses.

I paid my three bucks to get in the fair, and as I went in I asked a state cop where the show was. He gave me directions.

Bad directions. I walked for twenty minutes, and must have passed every building there. Twice. Except the one I was looking for.

I asked another cop and was given directions to the Colosseum. There was a horse show there.

I walked around some more, and asked again for

directions. The directions took me to the show – the other show, a redneck show. I asked for directions there, and for a map.

The map was almost as bad as the directions. I couldn't find the building that the show was supposed to be in anywhere on the map.

So I walked around aimlessly some more. It was dark, and I doubted that the show was even still on. I started looking for a beer tent.

As I was searching for the magical golden liquid, I saw a booth for one of the local radio stations, and asked them for directions. They gave me directions, and I walked... around in a big circle. So I whipped out the map and asked the guy to show me. He drew in the missing concert building, and put an X where his booth was.

Another fifteen minutes and I was at the show; or at least at a long walkway toward the show, where they were selling and taking tickets. Ladies, this is why men won't ask for directions!

I asked if the show was over.

"No, it hasn't started. They had some sort of 'technical difficulties' and there may not even be a show!"

I gambled my five bucks and got a ticket, and gave it to the lady at the gate two steps over, who tore it in half and gave me half.

I could hear a recording of Led Zeppelin as I walked up. I stopped at the concession stand, where they sold beer, beer, beer, and something from England that resembled beer, only dark and sweet. I got a beer: three bucks. I forgot that I had put the change for the five I gave them to get in the fair in my shirt pocket, so as I looked in my wallet it looked like I was only going to be drinking two beers. I made a mental note to drink slowly.

I sat down, and not two minutes went by before the Zepplin stopped abruptly and a new sound started in its place. People started cheering wildly. Four figures emerged from a big Winnebago, and the crowd cheered even louder, and Bics lit up all around. I don't know when I last saw lighters at a concert, probably back when Nazareth was still making records, before most of the people with the lighters were even born.

Here's a clue for you younger hippie wannabes: the lighters are supposed to come out *after* the band plays, demanding an encore. Although in this case, since the band was (luckily for me) so tardy, it was probably fitting. The meaning behind the lighters is, after all, "I'm fucking stoned and if you don't play (insert smash hit here) we're gonna burn this God damned place to the ground!"

The band reached the stage, the lead-in sound reached a crescendo, and the lights came up as the music simultaneously exploded.

It's been so long since I had that Nazareth tape out I forgot how good they rocked. After the first tune, the lead singer apologized profusely for the hassle and delay. Again, the crowd cheered wildly.

Several songs later, my plastic Budweiser bottle was empty, so I ambled back to the concession area and bought another one.

Folks were coming and going, and there were a lot of plastic beer bottles vended. I went back to my seat and started drinking... slowly.

Someone stepped up behind me and stuck a beer bottle in my face. I took it, and looked at the goateed fellow for a second... Tommie!

Tom is my former stepbrother; my dad was married to his mom a few years after my mom divorced him. I used to drink with Tom all the time, but I hadn't seen him in at least ten years. He was at the concert with his brother, and had recognized me despite my short hair and lack of spectacles, and in the dark. I don't know how.

I walked down and sat with him and his brother, who didn't recognize me at all. "I used to be your stepbrother," I told him. He looked puzzled. "When?"

The lighters weren't the only thing the young folks were trying to bring back. Thick, sweet smoke drifted up from the people in front of us. "I wish I had some of that," Tom said.

I replied, "back in the day they would have passed that around."

"Those days are long gone, my friend," Tom said. "I'll buy if you fly," he added, handing me an empty bottle and a twenty.

By the time the concert ended, I was stumbling drunk. It was probably the first time I ever kept up drinking with Tom.

The band left the stage, and the lighters came back. Including, this time, mine. I have a blister on my thumb now...

They came back on and encored with a couple of songs as fireworks went off across the fair behind them.

My "brothers" gave me a ride home. The only thing I didn't like about the concert was that Nazareth was selling CDs, and they wanted twenty bucks each for them. I'll just have to sample the tape and make my own CD.

Monday

I got to the fair in plenty of time, with plenty of money, and two beers under my belt. I wanted a head start on the beer, as they want three bucks for a bottle at the fair. I guess the folks who run the fair can't tell the difference between Budweiser and Heineken. At any rate, I don't even like paying bar prices, but bar price plus half again is robbery.

Nazareth had been five bucks, "Sweaty Teddy" was twenty. Nazareth had been in the "Multipurpose Arena," Nugent was at the Grandstand.

The five dollar show was better.

A lady from work was checking tickets for proper seating. "Moonlighting?" I asked. She just grinned.

The Fabulous Thunderbirds didn't play very long at all,

unlike a couple of years ago when they opened for George Thorogood. This time they only played perhaps a side and a half of a vinyl album's worth. Disappointing.

Nugent fans must be moronic cows. There were two beer tables, one at either side of the not very large concession area. The one on one end had lines ten people deep, while the other had ladies standing around yelling "cold beer here!" as if they were hawkers at a baseball game.

I like going to concerts with morons. I don't have to wait in line!

Nugent was good, played a lot of his best songs, and unlike the T-birds, played for a long time. It got too late for me, and I stumbled back to the bus and home.

I was late to work this morning.

Chapter 32: Car Bombs
Sun Aug 24, 2003 at 05:31:23 PM EST

Sorry there was no diary for the last week or three.

I've had stomach troubles, coupled with the blues. Why the blues?

Well, there are the obvious reasons. My broken van got repossessed a week ago Friday night. I got foreclosure papers served Saturday. I'm in the middle of divorce proceedings and will be filing for bankruptcy.

And if that isn't enough, I'm trying to get off the Paxil. I feel like the guy in the movie *Airplane*, "Sure picked a lousy week to quit [insert name of substance here]". Maybe I should go back up to a full dose... but I'm on my last bottle, and I have to see the doctor to get them refilled again. And doctors are the primary reason for my bankruptcy, besides X having left me in debt and overdrawn last year.

At any rate, I think what's got me the bluest is the fact that even though I got rid of the nerd glasses and got my hair cut, and even gained a few pounds, I still can't get a date!

People who aren't lonely can't seem to understand loneliness. "But your daughter's living there..." Well yeah, I have friends, too. But offspring and friends are no cure for the need for companionship.

I fear I'll never hold a woman again...

Last weekend I had stomach trouble, and stayed home all weekend, mostly sleeping. Except Friday, when I had an uneventful night at Dempsey's, and returned to find the van, not unexpectedly, gone. Repossessed by the bank.

Monday morning I had the liquid shits. I called the boss lady and told her I'd be in as soon as I could get off the pot. "That's too much information! We'll see you when you get in."

I got there about 9:00... and went back home at 10:00. Boss lady said I looked like hell, that I should go back home and get some sleep.

Married Lady is working full time now, so she spent the rest of the week prick teasing. I don't know if she realized she was or not.

Friday night I had some bills to pay. I took care of one, then drove to the north part of town to pay the other one. The asshole doctor, a really nice lady.

Oh, I'm sorry, that last statement might have been a bit confusing considering the previous context. I should have said she's a proctologist. A good looking one, too, and skilled. And of course, when someone's cutting me a new asshole I prefer skill to beauty.

The ass doctor closed up long before I got there.

It was hot as the car had no AC, and Dempsey's was on the way home so I stopped for a beer. Joe Frew was tending bar. "Hey, we don't want your type in here!"

"Hi Joe, howarya?"

"Good, you want a Rolling Rock?"

The sign said Bush was a buck fifty. I got a Busch.

"Any music tonight?" I asked. "Yeah," he said, "I'm playing."

"Well, I'll have to come back," I said.

"It's my old band. We don't play much anymore."

I drank my beer and drove home. I watched the sunset, drank another beer, listened to random MP3s and enjoyed the solitude. My daughter was spending the night at her mother's. X was somewhere in the Ozarks with "Faggot," as Patty calls him, and she was supposed to be keeping an eye on her autistic older sister.

At nine thirty or so I started walking up to Dempsey's. As I walked toward it, Joe and his band were walking around the corner from the alley. "How much did I miss?" I asked.

Joe laughed. "You missed everything." They went in as I stood outside and talked to Levi.

"My band's playing here tomorrow," he said. I promised I'd be back the next day.

Joe's old band was good, and sounded better the more I drank. I lost track of time, and didn't hit on a single woman. Of course, there weren't many in there anyway, even though people were coming and going all night

A young thin blond fellow with a short dark goatee, whose picture would have fit the K5 photo page well, bellied up to the bar next to me. "Oil 'ave a blow job," he said with a hint of a Dublin accent.

I laughed. "Dying to find out just what one is, eh?" I said. He laughed.

"They have car bombs, too," I added.

He looked at me. "Yeer oirish."

"Well, most of my ancestors were." He stuck out his hand, and I shook it. "I'm Steve."

"Oim Steve, too," he replied. "Ow 'bout that, two oirishmen and both named Steve! 'ave a drink with me?" he asked. "Sure," I answered. He ordered two car bombs.

I'd never had a car bomb.

Car bombs are a terrorist drink, invented by the Irish Republican Army during "the troubles", according to Steve.

The bartender poured two glasses of Guinness, and two shots of something brown and foamy from a mixing jar.

"Yeer supposed to drink the whole thing at once, now," he said, and raised his shot glass in a toast. We clinked glasses and dropped them in the Guiness, and downed them.

"Tastes a bit like a chocolate shake," I opined, and washed it down with the rest of my Busch.

"Ye *oar* Oirish!" he exclaimed. "Ya only hesitated a little in the middle, I was watchin'."

Levi seemed equally impressed with my drinking.

"I've been drinking all night," I said. "My first," Steve said. Ro, the bartender, called last call. I got another beer.

"Where's more booze?" Steve asked.

"The Station's playing at the top of the Hilton," Levi said. We all finished our drinks and wandered outside. Even though the Hilton is only a few blocks, everyone got into cars. Levi offered me a ride, and I was much too drunk to worry about how drunk he was.

"I wish I had some pot," Levi mused.

He had gotten me stoned a few times, and I'd never once gotten him high. And I had a couple of joints worth stashed at home since forever, waiting for when I could lure a female human into my lair.

"I have a little bit at home," I said.

"How do we get there?" he asked.

As we pulled up he asked "Is that a house or an apartment?"

"House," I told him.

"Wow, big."

He spied the guitars, the clarinet cases, the sax in its case, the piano... "Wow, nice piano," he said as he opened the keyboard and started playing. "Kinda out of tune though..."

We smoked the joints, and went back downtown to the Hilton.

The place was packed. It took half an hour to get beers, and by the time I got back to the table where everyone was sitting, my beer was empty. I went home.

I'd planned on traveling to Columbia to see Mike the next day. I woke up with a hangover, and took a Paxil, and aspirin, and a vitamin with a couple glasses of water. I drank a couple cups of coffee, and found a couple of roaches and some pot I had drunkenly spilled on the table the night before.

It's a good thing I was so drunk that I'd spill that,

because pot is a great hangover cure. I scraped up the spilled reefer and the roaches and rolled a doob.

I called my cell phone, and Patty said she didn't have a ride home. I told her I needed the phone, and I would drop by. I had her give me directions there. I'd only been at X's trailer once, and that was at night.

I drank another cup of coffee, and drove up to the gas station. I filled the car, put transmission fluid and steering fluid in it, and cleaned the windshield. I bought more tranny and steering fluid, a six pack, and some pastry for breakfast.

Yes, I know I should edit that sentence for clarity, but the vision of beer and tranny fluid for breakfast is an amusing one, and you know what I mean.

I went home, and ate my pastry and drank some more coffee. I poured the rest into my thermos, and started out to X's trailer.

The car wasn't running quite right.

I took the Chatham exit and went down the road. The engine started running even worse.

I smelled gasoline, and started looking for a good place to check things out. As I started eyeing the shoulder, a "WOOMP!!" sound came out from under the hood, along with thick black smoke. The engine died at the same time, and I wrestled the car to the side of the road.

Power steering and power brakes are great... until you have no power.

There were flames licking around the hood, and I tossed the thermos out and got an old coat from the trunk to try and beat the flames out. I pulled the hood release, and it came out by a foot. I ran around to the front and started beating at the flames with the old coat.

A guy stopped, and had a fire extinguisher. I emptied it as he called 911 which, the policeman later noted, were the last three digits of my vehicle identification number.

As I was losing hope of salvaging the car, I heard a siren. The fire department!

Nope, a cop. Chatham has a volunteer fire department, and it was Saturday.

By the time a fire truck got there, the car was completely engulfed in flame.

So much for visiting Mike.

Chapter 33: It's been such a long, long, long time
Sun Aug 31, 2003 at 03:30:35 PM EST

"All you touch and all you see is all your life will ever be" – Pink Floyd

Like a stray bit of star or an insignificant giant planet caught in a black hole's event horizon, it gets closer and closer, but never seems to happen. If you've seen my diaries before, you know how this is going to end...

Friday night was enjoyable, but for the most part uneventful. I typed a screed about the RIAA and how it is blatantly breaking the No Electronic Theft Act and possibly the Digital Millennium Copyright Act by downloading thousands of suspected songs of its members. I submitted it for editing, and walked on down to Dempsey's.

I was early, and the band was late.

Dempsey's is more and more becoming a haven for musicians and other artsy types; not just to play in, but to drink in as well. Joe Frew was there, and Levi, and a couple of fellows from The Station. The women there Friday were all with men, mostly with friends of mine.

The other Joe, one of the owners, was tending bar. Joe Frew, who does booking for Dempsey's, was annoyed, as the guy he booked never showed up. We drank, and talked, and played video games.

I've always been a retard at remembering peoples' names, especially when I meet a few at once. They all know my name and I know their faces, but damned if I can remember any names.

I've always been bad at remembering names. My weird brain lets me down. If I read it in a book, it stays in my head seemingly forever, no matter how unimportant and trivial. But if I hear it as speech it drains away from my neurons very quickly. My visual cortex must be overdeveloped at the expense of my audio cortex, I guess.

One girl was scribbling on the Illinois Times. I could tell by the way she held her pen she was an artsy type, nobody holds a pen like that without training. It's hard to meet a chick like that without thinking of the Dead Milkmen's *Instant Club Hit* ("You'll dance to anything....")

Joe said some friends were going to come by later and he'd see if he could get them to play.

Sure enough, they showed up around 11:30, and sure enough, he talked them into it. They didn't even charge him for the gig!

Several beers, laughs, and tunes later it was closing time, and I walked home. I logged on to K5, put the story to a vote, and went to bed.

I'd been tired all week. Maybe it was the heat, maybe it was the getting off of the Paxil, maybe I haven't been sleeping well, but when I woke up it was 5:00 PM. I don't believe I ever slept so late in my life.

I checked my mail, looking for the "your story was rejected" email, but it wasn't there. There had been half a dozen stories in the edit and voting ques, but now there was only one. Scoop must have been hungry, I guess.

My daughter asked if she could spend the night at her friend's, and I said OK. I used to relish the thought of her spending the night with friends, as if I met a woman I could take her home, but I've pretty much given up on that ever happening.

I fiddled around on K5 for a while, and noticed it was dark outside. I logged off, took a shower, and started walking downtown.

There was supposed to be a band from Indianapolis at Dempsey's. One of Joe's friends, a Jewish looking fellow, had laughed Friday about ripping them off; he was renting his mixer equipment to them for half their pay. The fucker. If he has a girlfriend I'm going to try to seduce her. Ripping off the poor, that's just damned evil.

As I was walking down the street to Dempsey's, I saw three women walking in. Two slim brunettes and a fat blonde. Well, this looked promising, at least there would be nice scenery. The band was running late, it was after 10:00, but they were just lugging in equipment. They said "hi" as I walked in, so I chatted a bit.

"All the way from Indy, I hear?"

"Yeah, damn it's a long drive, 3 hours."

Wow, they must have flown down the highway. Indianapolis should take more than three hours.

The question I always half-jokingly ask, "So, are you

guys any good?"

They laughed. "Hope so!" one said.

The only one in the bar I recognized was Mandy, tending it. Mandy's a farmer's daughter, and although she's not bad looking, and has a really nice body, she always has a serious look on her face. Workaholic type, hates it when it's slow. Her look tonight was downright annoyed.

I hadn't seen her in several weeks. I got a beer and asked her what was wrong.

"Fucking weirdos tonight, nothing but freaks. They're pissing me off!"

The place wasn't all that busy, but she did have a few clients. She went off to fill someone's drink.

The three girls who had walked in a block's length ahead of me were laughing. There was the fat blonde, who would have been a knockout if she'd lose half her body mass or more. One of the brunettes had a nice body, and a face halfway between beautiful and homely. I couldn't put my finger on what was wrong with her looks; perhaps the half Paxil I'd taken was affecting my vision. It does that at times. It had earlier, as I was walking; colors were brighter than normal, the darkness wasn't so dark, and things looked a bit unreal.

The third woman would have been extremely good looking, except for one blemish that stood out like someone had vandalized a Van Gogh with a magic marker – she had a pierced lip. And she seemed very intoxicated.

But of course she was intoxicated. "Wish me a happy birthday!" she said to nobody in particular.

"Happy birthday," I exclaimed loudly. She had cash in her hand. "Hey" I said, "it's your birthday, you get to drink for free!"

"Oh wow, I forgot, thank you!"

Before I could move over with them, some Latin Romeo moved in first. Damn!

I meant that literally. The fellow was Hispanic, and he claimed his name was Romeo. This seemed to tickle the girls.

Shit.

But they got tired of him quickly, it seemed. I suspected he was broke.

Birthday girl slithered over and put her arm around my neck, and thanked me again. "Dance with me?" she asked.

I don't dance, but how could I refuse? My dick was getting hard...

The band was still setting up, but the jukebox was playing. I danced with her.

"You dance funny," she said.

"That's because I don't know how to dance," I admitted.

She seemed to like that, and did an impromptu pelvic bump and grind. I don't think I've ever been so horny.

Somehow we wound back over by her friends, who seemed a bit left out. By now I would have even done the blonde, and fat girls are a turnoff for me.

Birthday Girl had a small tattoo on her right shoulder. It was too close for my old farsighted eyes to read.

Thoroughly enchanted, I offered to buy the three of them a drink. Romeo said, "buy me one too?"

I grinned. "You're the wrong gender!"

The girls laughed.

Birthday girl wanted to drink a tequila with me, and I told her sure, so long as they had salt and lime. I bought two tequilas, and blow jobs for Birthday Girl's friends.

Somehow Romeo got between me and Birthday Girl. Somehow, the enchantress made him disappear.

The four of us toasted Birthday Girl, and she wound up in my lap making out with me. I couldn't believe it! After a year, here was a woman half my age in my lap, her hands all over me and mine all over her.

"I want to take you home," I said.

And then it was over. Her friends got her off of me and toward the door. "Wait!!" I protested, "the music hasn't even started yet!"

"Give me your number!" she said.

I wrote it down, and made a point to make sure her friends heard me tell her to share my number with them.

The chick was so loaded I doubt she'll even remember me. They walked out the door and left me with a hard on.

I got another beer and finished half of it with a single swallow. So close, so close...

But I had felt a woman's body next to mine. Better than nothing!

I asked one of the guys from the band if they had a CD. Not only do I like collecting indie CDs, I felt bad for these guys. After gas and paying Joe's ripoff friend half their gig money for renting his box, they were playing for maybe minimum wage if they were lucky.

"Uh, yeah, we have a pretty old one. I think we have maybe two out in the truck. Four bucks."

I put four dollar bills on the counter and he went to get the CD. He almost forgot to take the money.

I talked with Joe's ripoff friend for a bit, and went back around the bar to talk with Mandy.

Mandy hadn't liked the birthday girl. This puzzles me, she couldn't have been jealous. I'd run across Mandy in another bar as a patron and tried unsuccessfully to hit on her.

Can one of you K5 ladies explain this to me?

The band started playing, finally. Some people started coming in. Women. Lots of women. Another birthday party for another birthday girl.

I didn't meet this one.

As Mandy was serving someone, two women sidled up next to me holding cash, a tall blonde and a short brunette wearing a long sleeve shirt and a pair of short shorts that revealed a beautiful pair of legs.

I got a case of asperger's and didn't know what to say. I drummed my fingers on the bar in time to the music. The young lady did, too. Still I sat there stupidly. They got their drinks and moved over to a table.

I mentally kicked myself in the ass for being such an ass

burger nerd geek dork wanker. Damn! I wish I knew how to pick up women. I could have had that one, if only I knew how. Damn damn damn damn damn! And shit!

"See that girl over by the videogame, the one with the short brown hair?" Mandy asked.

"Yeah?"

"She's a bitch!"

Mandy wasn't having a very good night. Seems the woman had bitched at her because a Dempsey's blow job wasn't the blow job she had expected.

A lot of the women there who should have been having a good time were frowning. They were the ones with men on their arms.

I doubt I'll ever understand women. Except in this case, I suspect that the Pietasters had the right answer: "Zantac. Because life's too fucking short!"

Well, at least I had a good time. So close, so close...

Poll
Wow, Rusty changed the poll options for more choices! Cool!
Yes 0%
No 0%
Maybe 20%
I don't know 0%
Who cares? 10%
What makes you think I have a clue? 0%
Forty-two 30%
Whatever 0%
G.W. Bush 20%
war 0%
peace 0%
piece 0%
lose 0%
loose 10%
 (this poll option is reserved) 10%

Chapter 34: What a long, strange morning it's been
Mon Oct 13, 2003 at 07:08:36 PM EST

The alarm clock rang annoyingly at 5:40, as it always does. I slapped "snooze" and went back to sleep, oblivious to the strange morning that was in front of me.

Several snooze slaps later and I was staggering to my feet. I stumbled downstairs and poured a cup of coffee from the thermos, and poured some of that white powder that's supposed to substitute for cow's milk in it. I went on down to the farthest corner of my basement, where the last working toilet in the house is.

When the house was new, it was the only toilet. Back in 1918 when it was built (state of the art, gas *and* electric!) people thought the idea of defecating inside your home was disgusting. Indoor plumbing and indoor toilets were new. Heck, both my sets of grandparents had outhouses when I was little. So because the idea of *shitting inside the house* was so... *ugh!,* they put the toilet in the basement next to the coal room, which was at least as disgusting as human waste.

I started a new pot of coffee before starting my second cup, and drank sleepily as the coffeepot gurgled. I went upstairs to shave, shower, and brush my teeth.

I got dressed for work, and drank another cup. I filled the thermos with the fresh coffee, grabbed a box of honey buns and took Patty's car to work, as she was off school for Columbus Day.

I got to work and parked. Wow, great spot today. I must have gotten here a little early. I went inside and the guard said to sign in. I showed him my ID, and he said "you have to sign in anyway. It's a holiday."

"Huh? I don't have to work today?"

"Well, there are a few contractors here..."

"Heh... in that case I'll see ya!"

I went back home.

About 8:30 the phone rings. It's Evil-X.

"Is Patty awake?"

I laugh out loud. Patty? Awake at 8:30 when she doesn't have school?

"Well, I have her permission slip."

"What permission slip?"

"For school."

"For what?"

"I don't know. She forgot and left it at my house."

"Well, do you want me to have her call you when she gets up?"

"I'm outside."

"What do you mean you're outside?"

"I mean I'm outside!"

"Outside of what?"

"Outside your house, where do you think? I have that permission slip."

I walked in the living room, where a looming shadow darkened my door. I opened the door, and there it stood.

"Uh, ya want to come in?" I asked, after Evil-X stood there dumbly for a minute like the door had never opened.

"You got coffee?"

Shit. I let it in, and looked at the paper. It was a permission slip I had signed for a school field trip.

I poured her a cup of coffee. As usual, she was Paxil's antidote, telling me how they were going to take my house away.

My God, but she's gotten fat and ugly. Uglier, I mean.

"I'll go wake Patty up." I wanted to escape. Damn, how I hate being a nice guy.

I knocked on her bedroom door. "Your Mom's here."

"It's 8:30. I'm sleeping! Tell her to come back later."

Poll:
Did you miss me?
No 5%
Hell no 5%
You were gone? 23%
Who the fuck are you? 23%
Why sure, sweetie! 41%

Chapter 35: Bar Fight!
Sat Nov 08, 2003 at 02:44:48 PM EST

NOTE: Penned Monday, posted Saturday

Bad moon rising?

Last weekend (OK, the weekend before last) was boring. This weekend was angst-filled for everyone except, it seems, me.

I'm blaming drugs on my lack of recent diaries.

I owe a very nice lady a phone call, but I have to call after 8:00 PM and Patty always has the long distance phone (free LD on the cell).

A month ago (plus a few days or so) I went to the doctor to get my Paxil refilled. I had been dosing down, and then quit for a week or two, thinking that it has been long enough that I should be able to get off of the damned things.

But then the first anniversary of Evil-X's leaving passed without my having as much as a date, let alone sex (except the one fifty cent oral), and it really got me depressed. So I went back to the Doc to get my prescription refilled.

She changed it and said she wanted to see me in a month.

I had been on the straight dose 20mg of Paxil; she put me on the time-release 37.5mg ones. I felt like a lifeless zombie, incapable of any emotion. Including the desire to log on to K5 much.

I didn't like it a bit.

So when I went back, I asked for the old ones back, and she wrote a new prescription. When I went to get it filled, I found out why the new time-release Paxil had been prescribed.

Kickbacks.

Apparently, Paxil's patent ran out. I got generic, and only had to pay seven bucks; the real deal cost me fifteen, and that was my co-pay; the actual bottle of drug was well over a hundred dollars.

Hooray that our patent system, unlike our copyright system, is really time limited like the Constitution proscribes. Thank God that the patent holders don't have nearly as good of lobbyists as the copyright holders, who "own" the copyrighted work forever, at least compared to a human's life.

So anyway, I went downtown to Dempsey's. No band. Interestingly, it was in the process of changing hands again; the guy with the expensive mixing board was buying it.

There not being any music, I just drank one beer and went home. OK, maybe I drank two beers.

Monday or Tuesday I walked home from work for lunch, and was greeted by an angering and depressing letter: the divorce hearing had been pushed back by X's lawyer. I thought of calling my lawyer to ask if it was legal to shoot lawyers, but that would have eaten into my retainer fee. So I didn't.

When I got home, there was another letter, from my lawyer. The hearing was now on the 24th, and it was a "status hearing", whatever that is, and I don't have to be there.

Friday night I went back to Dempsey's. One of the old owners, Joe, a large, muscular, linebacker-type fellow who obviously is no stranger to freeweights and steroids, was tending bar. No band.

I drank one beer and left, and walked down to Bread Stretcher's. I got two subs, ate one, and stuck the other in my coat pocket (BIG pockets!).

I walked on home, put the big sandwich in the refrigerator, drank another beer and went to bed. It was just as well I got to bed early, as I had gotten a letter from the city saying if I didn't cut the overgrowth in the alley behind my house down, the city would, and would charge me $275.00 per hour for the privilege. I guess they have a couple of lawyers cutting brush.

Of course, when I got up Saturday it was raining. And there was no string on my weed eater (I had stupidly let Evil-X borrow it).

I had Patty give me a ride to Dempsey's.

It looked to be another one beer night; no music. But it wasn't busy, and Mandy was tending bar and needed someone to talk to. So I stuck around to lend an ear.

She was upset; she had kicked her boyfriend out a week earlier. They had been together for years.

So, I stuck around and tried to make her feel better, talking to her and the bouncer, a heavy guy who appears to have more experience with a TV and potato chips than freeweights and steroids.

The new owner was to take over Monday (that's today).

Joe Owner came in. He was drunk. He was pissed. I somehow got the idea that he had been screwed over royally in the bar deal, maybe even losing his entire investment in the place. I don't know the details, though. But he was very, very upset.

He wanted his "goddamned remote control!"

Mandy didn't know where it was. Bouncer didn't know where it was. Joe got aggressive and physical, in a pushing match with Bouncer. Mandy was screaming and crying, already upset about breaking up with her boyfriend and obviously didn't need this.

As I contemplated stepping in and helping Bouncer (and surely getting my old ass kicked in the process), Joe turned his attention to a couple of large fellows at a table who obviously thought the whole show made Monty Python look somber and serious in comparison.

Bouncer was on his cell phone. "Damn it, I need cops here NOW! NOW, do you hear me? He's going to tear the Goddamned place apart! Get some help here!!"

Mandy was sitting on the stool next to me sobbing. Joe Owner left, maybe two minutes before four armed men in uniform came in. Bouncer talked to them, and took over Mandy's bartending duties until she could compose herself.

Things quieted down, the few folks who were in there left, and Joe Frew came in. He was looking for a name for his new band. So, what are your ideas for the name of Joe's new band? Joe is about the best blues singer I know. He makes a lot of the famous, recorded blues guys sound like shit.

Eventually the place closed. Mandy drove me home.

Chapter 36: Court Hearing
Tue Nov 25, 2003 at 09:54:17 PM EST

I have a foreclosure hearing next month. And another divorce hearing.

Thank God I have a sense of humor!

Back about a month ago my lawyer copied me in a "shit or get off the pot" letter to Evil-X's lawyer, stating "we're going to court on (whatever the hell date it was) to decide this divorce..." with, of course, a bunch of wherases and other mumbo-jumbo almost comprehensible lawyer nonsense.

Hooray! I had been goading my lawyer since I had hired her in June. Yeah, yeah, she was cheap and I was broke...

Anyway, the very next day I get a copy of a letter from X's lawyer to the judge saying he couldn't be there because of some convention or something in Chicago.

So the judge moved it up a month. This past Monday, to be exact. My lawyer said it was only a status hearing and I didn't have to be there.

Somehow a week or so ago I found Evil-X in my face as I always do, cursed as I am, who informed me that her lawyer told her she better be at the hearing!

I'm thinking along the lines of "holy fucking shit". Something like that. I also figured it wouldn't hurt to take a two hour vacation and a hike in the cold. After all, Satan Itself is arrayed against me.

So I tell the new boss lady (I'm on loan at work, did I mention?) I have a court hearing and need a two hour vacation and she says sure.

Monday I show up at work bright and early, and by the time I got to work, Patty had somehow wrangled the position of chauffeur. "Meet me at 8:30," I told her.

Eight thirty and my youngest daughter chauffeurs me to my first divorce hearing. She thought she had a right to be there.

I thought it was too cold to walk.

"Look," she says as we pull into the parking lot, "there's Mom's car." She parks next to it.

It's almost as cold as my ex-wife's heart as we cross the street to the courthouse. I ask for directions as I surrender my knife and go through the metal detector.

We ascend to the higher reaches of the building, and get

out to see huge windows. Six floors up. Very nice view, I was glad I wasn't afraid of heights. "Oh, you're afraid of water? Sorry, you've got the wrong courthouse. You want the one in the aquarium."

I noticed the braille on the elevator buttons and pictured a large blind man walking into one of those windows... I wonder how strong they are?

We walk closer to the courtroom and there it sits. Scowling, of course. I tried not to look. "Uh, excuse me, I have to go to the rest room..."

I really did. My bowels were, as they say, "in an uproar".

My lawyer was talking to the bailiffs. Someone please look up "bailiff" and see if I spelled it right. Yes, I've had a few beers.

Where was I? Oh yeah, my lawyer. "Can I help you?" one of the bailiffs asked. "He's waiting for me," she said.

Evil-X's lawyer had called my lawyer to say he wasn't coming.

So I chat with Patty and my lawyer until the judge comes in, and after the judge judges some other people he gets around to me, and actually pretty quickly, too.

My lawyer talks to him for two minutes and that's that.

Now there's another hearing in 3 weeks. The day before my foreclosure hearing.

I ask my lawyer how long before I have to move.

"Nine months. And don't pay any bills except your utilities!" She had already told me that since X had declared bankruptcy, I now had to since I was responsible for her debts. Even to the landlord she rented from when she moved out so she could fuck that other guy.

So anyway, why in hell couldn't we have done this a month ago?

As we were leaving the courtroom, and down the elevator, I had the pleasure of watching Patty deride Evil-X's choice of lawyers. She used lovely words such as "stupid" and

"incompetent" and she said it gloatingly.
Oh, I love my children so!

Chapter 37: I'm getting a final divorce decree for Christmas!

Mon Dec 15, 2003 at 09:33:45 PM EST

Please be advised that this is not the usual mcgrew diary. No drinking or chasing women in this one.

So, I went to court today for the dissolution of my damned marriage.

I'm pretty bummed. And pissed. There is no justice in Illinois, it seems.

No justice, no morality. The law is rock rigid, and is based on 1950 Ozzie and Harriet rather than the 21st century George and Jane Jetson.

But I'm ranting, and probably not making a bit of sense since you can't possibly have a clue what I'm babbling about.

So I'll start last week, when I got a letter Wednesday from my lawyer. The letter was a reminder of my Monday court date (wow, mcgrew got a date!).

It also had some crap about my debts and meager assets to fill out. And some stuff I wasn't sure I understood that I had to ask my lawyer about.

So I call the lawyer Thursday, and get squared away with the questions, involving a very humorous typo – they spelled my name "Hilda Mallory".

So I needed to fill this stuff out, and get it to her Friday night.

Work is moving me to another office five miles south, so now I need a car. By the middle of January, when the move happens.

The good news is that's where they moved an old boss who always treated me well, a more intellectual type with a PhD and two unrelated Master's. My knowledge of statistics is from a book he wrote, and two more he gave me. They had completely dismantled my unit, and had me "on loan" to another unit, Dave's.

Of course, after the dismantled unit was gone and its members scattered, they realized that the dismantled unit was necessary. So they just moved the office to where most of the people had been moved to. Boy, those guys that run things sure are intelligent, no wonder the economy is so good and unemployment so low.

Thursday night was to be a unit dinner after work, and there was to be a unit meeting most of Friday.

So, how long could dinner last, right?

I got home about 9:30. I sat down at the papers, and fell asleep. I don't remember going to bed, but the papers never got filled out.

Friday I got home from work and started on the papers. I finished right at five, and called my lawyer's Springfield office.

They were closing in a minute or two, but they had a slot in the door and besides, my lawyer got sick in court and had to be driven home by her husband. From the way they talked, I didn't think my lawyer would be in court Monday.

Mike had called from Columbia a week earlier and told me about a car for sale.

Charlie's mother's car supposedly needed some unspecified big budget items replaced, so Charlie paid Mike's brother $500.00 for an 88 Celebrity and had the brakes fixed, the alternator and fuel pump replaced, and tuned it up and cleaned it up.

Charlie's mom didn't want a different car. She wanted hers fixed. And the Chevy gone.

So I drove down there Saturday and paid $500 for the car. Mike would have driven it back for me he said, but it was slick and snowy and he was drunk.

It runs nice, except it needs shocks. Probably cost as much as I paid for the car. I left Mike's and drove home in the snow.

I got home fairly early. I ate dinner, and about 10:00 went down to Dempsey's to see if there was any music. There was; Joe Frew was playing.

And the one dollar Rolling Rocks are back! Woohoo!

Monday reared its dreary head this morning in anticipation of the pending divorce. I went to the courtroom, put my stuff in the tray, shoved my coat into the X-Ray box, and walked through the metal detector as half a dozen or more armed people stood around directing more normal, unarmed people.

I found my way to the same floor I had been on during the previous hearing, and found when asking that I was on the wrong floor.

I got to the seventh floor and found the courtroom, and sat in front of a very unattractive woman who smiled at me broadly, as if to say "fuck me now!"

I shuddered, and smiled weakly back and sat down.

The hearing was at nine, and by ten after I didn't see my lawyer or the judge.

Finally a bailiff said "all rise" and the judge said "sit down". The judge then spoke to lawyers and the court reporter and somebody said something about some guy in jail.

I asked the bailiff if I was in the right courtroom. He checked with the court reporter, and I was indeed in the right place. No lawyer.

They brought a long haired, bearded prisoner wearing blue jeans and a flannel shirt from a side door. The guy had spent the last three weeks in jail over a typo!

This fellow was adamant that his child support payments were taken out of his paycheck just like the court order said.

After the court reporter and a District Attorney and some other guys in suits who I couldn't figure out talked about and mulled over a piece of paper on the judge's bench, the judge finally said "but look here, this Court Order is obviously in error."

It seems from what I could gather, not being a lawyer and all, that they were only taking half the amount from his paycheck, but the payroll slip reflected what the judge had said.

"Calm down," the judge said, "you're getting out. But if you're not here on January fifteenth we'll put out another bench warrant on you."

They took him out a door on the other side.

"Is there anybody here for... mcgrew?"

I stood up and walked forward. Its lawyer wasn't here, either!

"Yes sir, uh, your on'er. I, uh, my lawyer's not here, I think she's..."

"OK, OK," says the judge. "Who's next?"

I sat back down, and some black fellow got divorced. His ex wasn't there, nor did he have a lawyer. It took five minutes.

I should have done that! Although you have to be separated for over two years before you can get divorced without your wife's permission.

My lawyer finally came in, along with Satan's lawyer. The black guy was free from slavery, and I was next!

The judge made me raise my hand and swear, although no bible was evident to swear on.

The Air Force, marriage, divorce... I hate raising my right hand!

My lawyer asked my name, age, where I was married (the Old Cahokia Courthouse, oldest court house in or west of the Mississippi Valley) and was I sure that counseling would not make me want to change my mind.

"We tried counseling. That's when I found out about her adultery, which is in fact what our 'irreconcilable differences' are," I said.

"Oh," the judge says.

"I have no further questions, your honor."

"No Questions," Lucifer's shyster said at the judge's nod.

And it was over. There is to be one more hearing before the first of the year, and I'll be completely single, after over a year after she left. And then speaking with my lawyer afterward, Evil-X gets part of my pension! Yep, that's law. And no child support, since Leila's living with her mother and still going to high school, even though she's 18.

The bank will be taking my house at a completely unrelated hearing tomorrow morning. They already repossessed my van (which had a broken transmission anyway).

But... freedom! Liberty! At the cost of most of everything I own, at the cost of personal bankruptcy, at the cost of about fourteen hundred bucks in legal fees IF I don't

fight for custody...
    I took an extra happy pill when I got back to work. It didn't work too well.

Chapter 38: I'm back. And I hate technology.
Fri Mar 19, 2004 at 07:53:38 PM EST

...especially anything that has moving parts. Like cars... and CPU fans.

About 20 minutes after I posted my last diary (OK, I don't really remember how long) the computer stopped working.

No prob, I tell myself. Whatever's wrong I can fix. I mean, I've got piles and piles of discarded computer parts in the basement. Whatever's wrong with it I can replace easy.

So, I open it up, and the CPU fan is covered in dirt and isn't moving.

So I get an old hulk, with a 120mz CPU, swap hard drives and... well, they didn't have 30 gig hard drives back then. It just plain isn't going to work.

What's more, the battery seems to have died and the CMOS doesn't seem to work anymore; it quits about the time it should be looking at its drives.

So, I tell myself, screw it. I've got stuff to do. I'll get back to the damned computer later.

The car I bought from Mike's friend Charlie runs for about two weeks and quits. In the pouring rain. In heavy traffic.

Luckily, my daughter was with me, so I had someone to steer while I pushed. I get it off to a side street, and get a tow truck to take it, me, and my daughter home.

The next day, I push it to the repair shop around the corner.

The fuel injectors are bad, and it's going to cost over a thousand dollars to fix.

Damn!

I hate moving parts. Cars used to have carburetors, and the only "moving" parts were adjustment screws, which never needed adjustment but stupid people adjusted all the time, but otherwise, carburetors almost never went bad.

I finally found a place to change the injectors for eight hundred bucks.

Evil-X said she was going to take the TV. It had come from her dad, who I had told could have it back any time. So now I'm going to have to spend more money on even more technology.

I hate technology. Because I'm a cheapass.

I visited my sister at Christmas, who showed off her new TV. A fifty two inch wide screen LCD. Boy, those Playstation 2 pixels are GIGANTIC! My oldest daughter wanted a Playstation, so I bought her one for Christmas. I bought my youngest a new car stereo.

Since I've never, ever had a TV die a natural death although I've had them struck by lightning, peed on, and dropped, I decide that I want one I'm still going to enjoy when I'm even more ancient than I already am.

And after seeing my sister's gigantic TV, the 27 incher I was used to wasn't going to cut it.

"You think it's too big?" she asks.

"There ain't no such thing as too big a TV."

"That's what David says." David's my nephew, her son.

So being the cheapass that I am, I shop around, and ask shop owners what the biggest TV they have for a thousand bucks is.

Yes, I spent twice on the TV what I paid for the car. The biggest anybody but Circuit City would admit to was thirty six inches, so I got the flat screen forty two inch "widescreen-enhanced" (although it's a standard aspect tube; winding through the menus you can get 720p out of it if you're playing a DVD) Trinitron. Its screen is about as tall as my sister's widescreen, although hers is about 50% wider.

But she paid three times what I did, so I'm happy.

I mean, I'm a cheapass. I hate to spend money.

So, I occasionally tinker with the old computer junk, trying to, if not make a silk purse out of a sow's ear, at least something I could get on the internet with.

Jonesing for the internet, I finally broke down and bought a new motherboard and some memory.

And a video card with a TV output so I could plug it into that bigassed TV set.

Then, SBC calls wanting to hook me back up with DSL.

Mind you, I still had no internet box, although I could play Duke Nukem (the original side scroller) and Solitaire.

I bit, and they would have the equipment to me in a week. "But I already have a DSL modem..."

"But it's FREE!"

What the hell, just what I need, more electronic junk cluttering my basement, which I'll have to move shortly, as I'm losing my house to the bank.

So the parts come... and out of a half a dozen old cases, the MB wouldn't fit in a single one. Somehow I wrangled the supplier into sending me a new case for free.

So as it stands, the new box is sitting here with the side off, two floppies inside, of which only one works because there's only one floppy power cable, two hard drives, only one of which works because I totally and stupidly screwed my Linux drive.

Never do a FDISK/MBR when your primary drive has Linux and LILO. But that's what I get for building a computer when I'm drunk.

And two CDs, one of which is a burner and the other which (surprise) doesn't work, because I can't find the CD (or floppy?) the drivers are on.

But I'M BACK!!!

And the divorce was finally final the last day of the year.

And I've been off of the Paxil for almost two weeks. Damned near as bad as giving up cigarettes, with the same result: uncontrollable, insane, rage.

Speaking of which, that damned X still hasn't got this TV out of my living room yet.

But I'm better. I miss the cartoons... I hope it doesn't screw up my diary style too much.

And probably a bunch of other stuff I don't have the room to write right now.

I missed you guys. I wonder if any of my K5 harem still love me?

Chapter 39: The parts order from hell
Fri Mar 26, 2004 at 09:23:17 PM EST

So, I'm sitting at my kitchen table happily typing away when the damned computer locks up.

It's not supposed to do that, I was using Mandrake 8.2 and KDE!

So I cuss and rant and threaten it and call it names and try to think of a way to blame Ashcroft and Rumsfield who, being absolutely evil, makes an excellent head for the Defense Department. Can't think of any. Shit.

I hit the three fingers, and KDE sits there frozen like Evil-X's soul. Damn. I hit the reset button, and it goes black.

And stays there. So I cold boot it and... nothing.

So, I open it up. The CPU fan isn't moving.

Of course, like the way that any cigarette smoking Hanford employee who dies of cancer at age 97 was killed by the tobacco company, my CPU was fried by overclocking.

Yeah, read that sentence again...

Anyway, this is the second Celeron this box has had in it, and both died the same way: their fans stopped.

In over twenty years of computing, I have never once had a power supply fan go bad. In fact, in all my life I've only seen one fan of any kind stop, and it was a forty five year old window fan with a blown capacitor.

So here's the second chip fan offing my CPU in only a couple of years. It's a conspiracy, dammit!!

Being around Christmas, and having just bought a thousand dollar television, I just let the computer gather dust for a while. I mean, that CPU frying was surely God's way of telling me to set it aside for a while.

Speaking of which, I read that Pat Robertson said that God told him that Bush would win again.

So, when Kerry [insert appropriate sports term here] him in a fucking landslide, does that make God a liar? Right wing Christians rejoice, you don't have to go to the polls this year! Bush has God on his side and doesn't need your vote.

I forgot what I was talking about.

Oh yeah, the computer. Anyway, After paying for a thousand dollar TV, a Playstation for my oldest daughter and a nice Jenson car stereo for my youngest daughter and an $800 repair three weeks after I bought the $500 car, I was a little short for computer parts.

Finally I catch up a little, and decide that dammit, I'm not going to replace that fan and chip again. They're Jurrasic age PC parts; an old 400 mz Celeron.

Nope, I'm going to buy a whole new motherboard!

Of course, I'll need memory for the new board. And hell, it would be nice if I could watch these AVI music videos they put on some CDs on that bigassed TV set. So I want a video card with TV out, too.

So, I call my supplier. I'm not going to name names, because this is the first time I've ever had a bit of trouble with them. Their order takers are more knowledgeable than a lot of places' tech support people.

Until this time. What's worse, the guy didn't sound like he should have been saying "I am. We told it, I am. Sofa king, we told it."

Have someone read that sentence to you out loud.

At any rate, I tell the guy about my dead Celeron and how I want to upgrade the motherboard, and get some memory, and get a video card so I can plug it into the TV. He tries to sell me a supercomputer cluster, and I say no, I'm not much into computer gaming any more so a pretty low end one would do.

He figures the cost, tax, shipping. Of course, the God damned UPS won't ship to a residential address on Saturday. Dumbasses. That's when people can be home! One of you rich guys should start a competing company that fills this niche, you could get rich. Uh, richER.

So he tells me it will be there Friday. I take Friday afternoon off to wait for the new computer.

No computer. I call the supplier. "Oh, it was back ordered". Nice. They had my phone number, they could have called me, but I wasted half a vacation day because they couldn't be bothered.

Seems like the last time something was back ordered, they called me and apologized, and kept me from wasting half a vacation day.

"OK," I say, so far being nice and not admonishing them about the call. "How about delivering it to my work?"

So Monday I tell the guard I'm expecting a UPS delivery and make sure he knows where I sit. It's a big building, and I was only there for a temporary assignment.

No package.

Oh yeah, the almost obligatory Paxil twist to a mcgrew story ("-1, no tripping with Paxil and beer mentioned!")...

I should edit that last sentence, it's really ugly, isn't it? But anyway, quitting serotonin reuptake inhibitors is quite like giving up what the Brits call "fags".

Yes, son, when you hear that guy with a British accent in that pub talking about how much he hates fags, he's not trying to pick a fight with your limp wristed ass. Nope, he's bitching about the cigarette smoke.

Oops, my apologies. I should be more sensitive. That should be "limp wristed *arse.*"

I know how hard it is for an Englishman to give up faggery (is that correctly stated?) as I used to smoke cigarettes myself.

Oops... er, SHIT; I was going to post a link! Does anybody have a link to that smoking story? The K5ARP portrait was priceless, I can't lose that!

So unlike Rusty, I've been on a very short fuse lately. You guys are lucky I'm not him, or K5 would have been a sheet of radioactive glass. I mean, some things skirt the line, but some things dance yards past it and do little victory dances while flipping you the bird and flinging boogers at you.

Ur, shit, I'm OT again. I was talking about Paxil... and I stopped taking them about two weeks ago.

Some people cry. Some people commit suicide.

Like cigarettes, whose nicotine affects serotonin reuptake, withdrawal symptoms can be blind rage, as in my case.

I'm proud of myself. So far I've managed to stay out of jail, despite a couple of almost bar fights. Actually, there was one bar fight but I managed to stay out of it. I'll have to fill you all in on that in another diary, I guess, this one's getting really long and the story's nowhere near finished yet.

So I'm really starting to get pissed by now. I mean, pissed like a Palestinian. No, even madder, because those bomb-strappers ain't going through Paxil withdrawal.

And they never met Evil-X, either. Is proof of Satan also proof of God?

So I call the supplier, and give the lady a hard time just because she works the same place as the asshole that took my order, and she says she'll call me back.

She calls me right back, and says that UPS tried to ship it but the building I was in didn't exist. So I get the UPS number and harass them.

She says that the driver said that he tried to deliver it, but they didn't know me. I politely called bullshit.

"Your driver's just plain lying." I then explained how I had alerted the guard first thing in the morning. And I told them that they could get my parts to me by 6:30 at my house or they could ship the God damned thing back to the supplier and I'll go to the store in town and just buy a new damned computer. I mean, it just isn't worth the hassle.

To their credit, they had it there by 6:00, and the driver was apologizing profusely and making excuses.

So, I open it up, and go to install the motherboard...

And there's no way in hell it's going to work in this case! No mounting holes line up, and all the i/o ports are soldered on, so that it obviously needs a proprietary case.

I call them back, catalog in hand. And while on hold (they didn't use to have me on hold like this either) I notice a combo: a motherboard just like the one I paid $125 for, with a case, for $125.

The movie *Airplane* kept popping into my head ("sure picked a lousy day to quit taking Paxil").

So she'll have a case sent to my work.

This time it was actually delivered. I got back from lunch and it was sitting on my chair.

Once home I decide that there just wasn't any challenge in building a computer, so I decide to get drunk first.

It still wasn't a challenge.

However, when I went to boot the thing, neither Windows nor Linux liked the new hardware. Linux just took forever booting, and Windows refused to boot at all.

So I started it with a DOS floppy, and DOS happily

displayed all the files on the C: (or as Linux sees it, hdb) drive.

I try to reload Windows, and get a cryptic error message. Something about the boot record... of course, the boot record must have gotten corrupted somehow.

And we all know the answer to a corrupt master boot record is FDISK /MBR.

Oops. Shouldn'ta drunked that last beer. Shit. Windows is on the second drive, Linux is on the primary drive. I had killed LILO, the Linux bootloader. There was no way this drive would live again in its present incarnation. I would have to find the Mandrake CDs and reinstall LILO.

The Mandrake CDs are nowhere to be found.

Now I had to get Windows going. I unplugged both drives and plugged the Windows drive in as the primary disk. This time, after another floppy boot, I was able to reinstall Windows.

Then I found out why the phone company sent me a new DSL modem and cables and filters when I already had them. The old stuff wouldn't work with their new stuff.

No problem, as the new stuff was on the table in an unopened box. I was soon zooming around the internet on my fast new computer, and of course the first place I went was...

Hell no, not K5. I went to get some Mandrake ISOs. "As soon as I get Linux running," I tell myself, "I'll put the video card in."

As Mandrake is downloading, I set out to delete spam. Spam spam spam spam spam spam spam spam and yet even more spam.

It took longer to clean out all the spam than it did to download three CDs! But after the electronic pigshit was cleaned off of the virtual carpet, there was an email from the supplier telling me about the back order.

Yeah, geniuses, it's really easy to check my email with a broken computer.

I do the upgrade install, and it's hosed. I can't get KDE to come up. So I reinstall as a new installation. Wallah! Can't get the DSL to work but WTF, that'll come.

Time to put in that new video card and plug it in to the TV. I've got Reefer Madness on the computer and want to see it on the movie-like TV screen.

The card is an AGP card. The motherboard has no AGP port.

Of course.

So I called the supplier and got the same clown that sold me the shit. And I gave him a hard time in spades. I told him I didn't say "I want part number x and part number y," I said I wanted a motherboard to replace a 400 celeron and a video card to watch it on the TV; he picked the parts and I paid for them, and he didn't deliver what he sold me.

He started arguing, and I just said "OK, I've had it. Now you're rudely interrupting me. That's it, I want to talk to your supervisor."

"But I..."

"Look, I've been buying your stuff for fifteen years and never had this kind of God damned clusterfuck. And then been argued with. Now put your supervisor on the phone!"

"Well, we surely can come up with some sort of solution..."

"You're goddamned right you can! You can send me what I paid for; what I asked for and paid for. Send me a PCI video card or an AGP motherboard. And I don't expect to pay for shipping or anything else, either."

"But we can't..."

"Put your supervisor on!"

"Well, maybe I can..."

So a new motherboard, with AGP port and slightly faster processor, was supposed to come today.

It didn't. It's backordered; It's supposed to be here Saturday, overnighted.

So if you folks will excuse me, I'm going down to the bar and drink and listen to music and ogle at women.

And try to stay out of jail.

Poll:
Did you miss me?
Thank God you're back, I almost committed suicide! 10%
The days were so dreary without your posts... 0%
WTF, hell yes I missed you 20%
Sure, why not? 10%
I guess 10%
Huh? 10%
Miss YOU? 0%
Yeah, I miss chancre sores, too 0%
Shit, you're back? I'm leaving! 0%
Die, asshole 0%
Who the hell are YOU? 40%

Chapter 40: Barfighting and other, less exciting stuff
Wed Mar 31, 2004 at 09:17:53 PM EST

OK, so I promised you folks a story about a bar fight. No, it wasn't the diary where I talked about Delroy, as I didn't even go in that bar. I had no wish to have a second, third, or fourth asshole.

A woman I worked with moonlights as a bartender at a grimy little run down bar between redneckville and the ghetto, right next to the tracks. The tracks closer to the ghetto. It's not far from my house.

Now, it's a bit strange, because all the bars that line the track in this particular part of town are all redneck bars.

So I'm talking with the lady, and a young chump at the other end of the bar's cellphone goes off.

"Dirty deeds done dirt cheap!" it chimed gayly. I laughed out loud. I wondered to myself what this moron paid for that ring tone. I didn't have to ask, as he was only too happy to tell everyone there how cool his ringtone was, that he paid $3.50 for it.

I laughed even louder. He took offense. "Well, I didn't mean to offend you..." I started. "Well you did!" he interrupted.

"But," I continued, "I just think it's really stupid to pay good money for something that should be free. I bet you buy bottled water, don't you?"

Stupid fucking drunks. One of the few advantages of being an old fart is that you cannot lose a bar fight with a young man!

You may, or probably will, get your old ass kicked by the young punk, but when the cops show up guess who goes to jail? And that guarantees that you can win a civil suit, and watch him cry as his SUV is auctioned!

He didn't quite get the bottled water thing. "Huh?"

"I mean," I said, "I have to work for my money."

"So what do you do? Just what have you produced?" he retorted.

I told him. He was then offended by where I work. In my own unique way I explained just how he benefited from what I do. Then Larissa, the bartender, chimed in, glaring at him.

"I work there too, asshole," she said.

Somehow things were smoothed over without the necessity of fisticuffs, to my amazement.

I showed up there a couple of days later, and the guy apologized up and down to me for his previous behavior.

So Friday, I decide to go to Boone's Saloon, where there is supposed to be a retro rock band. I went, paid the three dollar cover, bought a single beer and was mostly bored. The band took a break and I left, and walked down to Dempsey's.

There was an excellent band. I got a beer, and couldn't find a chair for a while. I found one and sat at the back for a while, stood for a while. I noticed a fatass hassling people. Fucking drunks! A few left.

That let a barstool open and I sat down, and got a second beer. A few folks I knew walked past and said "hi". I settled down to my beer.

Fatso, with a kind of "rassler" build, walks past and pushes my chair a full two feet. I ignore the cockbiter, trying hard to not let the Paxil withdrawal ruin my night.

Fifteen minutes later, it happens again. This time I give him my Clint Eastwood glare. He pretends not to notice that anything has happened. I get another beer.

He walks past again, this time just bumping me. "Say, Bud, could you scoot in a little?"

I give him "the look" again, with a bit of disgust thrown into it. "Sorry, Sparky, any closer and my dick'll be up against the bar." I proceed to move the chair *away* from the bar and ignore him some more.

Twenty minutes later he's in a fight with some guy right behind me. Then two other guys try to restrain Fatass, and as I'm about to get up and "help" (like, beak fatass' kneecap or something so he calms down) a third guy gets knocked off his feet, hitting the bar with his head.

I tried to help the guy with the busted head, who didn't seem to think it was much of a problem.

Drunks. He certainly felt it the next morning, I'm sure.

The cops showed up by then, and Fatass was gone. The owner assured me a few days later I wouldn't be seeing that guy in his bar again.

And the moral of this story is, if you can't stand being laughed at, better leave when you see me enter the bar.

Chapter 41: Evil-X
Tue Apr 27, 2004 at 06:25:23 PM EST

Sunday morning as I was drinking my coffee, the phone rang. Satan was on the line.

"I'm going to come over this afternoon to get my stuff."

I had piled the TV set that I had replaced with the flat screen 42 incher (that's over a meter diagonally for those of you in the civilized world) by the door. She had been threatening to take it since she left; her father had given it to us. It was covered with other junk that I had no want for. So today she was finally going to get it. Not a good day; Tuesday I have a (final?) foreclosure hearing. I was already frantic, terribly blue, and worried sick.

"Today's not a good day," I told it.

"Well, it's the only day I have somebody to help me with it."

That made it worse. In my present, undrugged mood I was capable of murder. I feared that I would snap. So I phoned my youngest daughter, who lives with me but was, as usual, running around with her friends.

"Your mom's coming over to get that TV and stuff this afternoon. Would you call her and have her let you know when she's coming, so I can leave? And would you be home to make sure she doesn't steal any of my stuff?"

Patty says "sure". About one my cell rings. "Mom's on her way, she'll be there in fifteen minutes".

So I walk out the back door, and down the four blocks to Track Shack, where they have "all you can eat" chili dogs for a buck.

The bartender there wasn't a supermodel by any stretch of the imagination, but she was more fun to talk to than some guy. And there was a baseball game on the TV.

A few hot dogs and beers later, my pocket rings.

"I think she left, she's not answering her phone."

"Huh? You weren't there to make sure she didn't steal anything?"

"Don't worry, she promised not to steal anything." My heart sank, and all of a sudden I didn't feel well at all. This is the thing who, if it promises that the sun will rise in the morning you can be sure that the sun will never rise again. If it promises fire, prepare to freeze.

I couldn't believe that my daughter, who knew this evil thing all of her life, could listen to her mother's assurances. When Evil-X says "I promise," it means "no way in fucking hell!"

Patty asks for money. Of course. She and her friend come to Track Shack to get money, and she gives me a ride home.

We get home and there is a mess where X's TV had been. Of course, I had expected it to leave a mess. It is, after all, completely evil and cold-hearted and has no thoughts or feelings for any human being, least of all me.

There is a huge mess in the pantry, where a broken table its dead mother had left it used to be. Crap all over the house all over the floor. She had knocked a stack of CDs and DVDs off the DVD player and left them in the floor.

The piano was gone.

"Patty, she took the piano!"

Patty says "It's OK, I told her she could take it."

"What????"

"Well, look, this way you don't have to pay to have it moved, and she'll have to pay to get it tuned."

Right, like that will ever happen. X doesn't play piano, or any other instrument. Her only reason for wanting it was to deprive me of it.

Patty promises to get us an electronic tuner for the guitars. Being her mother's daughter, I know exactly what that means.

Patty leaves, and I walk up the stairs to use the bathroom.

The table holding the phone and lamp is gone. The phone and lamp are on the floor. My bedroom door is open – she had gone in there and trashed my bedroom, taking one of the dressers, leaving one drawer behind, on the bed. The top of the other dresser is now covered in junk.

I'd had it. Even a loser like me has his limits, and mine had been passed in spades. I called the police. After hanging up, the phone rang again. It was my daughter. I told her about all the missing stuff, and that I had called the police.

"Call them back, don't have Mom arrested! I'll get the stuff back."

"No, they're on their way. I've had it with your God damned mother!"

Presently a policeman shows up, and I explained the situation to him. He asks to see the divorce papers, which as I'd told him state that X already had all her stuff, signed by her.

The cop says I shouldn't have told her she could "get her stuff." Figures. No good deed ever goes unpunished.

Evil-X drives up in her shiny white PT Cruiser, which stands in stark contrast to the two old junkers in my driveway. The cop walks to the street to talk to it, and my daughter is talking at it, too. I proudly quell the urge to take the cop's gun from him to kill everyone with.

X gets the table out of its car, and Patty brings the table in.

Between Patty and the cop, whose parents had been divorced and who had gone through what Patty is going through, I'm convinced not to press charges. The evil demon leaves an a cloud of noxious fumes; tobacco, not the expected brimstone.

I get another beer out and start drinking. By then I was pretty loaded. When I woke up, it was dark. The clock says 9:30. I drink another beer, clean off the bed, brush my teeth, take out my contact lenses, get undressed and get in bed.

It was like laying down on a pile of ice. The Evil One had taken the comforter off of my unheated water bed.

I went downstairs and laid back down on the couch, praying to God to kill the evil demon and rid us all of its evil influence. I finally got to sleep, drunk and lonely.

Chapter 42: 420
Sat Apr 24, 2004 at 08:38:19 AM EST

Yesterday was 4-20. I was prepared.

A-9 was launched. Amazon.com wasn't prepared, Google it ain't.

And my main web site is still missing.

I had procured some killer, just for the occasion of yesterday's celebration.

It wasn't nearly as good as last year, but last year there was a complete and total alignment of everything. Easter was on the 21st, and Perfunctory was playing at Dempseys. And Shorty made sure everyone there that wanted got a hit or two.

But that was last year.

Monday night I'd gone downtown, and couldn't find a single soul that I knew. I went by Dempseys, where there were three fat kids at the bar and a fat kid behind the bar, none of whom I'd ever seen before. I liked it better when Rier hired beautiful women to tend bar. The only one still tending bar is Kristen, who used to own the place about three owners ago, and she only works Wednesday and Saturday nights.

So Monday I'd wound up at the Firehouse, a "new" bar. It's not really new, it just got new owners. It used to be called "Jake and Elwood's" and was actually a pretty crummy, overpriced, no-entertainment college kid and yuppie bar. The only thing that made it stand apart from any other bar was the plexiglass statues of Jake and Elwood Blues above the front door.

One night I noticed Jake and Elwood were missing, and went inside to find it had actually developed some character. Three local firefighters had bought it, and renamed it to "The Firehouse". It's now decorated with firefighting equipment, much of it charred and/or melted. The door handles are fireaxes, there is a fireman's pole in the place that stops at the ceiling, where people have climbed up and written their names in magic marker.

The beer tap is a fire hydrant.

I was actually hunting for either Joe or Dave, both of who "owes" me a CD. Couldn't find either one. Joe had played at the Firehouse on my birthday, and they had recorded the gig. Joe sometimes hangs out in the bars he plays in, but no luck. I drank a beer and went home.

Since last night was 4/20, I figured I'd find somebody.

But first I had some groceries to buy, and a DVD to attempt to return to Walmart. There are some incredibly dumb people in Hollywood!

A week or so ago I'd picked up the DVD version of Kung Fu's first season. Playing the premier movie, it struck me that it was in wide screen format. Huh? This was a thirty year old TV show, why wide screen? I'd remembered something about all TV being shot in 35mm in the '60s and '70s, so perhaps this was in its native format with extra real estate that had been clipped for TV.

I had the shows on tape, so I stuck one in to compare.

The top of each frame was sliced off in the DVD version.

I can NOT understand people. My dad goes postal about wide screen DVDs; he hates them. He feels like he paid good money for that picture tube and wants picture on every inch. Personally, I want to see the whole picture whether it will fit on the screen or not; I want wide screen when I can get it, because you get the whole thing as it was played in the theater.

If he were a fan of that show, this DVD would be one we could agree on.

However, I'd lost my receipt, and there weren't any full screen copies there. In fact, there were no copies left at all. Drat!

When I returned *The Long Riders*, a very good, very violent, historically accurate portrayal of the James Gang, I had no problem. And what was wrong with it?

Well, despite the fact that there was no mention of censorship, the cover noted an "R" rating, and again before the movie started it had the "R" rating, it was, in fact, no longer an "R" movie. You could have shown it as it was on the DVD on prime time broadcast TV and nobody would have complained. The scene with the titties was cropped to excise the boobs. The scene where the farmer and his pigs are killed is toned way down. The explosion that kills the fifteen year old boy even had his screams removed. It was sanitized, made boring.

Yet these are the same people who leave Arnold cutting

his eyeball out in the TV version of "The Terminator".

I probably shouldn't even mention the brutal slashing that Spielberg is doing to the DVD version of Star Wars. You know, where the alien didn't shoot first, or even at all, in 1978 but now does, while Harrison Ford boredly ignores the alien's shot that hits four inches from his head. Nice of him to trash his own movie.

I'm glad I still have the tape of that western. It's a damned good movie. The watered down TV version is just boring. I'm glad they gave me my money back on that one, but I would surely like to have an uncut version, uncut as in "exactly as it was shown in the theaters".

So I put the groceries away, roll up a fattie of the expensive greenery, and head downtown.

There are a couple of guys standing outside, playing guitar and mandolin. There is a fellow putzing around with the amps and stuff inside, and a couple of chicks with guitars. One of the fellows in the band looked familiar, and I at least knew the bartender.

Shorty showed up, and I told him that when he saw me heading for the alley to follow.

Then Dave and his girlfriend showed up. She is one of the 1 in 365 people whose birthday is on the famed 4/20. Lucky girl.

"Having a birthday on Christmas would be cool," she stated. Nobody agreed. Having a birthday on Christmas negates your birthday. Plus, in Springfield you drink free on your birthday, and the bars are closed on Christmas. "Well, the fourth of July then." That was agreeable.

"My wedding anniversary was on the fourth of July," I mentioned.

"Was?"

"Well, yeah, I'm not married any more."

Eventually the band decided to come inside and play. Not bad, and I'm glad they started at 8:00, because I have to work.

So, Shorty follows me to the alley when the band takes a break, and so does about a dozen other people. It turned into a pretty good party, as I wasn't the only one to come prepared.

Even if I no longer take Paxil. And speaking of which, I'm sure this isn't nearly as interesting as most of last years' diaries, but I have a ton of stuff on my mind, not the least of which is finding a place to live before the bank takes my house. I have another foreclosure hearing next Tuesday.

I'm really bummed about losing the house. Cross your fingers; maybe when the move is done I'll be able to write like I used to.

Poll
Best Illinois Band
REO Speedwagon 0%
Chicago 0%
Head East 0%
The Gunga Dins 0%
The Station 0%
The Oohs 0%
Black Magic Johnson 0%
The Debbie Ross Band 0%
The Jungle Dogs 0%
Other (write in) 100%

Chapter 43: Patty's friend at K5
Fri Apr 30, 2004 at 05:40:46 PM EST

The phone rings this morning. It's my daughter, calling from school. She'd slipped and fallen in the basement doing her laundry last night, and wanted my permission to leave school to go steal some drugs from her mom's house.

"Sure."

It rings again, shortly before lunch. It's Patty again.

"Can I eat lunch with you?"

"Sure, meet me at Frankie's. If you're not there waiting for me you go hungry, I only have an hour."

"OK."

I don't like Frankie's. The jukebox is usually playing sucky music, either hip-hop or country. Bleh to both. Their Rolling Rock is outrageously expensive, priced as if it were an import. Their jukebox costs more than any other jukebox in town.

And Frankie is an asshole.

But they have all-you-can-eat walleye for about three or four bucks on Fridays.

So she's waiting for me in the parking lot, and we go in and sit down. Ten minutes later we still haven't been waited on. Some people come in and sit at a nearby table. A waitress finally takes our order, then takes the orders of the people who just came in.

"One of my friends goes to that Quro shin, corrosion, whatever it's called. He reads your stuff there," Patty tells me.

"Huh? How did he know I was your dad?"

"He didn't, but he mailed me a link to something there and I saw your thing about Mom."

"Yeah?"

"Yeah, one of your friends made a comment that I didn't like, so I flamed him in a comment."

"You have a K5 account?" I ask.

"Account? No, I just made a post."

This confused me for a bit, until I realized that the browser is set to log on to K5 automatically; or at least, it's still logged in if I don't log out. She had made the comment under my ID.

"Don't worry, I signed it with my name."

"Well hell, I guess it's OK unless you crapflooded or something. Who was it you replied to?"

"Elevator something... I don't remember."

"Cruel Elevator? That's not my friend, he's just a troll. And you bit. Boy, did you bite! How many times have I told you not to feed the trolls?"

The people who came in after us got their food and started eating. The waitress comes by. "Need another beer?"

"No, just this one. I have to go back to work. In twenty minutes, in fact. Have they caught those fish yet?"

We got our food about the time the people who came in after us were leaving. Probably tourists who had all damned day.

My tip was far less generous than normal. I was almost late back to work.

The Station is having their CD release party at Dempsey's tonight, so there will likely be another diary tomorrow or Sunday.

Poll
I should:
stop drinking 0%
drink more 25%
buy some pot 0%
just say no 25%
get a life 50%
other 0%

Chapter 44: Redneck Friends
Sat Jun 12, 2004 at 11:32:45 AM EST

So, here we were, Mike and me and his twelve year old son, sitting in a bar at ten P.M. eating fried chicken and drinking beer.

Well, Mike and I were drinking beer. Matt was drinking Pepsi.

If that ain't redneck I don't know what is. Maybe if Matt had been drinking beer too, that would have been more rednecky.

Note: I tapped this out in a text editor a couple of weeks ago, as I've been without the internet. Perhaps a comparison between DSL and cable will be a later diary. Also, I might write up last night's Perfunctory show. I think the band was drunk.

Chris and Donna are so redneck they make Mike and me look like urbane sophisticates. Chris was at Mike's house a few weeks ago.

God, I feel sorry for Chris. Donna's a hottie, if you're turned on by ultra-skinny chicks, but other than that she's worse than even Evil-X, if you can believe that.

She's a stone cold alcoholic, drinking from whatever time of day she deems "morning" until she passes out at night. She doesn't cook, she doesn't clean, she doesn't shop, she doesn't work.

She doesn't eat. At least, not much anyway. All she does is smoke cigarettes and drink cheap beer.

"I haven't had any pussy in three months," Chris laments. Meanwhile, according to him, every other guy in the little redneck town they live in is getting some of it. He told us of the guy she was banging whose dick was covered with warts.

"So why the limp?" I ask.

"Look at this." He pulls up his pants leg, and there is a big, raw, ugly wound. "Fucking bitch stabbed me with a paring knife!"

Mike and I just kind of stared at him incredulously. "What did you do to piss her off?" Mike asked.

"She was drunk and I wouldn't let her have the car keys."

Like I said, poor Chris.

Robert the Farm Boy shows up. "Hey, I got some killer sensie, want some?" Robert has a wooden leg and grows some fine, fine dope.

He pulled out a huge, ten inch long and two inch in diameter bud. My eyes got big and my mouth watered. "Forty bucks," he said.

"Damn," Mike replied. "I just can't afford to smoke the shit." Lucky for me Mike was on his seventh beer and his math wasn't that great; anybody else would have asked a hundred bucks, maybe two. Hell, I don't know prices these days as I haven't been buying it, maybe five...

"I'll take it," I said. Damned thing must have been two full ounces. Ever see the movie *Nice Dreams*? I wonder if I'll turn into a lizard now?

I rolled up a couple, and we all walked down to Mike's barn and got wasted. Fuck Paxil, the killer bud is lots better.

The hog pen is pretty close to the barn, and the wind was going in the wrong direction. Damn, but Mike's pigs stink. They sure taste good, though. We staggered back up to the house, and Mike put some dead pig on the barbecue pit.

The Redneck P.E.T.A. is "People Eating Tasty Animals", Y'all. YeeHaw!

I finally found an apartment a few days later that would let my daughter keep a couple of her cats. I got lucky, she gave the males, who piss all over everything, to her sister who lives in a trailer in Chatham. By herself now, as Evil-X abandoned her (again) to move in with her boyfriend.

The apartment was finished on Friday night, and I wrote a check and got the keys and started moving. Mike and Matt came up in Mike's pickup truck the next day (Saturday) to help me move the big stuff; washer and dryer, fridge, furniture... I'm getting too old for this shit.

They didn't get up there until afternoon, and we got done after dark. I'd promised Mike and Matt dinner, so we went down to Gloria's kitchen, a little redneck bar.

We got there right before the kitchen closed.

"Damn, this is good chicken," Mike exclaims. "I can't believe they're still cooking at ten o'clock!"

Poll
Gayest song ever
Queen's "I Want You To Be A Woman" 100%
The Queers' "Beyond the Valley of the Assfuckers" 0%
Whatever song the band at Pops was playing when I left 0%
Other (post) 0%

Chapter 45: No Paxil for me, young man!
Mon Jun 14, 2004 at 08:34:36 PM EST

Drugs are bad, M'kay? Remember that the next time you sprain your ankle, or the doctor tells you that you have to take Statins for your cholesterol, or AIDS drugs because you're a gay hemophiliac diabetic needle junkie. Like Nancy said, "just say no."

OK, maybe not all drugs are bad, but it would be nice if our "health care professionals" would give us more of a lowdown on the dangers of the drugs they prescribe.

Like for example, when they say "Hmm, you're really bummed, dude. Wife left you for a fat ugly unemployed loser with a little dick? No wonder you're bummed. Here, start taking these. You might get fat, but you won't be bummed out and they'll keep you from getting so horny." He (or in my case she), as well as the scientific community who writes about this crap, should probably add "when you stop taking them, you're not going to be the same as you were before you started them."

Like LSD, Paxil changes you forever. At least the people pushing LSD will warn you of this. The people pushing legal, prescription dope don't.

I haven't taken Paxil for almost two months, but when I drink, sometimes the cartoons still come out. They're just more photorealistic cartoons now.

I met the "lady in red" from *The Matrix*. Not the actress who played her, but the actual character. She put on a little weight since Neo saw her in his training session with Morpheous.

It sucks where I live now. There are only three bars within walking distance, two run down little redneck bars and one fancy high priced joint. None of them has live music. The music is mostly downtown, and I'm over two miles away now, far too far to stagger when you're wasted. So now I can't get wasted on the weekends, at least downtown.

Bummer.

Anyway, I saw in the "Illinois Typo" that Perfunctory was playing at Dempsey's Friday.

I'm not really much of a deadhead, but for some reason I wind up having a real good time whenever I go see this band. Maybe it's the other people in the audience?

So, at any rate, unlike past summers when I would get a head start on the bar beer with some much cheaper grocery store beer, I held off until 8:30 or so, when I drove downtown to Dempsey's.

The band was setting up when I got there. They appeared to be not very steady on their feet. I drank a beer, and they still weren't playing. I got up and walked down the street, thinking I'd stop at Bread Stretchers for a fifty cent per bottle cheaper beer, as that damned Rier stopped having the dollar Rolling Rocks and was now selling them at $2.25 like the rest of his domestics, higher than anybody else in town.

I haven't been spending nearly as much time at Dempsey's lately.

Bread Stretchers looked like they were setting up for a tenyboppper show. I kept walking. The Firehouse was having a DJ, but since he hadn't started I went in and got a beer. At a quarter cheaper than Dempsey's, I might add, and walked back down.

There was no pretty bartender at Dempsey's Friday. Rier and some other guy were tending bar.

Damn.

The band was playing when I walked back in. I got another beer, and found a stool. It wasn't nearly as busy as usual on a Friday. The band wasn't playing as well as they normally do, either. I think they got a head start on me when it came to the night's drinking.

I looked around, and there was "teh lady in red" from the Matrix; the program that Mouse wrote for the training program to distract new recruits.

She gained a little weight. Mouse's programming skills were deteriorating, it seems.

She was with some skinny little short guy from the band, or at least, appeared to be. I sipped on my beer, not wanting to hire a cab to go home in.

A man walked in with one of the homeliest women I've seen in quite some time hanging on his arm. She sat down next to me and smiled, he walked up between us like he was afraid I'd take the ugly bag away from him. I scooted my chair over to give him room, and he thanked me.

The lady in red, who appeared to be with the band, walked up to the bar next to me and ordered a beer.

Note to Mouse: you really should have her drinking wine. Beer makes you fat.

She turned to talk to me, and I conversed with this attractive program. No, she wasn't that fat, just a little on the heavy side, for a computer program. I guess Mouse must have gotten a job with Microsoft. She then went back to her seat with the fellow who resembled her programmer, at least in height.

Now, pay attention, K5 geeks, I'm about to reveal to you why you can't get laid.

It's not because you're a fatass from sitting at the computer all day eating pizza and drinking Jolt. No, I see fatassed bastards with attractive women all the time. It's not because of your ugly face. Indeed, It seems that women are attracted to butt ugliness.

No, it's because the part of your brain that is supposed to go toward being able to tell when a woman is flirting has been hijacked for other purposes; say, understanding the behavior of neutron stars, or knowing when to loop and when to branch.

It occurred later that she had been flirting. I could have gotten laid. In the things that matter in life, I'm the biggest fucking retard on the planet.

The Lady in Red left with some fat ugly nerdy looking guy.

Like always, I went home alone, especially annoyed because my daughter had said she was spending the night with her mother.

And speaking of Patty, she doesn't like the new apartment. The first night there as I was showing it to her, a snake slithered across the doorstep as we approached, and a spider scurried out as we entered.

Looking around, she whined "my old room was bigger than this apartment!"

The next evening, Saturday, I decided to drive down to St. Louis and party with old friends. I couldn't find any.

First I stopped by Jeff's. Jeff wasn't home. I called Mike, who didn't answer the phone. I drove by Johnny's, and there was no car in the driveway. And so on and so on. Nobody home.

Damn. I drove out to Mike's, thinking maybe he was just in his barn or feeding the animals or something.

Nope.

So I decided to go to Pop's Saloon, where I hadn't been in years. In fact, it wasn't really the same place, as the old Pop's had burned to the ground several years ago and been rebuilt about 200 yards away from the old one's ashes.

I paid six bucks to get in. That's twice the cover I'm used to paying, when I even have to pay a cover at all.

The place is huge, and it was nowhere near crowded. The band sounded like shit. The singer couldn't hold a tune if you gave him a bucket and a pair of vicegrips. Luckily, I'd walked in at the last song.

The audience was young. For my six bucks I got a fluorescent green band around my wrist. Apparently, they allow kids in this bar but the kids can only drink if they have the arm band. Unlike B.B. King's bar in Memphis, where my then sixteen year old daughter was served, and brought me the shot glass as a souvenir.

"What'll ya have?" the guy behind the bar asked.

"Rolling Rock."

"Um, don't have it. Heineken is about the closest," he said. At least he knew the difference between a lager and a pilsner. Some bars in Springfield have only pilsner beers (usually the more redneck bars).

I paid three and a half bucks for a can of beer. A damned can! Wow, this place has no class whatever. Even the redneck bars in Springfield have bottles, but they don't have bottles because cans don't make as good a weapon as a bottle.

At the bottom of the can the next band was all ready

to play, so I bought another can, wandered over to the "merch" table and bought a five dollar CD, which still sits in my car's front seat, unwrapped.

The band started up. They were technically proficient; the gay-looking singer could hold a tune, and in key, unlike the previous band.

But they still sucked. It was the new commercial sound, the minor key whining of an emo wannabe, the same shitty sound you hear on the pop radio stations. Ugh.

"Mind if I sit here?"

"Sure," I said, and looked up. It was some guy about a foot taller than me and twenty pounds lighter. Like the Lady in Red, I've gained a bit of weight since you've seen my picture.

Black hair down past his shoulders, and face made up like he was a member of Kiss or something. "You don't look very happy," he said.

"It's this minor key music," I replied. "Plus, you're not a woman." I drained my beer and went home.

Chapter 46: Stars and bars
Mon Jul 05, 2004 at 04:46:40 PM EST

A new bar, a likely ass burger girl, an old bar, a couple of old friends.

So a week or so ago I decided to try out this new bar. Now, when I say "new" I mean brand spanking new. There didn't use to be a bar there at all, and they gutted the place and built it into a bar called... Somebody's Sports Bar? I don't know, I think it starts with an S. Not really a memorable name.

At any rate, it was a pretty big bar, and pretty crowded. Impressive, as it was in the middle of the week and there wasn't any music or anything, just a ball game on the TV. The only noise was from people, and you almost had to yell to be heard. I sat down at the only empty stool on the bar, next to a not bad looking woman with glasses. She seemed to be with two other women sitting on the other side of her.

I couldn't get eye contact with the woman with the glasses; she seemed to be paying studious attention to the other two women, while not saying anything. The sign said Moosehead for two and a quarter so I got a Moosehead. I hadn't taken two sips when my phone rang.

I answered it; it was my oldest daughter. I walked around where it wasn't quite so noisy, talked for a few minutes, and went back to the bar. My beer was almost finished, and geeklady was holding an empty beer bottle, still avoiding my gaze, sitting back to where I couldn't casually glance over at her.

The fellow on my left finishes his drink and the bartender hands him another one. "I must be invisible!" the woman exclaims. The bartender points to my almost empty beer, and I hold up two fingers. I pay for the two beers and hand one to the invisible woman. She smiles. "Thank you."

I tried until the end of the beer to get her to converse, and finally gave up and went home.

So, Mike calls Saturday, "come on down and help eat this pig."

Speaking of pig, on the way down I saw Evil-X in her PT Cruiser. Happy Anniversary, whore.

So anyway, back to the pork.

This was no ordinary pig. This pig was a man-eater, who

had bitten Mike and both his sons. I guess the grill was Mike's revenge, sure was a tasty piece of meat. By the time we finished eating it, mike was passed out in his chair.

Mike likes beer. I didn't mind too much, a former neighbor was playing at Dempsey's and I wanted to get back to town. Mike's wife asked me to come back next week to set up their new computer. I'd probably be there anyway, as I've been driving down there every week as it was.

Back in Springfield and it's still only eleven. I drive to Dempseys and go in. The band is on break, the building is crowded, and Mary and Kristin are tending bar.

Mary is the owner's mother. "Hi!" she says, recognizing me. "Boy, this sure is a great band!" she exclaims in wide eyed awe. She's right, they are good. Ed, the singer, used to be a union carpenter, but finally quit pounding nails because he was making a lot more money singing. They don't have a web site or a CD, they just play gigs, and pack them.

I tell Mary yeah, they are, and tell her I've known Ed for a few years. "We're, uh, out of Rolling Rock," she says. "Well, there's some back there but it's warm."

"Well hell" I say. "How about a Busch?"

She opens the cooler, and a crestfallen look goes in her face. "Uh, we don't have that either."

I was speechless. I must have stood there slack jawed.

"How about a St. Pauly Girl?" she asks. She only charges me for a Rolling Rock, and I find a chair. Ed walks past and sees me, and stops and chats for a couple of minutes before going on stage.

There are some seriously unattractive women in Dempsey's tonight. Packed as it is, there are no really good looking women. I finish my beer and go up to the bar for another.

Kristin charges me for a St. Pauly Girl. I don't tip her tonight. Instead, I drink it and walk down to The Firehouse, where Posamist is playing. Disappointingly, they redid their page, so its index is no longer a picture of Allie's ass. My guess is that this probably has something to do with the fact that Allie works at Dempsey's, and Posamist is now the house band for Boone's Saloon.

And Joe and Ryer had some sort of falling out. Ryer would only say it was "artistic differences". At any rate, I haven't seen Joe at Dempsey's since then, either playing or drinking.

I get a Rolling Rock and listen to the music. The Firehouse isn't quite as packed as Dempsey's, but it's bigger. And there are, happily, very good looking women there.

And sadly, none seemed the least bit interested in me. As usual.

Chapter 47: July 4 – the lost diary
Thu Jul 15, 2004 at 07:38:56 PM EST

When I wrote the last diary, I actually wrote two of them, one covering the second and third of July, and one the fourth. I stuck the one for the fourth in a floppy and... I lost it.

It was just plain gone, slipped through some kind of space-time dimensional field or eaten by a hungry ghost or something.

Anyway, a week later I'm doing my laundry and found it inside the washing machine. Must have been inside a shirt pocket.

There was an article too, but the floppy couldn't be read there. Since there are about ninety stories in the queue right now I guess it doesn't matter much.

Independance Day

I thought I was so damned smart...

You don't have to be married to know that there are two days in the year that a married man must never, never, ever forget. One is his wife's birthday, and the other is his wedding anniversary. Woe be to any man who forgets either of these important dates.

I was married on America's bicentennial, a date I was sure to remember. What a dumb move. I just had to pick a day that was impossible to forget...

Actually, it was on the 3rd, as July 4th, 1976 fell on a Sunday, when the judges aren't working and the preachers are. So we made the big day the day before, a Saturday.

In the spirit of the nation's bicentennial birthday, we were wed in the oldest courthouse in or west of the Mississippi valley. The old Cahokia courthouse is older, even, than the country whose birthday we were being married on.

Every year on our anniversary there were fireworks. I wish we had picked a different day.

I never once forgot my anniversary. Not once. What's even more impressive was I never once forgot my wife's birthday, either. Of course, you can probably guess that she forgot mine more than once. Hell, she forgot our kids' birthdays before.

Why is it OK for a woman to forget anniversaries and birthdays, but not men? We sure have a double standard going here. Like I've said, men are stupid, and I'm probably the dumbest one on the planet.

And women are evil. And their leader is my former bride, Evil-X, also known as "Satan".

This was the first anniversary in over a quarter of a century that I was legally single, although last year we were separated and the year before she claimed to be working, although I think she was giving my fireworks to her new fool rather than working. I was a little blue and lonely in the morning Sunday. I need a girlfriend.

Preferably one half my age. Those Russian girls who keep sending me wedding invitations via email don't count. I need one I can actually touch.

I was determined to forget my anniversary, and celebrate my country's anniversary. I planned to do this, of course, with beer. How else?

Now, New Year's Eve is my real independence day, as that was when my divorce was final. I spent that evening at Dempsey's, as close to where they set off fireworks as you can get. I planned on spending the evening of July 4th there, too.

I went in an hour or so before the fireworks were scheduled to go off, and asked for a Rolling Rock. There still wasn't any cold! I told the bartender to put some on ice and I'd be back, and walked down to the Firehouse.

The Firehouse used to be "Jake and Elwood's" before being bought out by three Springfield firefighters. When it was Jake and Elwood's it was just an ordinary bar like any other bar, with the only theme being the statues of Dan Ankroyd and John Belushi wearing black suits and sunglasses over the front door. They really themed "The Firehouse" up well, though. Its door handles are fire axes, its beer tap is a hydrant, with another non-functional hydrant on the floor by the door. It has a fireman's pole that goes nowhere, just standing there like a ceiling prop. There are charred remnants of firefighting tools on the walls, and photos of buildings burning down.

I got a Rolling Rock. Somebody put money in the jukebox and Johnny Cash started spewing from the speakers. "I shot a man in Reno, just to watch him die..."

Wow, that Cash fellow sure wrote some friendly, family styled lyrics, didn't he? Too bad the trash they sing these days isn't wholesome family entertainment like that!

It seemed that the only ones in the bar were couples. Including two women who were kissing and groping each other. Damn it ladies, it's OK for men to be gay. In fact, I encourage all heterosexual men to go faggy and let me have their women.

If I were a woman I'd have to be a lesbian.

I finished my beer and walked back on down to Dempsey's. Ordinarily I'd have stayed away out of principle, Mary should have stocked the beer Saturday night, damn it. But the sidewalk in front of Dempsey's gives the best fireworks show.

Besides, that beer should have been cold by now.

Rier (whose name I can never remember exactly how to spell) was checking IDs at the door. His parents were walking up from the opposite way down the sidewalk, and a couple of guys were walking up behind me. "Dude, better check those two, they look kinda suspicious," I said, pointing at his parents. He grinned.

One of the other people coming in said "yeah, man I know she's not 21!"

Rier groaned. "That's my mom, man!"

Although there were a lot of couples in there at least I wasn't the only seemingly single person, as there were a few groups of people. Including three women who looked like they were having foreplay for a threesome. WTF was it with lizzies on the 4th? I guess God's up there laughing at me again. I don't mind, if He's happy I'm happy.

I drank my beer and got another. People were starting to go outside in preparations for the fireworks, so I did too.

"You can't take that beer outside" Rier said. I simply gave him a dirty look and pointed to a group of a half dozen people swilling from brown bottles. He scurried off to harass them; I downed the beer and threw the bottle in the trash.

The fireworks were very, very good this year. They rivaled the 4th of July fireworks at Disney World, and they go all out on Independence Day there.

My tax dollars at work. All the streets have crater-sized potholes, the sewers flood when it rains too hard, few of the walk/don't walk signals work, quite a few traffic control signals ("red lights") have at least one light burned out, there is a perceived racism problem (only three of over a hundred city firefighters are black) and 6th street's dotted lines are still as crooked as any politician in Illinois, but they can afford half a million bucks for a fireworks display. Or two – they shoot them off down by the lake, too.

At any rate, it was a real good fireworks display. I went in and got another beer. "Staying for the long haul?" Mary asked. "Might as well" I said, "I don't have to work tomorrow."

But I didn't. I got bored, finished my beer, and left. I hate kareoke, and it seems that every damned bar in town (at least the ones that are open) have kareoke on Sunday.

I think Rier's singing was what did me in.

As I was walking back to the car, I heard what sounded like live music. On a Sunday? I followed my ears...

There was a band playing outside, in the YWCA parking lot at 5th and Capitol, half a block from where the Governor used to live. No, not the present Governor, he's too damned good to associate with the downstate redneck riff raff like the previous Governors did, all living in the Governor's Mansion at 5th and Edwards. No, this guy's Chicago all the way, and like everybody else in Chicago, thinks Illinois' southern border is Interstate 80.

I don't think he'll be in office a second term. He has a knack for pissing everyone off, not just rich people and Republicans as Democrats usually do. No, this guy pisses off Republicans, Democrats, business, labor, women, men, children, and their furry pets. The state's employee union, who has backed every Democratic candidate for governor since they had a union, claims that next election they're going to back a different Democrat in the primaries, and if Blagoyabich (or however the hell you spell his name) wins the primary, they will back the Republican for the first time in their history. I guess he really pissed them off.

The last Democrat to be Illinois Governor was in the early 1970s. He went to prison as soon as his term was up.

Had the absent Governor actually deigned to live in the Capital city, rather than moving it in a defacto manner to Chicago, he could have opened a window and heard the live music. His loss. Just stay the hell in Chicago, Governor.

In fact, I know how to cut Illinois' crime rate by 95%, increase public school test scores by 90%, reduce unemployment to practically nothing, and a host of other measures that would make Illinois #1 in about everything except population and area. All they have to do is give the Chicago area to Michigan, and give East St. Louis to Missouri.

I don't know who the band was, but I've heard the songs on the radio before. Just not for a really long time... I think it was the "Oak Ridge Boys" or somebody.

It didn't get any less boring. I was home before 11:00, and in bed before midnight.

Well, not actually bed... I left the bed at the foreclosed and reposessed house. It was "our" bed, the one we bought after that really bad car wreck when we had to have a waterbed just to deal with the pain of our injuries.

The one she made love to half a dozen other men on while we were married.

The pain bed.

I've been sleeping on the floor for the last month. I think I'll go buy a couch tonight.

Chapter 48: Bar stories
Mon Jul 26, 2004 at 06:29:49 PM EST

This particular diary will attempt to tie together a few disparate visits to different bars at different times and make a coherent whole out of it. More likely I will experience the same abject failure at writing anything the least bit interesting like you've seen in the last several diaries.

There are quite a few differences between this summer and last. For one thing, I'm not such an emotional cripple as I was last year, although I'm still psychically limping a little. Most of the time I'm in good spirits. In fact, when I get a touch of the blues it's over losing my house, or that animation I did on paper 25 years ago and never finished getting into the computer that was lost in the move, or the loss of that Doors tape. I also think I might have lost that painting I did when I was sixteen, the one my Grandmother loved so much. Evil-X was a nightmare, but I've gotten up, brushed my teeth and drank my coffee.

Secondly, I'm not on Paxil, that silly little drug that kept me constantly amused. When I first got off of it I was not the least bit amused. In fact, part of withdrawal for me was a feeling of rage. Rage against everyone, anger at the least slight. Kind of like giving up cigarettes.

Thirdly and most importantly, I'm no longer walking distance from downtown, meaning I can't get shitfaced drunk while listening to live music, unless I want to spend fifteen bucks or more for a cab.

Boone's Saloon

I've mentioned Joe Frew and his band, Posamist a few times before. They're the "House Band" for Boone's now, playing there every Thursday night.

I stopped at Bread Stretchers' and got a sandwich and chips and took them to Boone's, as Boone's has great food, but only in the daytime. The kitchen closes at 2:00 PM. They don't do dinner, only lunch. I got a beer, sat down on the empty side of the brick wall (not that they were all that busy) and ate my supper.

The band started playing as I finished eating, and enough people had come in that I missed my chance at a bar stool. I sat at the table in the front corner and sipped my beer, watching the young pretties.

A stool opened up and I moved to it. It seemed, like it

always seems lately, that there were nothing but couples.

I spied a strange looking woman standing by herself, looking both defiant and uncomfortable. She seemed oblivious to the music, although she stood facing the band.

I couldn't put my finger on why she seemed so strange looking, and still can't. There are some really weird looking people in this town, which is why so many of them looked like cartoons when I was on the Paxils, I guess, but this woman wasn't the least bit ugly. In fact, she had an attractive face and a nice figure, but something was out of place, and I couldn't put my finger on it.

Of course, I would have liked to put my finger *in* it...

As I was about to get up and walk over and hit on her, she walked over and put her arm around some guy who remained oblivious to her. Obviously, these two were married. For now, anyway.

"I'm Joe motherfucking Frew, how the fucking hell are you?"

Wild cheers from the now half-drunken crowd. "Social!" glasses and bottles raised in the air, the crowd screaming. "Hey, we have free CDs at the bar over there, just talk to Matt's lovely girlfriend."

I think the cute little blonde bartender, whose name I don't know, had been flirting with me. I wish I could tell, I'd surely like to know that young lady better!

But at any rate, this was Thursday, so when the band took a break I walked up and said "hi" to them, and went home and went to bed. Damn, but I hate the alarm clock.

The Firehouse

Once again, I missed my chance.

One evening last week, not sure what day, I went by the Firehouse for a beer. It was mostly empty (the bar, not the beer, at least until it was finished), but there was a fireman there. You could tell by his conversation with the bartender, another fireman, that he was a fireman. He was with what I assumed was his wife. She looked familiar, and I couldn't put my finger on where I'd seen her before. I got a beer and started drinking.

She was a lovely young thing; thin and shapely, with dark hair and dark eyes and that fake looking salon tan the young people all seem to waste their money on these days. I guess white skin is out of fashion, with all the white kids getting dreadlocks and deep salon tans and dressing like rappers with their pants hanging halfway to their knees and talking in ebonics, despite the fact that none of them would have the balls to drive through the slums with their doors unlocked.

But this was no "wigger." This young lady was wearing an evening dress and high heels, despite the fact that it was only a little past six. Her hair was conservatively cut and coiffed (is that the right word? A word at all? Did I spell it right?) and her face was conservatively made up.

Well, it would have been conservative, except for where she seemed to have a bad aim with the eyebrow pencil. She was well more than half way to passing out.

"Hey, I know you!" she exclaimed. "I made you your first martini!"

Now I knew where I'd seen her before, on the other side of this very bar. "You're right, that's where I've seen you before." I had been in there a month or two earlier, and when talk had gotten to alcohol and various drinks, I'd mentioned that in all my years of drinking I'd never tried a martini, so she made me one.

I hated it. Yech! How do you faux sophisticates stand drinking that swill?

I noticed her ring was on her middle finger, but she seemed to be with the fireman.

We chatted, I drank my beer, and another.

I finished the beer, told her it was nice seeing her again, shook her hand in preparation to leave, and could tell by her expression that I had fucked up yet again. Here I've been praying for a pretty young thing half my age, God delivered, and I was too damned stupid to recognize the gift when I saw it.

Damn!

Rierpalooza

Rier Delandy's mom and dad bought Dempsey's for him last year, so he decided to celebrate his 23rd birthday this year with a toga party at his bar, open to everyone. "We're gonna have a kick ass band, and beer for a buck and a half!" I'd promised him I would show up.

So after getting back from my mother's and dropping my daughter off at her trailer, I cruised downtown to Dempsey's. By this time it was past ten, so the band would already be playing.

Rier's dad was at the door checking IDs, and the band was playing some disco shit. Gad but I hate disco, why couldn't the Gibb brothers been bricklayers or something? I talked with Rier's dad for a minute, and went in and found a stool.

"The usual?" the bartender asked. "Yeah" I replied, and he disappeared in the back. I pulled out two ones. "Two and a quarter" he said. I gave him a quarter. Halfway through the beer I saw the sign – Bud and Bud Light for a buck fifty.

Fucker! No tip for YOU tonight!

Rier's mom was talking to some skanky looking guy with a beard. He seemed to be hitting on her, and she seemed to be trying to be polite.

This is why I won't hit on women while they're working. She saw me and said hi and extended her hand. I shook her hand, said hi, and saved her from the wolf. Rier's dad owes me!

I bought a Bud and drank it. Not only could I not get drunk, as I was driving, but this band really really sucked. Yes, they were technically proficient, but they played nothing but covers of bands I always change the station when I hear their songs on the radio.

Apparently I wasn't the only one who thought their choice of tunes rather shitty. I half heartedly clapped a little on some of their less sucky songs, but didn't applaud much, and neither did anyone else. The band finished one song with no hint that anyone in the audience had ears, and remarked "That was our last Michael Jackson song."

I yelled "Yeah!!" at the top of my lungs and cheered wildly. Laughter from around the room, with more applause from others. Rier, don't book those losers anymore, OK?

I finished the Bud and walked to the rest room. Rier was walking in, then right out. I'd seen him and wished him a happy birthday earlier.

"Full house?" I asked. "Yeah," he replied, "I think I'll just use the alley." I followed him out the back door. "I'd buy you a drink if this was anybody else's bar," I said.

"I quit drinking," he replied. "About three months ago."

On the way home I stopped at a little redneck bar walking distance from my apartment. I don't know the name of the place. I went in and ordered a draft.

Halfway through my beer the fellow next to me, looking over at the pool table and spying a black man staggering out of the men's room, exclaimed "where'd that nigger come from? Who let that God damned nigger in here?"

If I hadn't guessed before, this would have been a really good clue that this was a very redneck bar, despite the fact that ACDC was playing on the jukebox.

"I hate niggers," the fellow repeated. "I can tell," I answered, looking him in the face and thankful for my green and yellow eyes.

"Is it a crime to hate niggers?" he asks. Um, yeah I think so these days... but he continued without my saying anything. "I've hated niggers ever since I was in prison. Know what I went to prison for?"

I was wishing I'd just passed this place by and gone home. "Probably something that shouldn't even be illegal," I said, trying hard to be diplomatic.

"Bank robbery," he says.

"Well," I replied, "I can see why that ought to be illegal..."

"Hey," he interrupted, "where'd that nigger go?"

"Dunno" I said, "Maybe he left."

I finished my beer. "I have to go, too."

"Oh, I'm sorry, did I run you off?"

"No, I'm out of money," I lied.

Fucking trolls!

Poll:
if I publish this boring mess after it comes to novel length and some kind of conclusion, how much are you willing to pay for a copy? And a pop quiz: Which poll option comes from a rock song, and what song?

One hundred English pounds! 0%
Fifty bucks, but it has to have dirty pictures 0%
Twenty five dollars 0%
Fifteen bucks and not a penny more 0%
Five bucks, I only buy paperbacks 26%
Pay??? 33%
Fuck you, this shit sucks 33%
Other (post) 6%

Chapter 49: DOOMed
Wed Aug 04, 2004 at 08:57:53 PM EST

I'm in a REAL bad mood. I've had a REAL bad day.

It started out well enough, pretty much like any other day, with the alarm clock rudely calling me to work.

Work... Jesus, I wish I was independently wealthy so I could buy an island somewhere and never have to deal with the species homo sapiens ever again. But this morning, even work started out OK. I spent an hour in the office, then told the acting boss (the real boss is on vacation) I would probably have my brakes fixed after my appointment and didn't know when I'd be back.

I had an appointment with some government bureaucrats to see if I could get child support. Fucking bitch should have stayed out of my retirement money.

I was lucky I wasn't in Europe, because it was a beautiful 70 degrees. Very lucky, as 70 degrees in Europe would be a hundred fifty eight here.

I was in an excellent mood. I greeted the guard at the door, gave him my name and signed a sign-in sheet, and waited about 20 minutes for a government caseworker.

She was pleasant, and had me fill out a government form and sign more papers than you have to sign to buy a house. I was there about an hour.

I left, and took my car down to the garage. I told them I needed the brakes fixed and the oil changed, and to see if they could find out where all the oil was leaking. If it's that big main seal at the bottom that costs a ton, I'll keep dumping oil in it. If it's a valve cover gasket then fix it. They told me they'd call me to let me know what it was going to cost, and gave me a ride home.

My daughter was still asleep. I woke her up and asked her if she had to work today. "Yeah, from eleven to two."

Damn. I was going to use her car. Well, I'd drive her to work and could she get a ride home?

I dropped her off at the mall where she works, and drove a quarter mile to Best Buy. I wanted DOOM.

Some Best Buy kid greeted me at the door, and I asked him if they had DOOM. "Yeah, they have a big display in the middle of the store." I walk down there, and there are four five by four foot cardboard shelves making a cube, all filled with mostly empty.

Christ, this game is selling. The display looked like it would hold a few hundred copies of the game, and there were only a couple dozen there. Yeah, maybe it's a marketing illusion designed to mimic popularity by not stocking very many, but there is a small crowd of people plucking copies like they're getting paid for it. Most of them are old fucks like me.

"I wonder if my new computer will play this thing?" I wondered out loud. "Well," some guy says, doubt in his eye. I could read his little mind, "Gee, mine's not brand new!"

"How fast is your processor?" he asks. "It's a 1.8 ghz PIV," I reply. "Hmm.... what kind of graphics card?"

"NVidea, but I couldn't tell you what model. No matter," I said, "If I don't have enough computer I'll just buy some more parts." I took it to the cash register and paid for it, just short of sixty bucks.

Fucking elitists, expensive as hell and you need a brand new computer to play it, and they still make money hand over fist! It boggles my mind.

So by this time it's close to when I normally have lunch. Now, last year I was on a temporary assignment really close to Boone's Saloon, and got to eating lunch there every day. They have damned good lunches, the help is all pleasant and the service is good. But the food is excellent. If you're ever looking for somewhere good to eat in Springfield, there are a lot of very good restaurants, but mostly the bars have better food and lower prices.

Best of all, Boone's has about a dozen different kinds of beer on tap, from Busch to XX.

I ordered a pilsner and a blackened prime rib salad, the special today. Now, before you think this is some snobby dump, it's not; the pilsner I ordered was Busch. And the salad was about five bucks, a huge bowl with plenty of meat.

I may sound like I'm singling out Boone's but all the

bars are that good. I've been eating at a different place lately, since I'm too far from Boone's. Top Cats is every bit as good, plus they have all you can eat walleye on Fridays. Of course, so does Frankie's, but I dislike Frankie and hate his shitty little bar. Even if their food is good. The service there sucks; I hear it's because he treats his help like shit. Businesspeople, let that be a lesson to you.

I open up the DOOM package, and start reading the fucking manual (or "FM" as they call it at slashdot). My salad comes, so I put the FM down.

"Wow, DOOM 3 is out?" the waitress asks. Pretty little thing, not old enough to pour beer. "My brother had the first DOOM. That was a fun game!"

I talked about DOOM with the pretty little waitress for a minute, and she went to wait on a different table and I ate the salad. The prime rib seemed more plentiful and with bugger hunks than I remembered. Too bad they closed down a few years later.

This was a wonderful day. I finished my lunch, left a tip, paid and walked outside...

...straight into the ovens of hell.

The 70 degrees Fahrenheit seemingly had turned into 70 degrees Centigrade. It's Illinois in August, where Satan comes to warm up when hell gets too chilly.

I got in Patty's car, and holy shit it's hot! She doesn't have an air conditioner. Damn. Or maybe damned.

I pulled out as the light turned green. And almost got slammed by someone running the light. My day had turned a corner, and not a good corner, either. The guy who ran the red light was one of the better drivers I encountered on my way back to work.

But I got there. And not in too good a good mood. I was glad to be in the air conditioning... damn, though, I was still hot.

There was a note on my chair. As I was puzzling over it, its author came in. I'd gotten some of the "controls" in the "experimental" group. Oops. Oh well, easily fixed.

"But you have the experimentals listed in alphabetical order." Yep, standard operating procedure.

"But these are time-dependent!"

"You didn't tell me that!"

"But why did you change the order??"

"So people could find the items easier when they see this dumb report. And for me to find bad data because I'm suspecting there are some really bad data in there."

"Well, it has to be in the order you found it on this one document!"

She never could explain why SOP wasn't being followed. The bottom line was I was going to have to redo the whole damned thing, and I had been so glad to be done with it. My mood went from not good to fucking pissed. Shit! Fuck! Son of a bitch! Goddamn it!

"I'm pretty darned frustrated by this," I said.

I studied it for a couple of minutes, wondering why I ever quit smoking, and remembering how God damned hot it was outside, and how God damned cold it gets in the winter, and how you second class citizens (AKA "smokers") have to go outside every hour. And figured maybe I could move some rows around or something and fix it up...

A couple hours of mindless drudgery later, and she comes back in.

"Now I'm frustrated!"

"What?"

"That document that was supposed to have the right order was in the wrong order."

Somehow, I made it all the way to four o'clock with not only not murdering anyone with my teeth, but without even being brusque or rude.

But before that happened, my cell phone rang about three. It was the garage, and they'd been trying to get hold of me all day. God damned cell phones... Now it'll be tomorrow before I get my car back. But at least there was some good news: I only needed pads on the front, and an inexpensive seal for the leak.

I stepped out at four, and it was hot. Didn't seem quite as bad as earlier though. At least, until I'd driven a few blocks,

Smoke came from under the hood. The smell of rubber; the car wasn't on fire, thank God. But Patty's going to need a belt or hose or something.

Sweat pouring down my jowls... when I was skinny I never sweated. Now I sweat like a horse. And the heat isn't helping my mood either.

A city vehicle, one that drives cripples and blind people around Springfield cuts me off, nearly taking my front bumper. I lay on the horn, signal, get over, and pass him. He proceeds to speed up, and drove three feet from my bumper all the way from 6th street to McArthur. #131, if you happen to be an SMTD supervisor or Mayor Davlin or somebody. You sure hire some incompetent assholes, you know that? And guess what, I can't vote against the driver of #131 this fine 4:10PM August 4 2004 in Springfield, Illinois, or his supervisor, but damn it I can vote against your damned ass, mayor. And I plan on doing so. Fucktards.

I put some gas in Patty's car, and put air in one of her tires, thankful that I didn't buy them in Scotland where they were invented and where I'd be forced to call them "tyres".

And of course, I bought a six pack of Rolling Rock.

I get home and immediately drink two full glasses of water, and open a beer, and tear the cellophane from DOOM's CD jewel case. I stick the CD in, and it says...

"Now installing the DOOM 3 Installer..." which I find mildly amusing.

Then it says "In order to run the DOOM 3 installer you must reboot your computer. Do you wish to reboot now?"

What a stupid fucking question. I'm trying to install a fucking game I've been waiting years for.

After the reboot, the installation screen comes up, and I'm impressed. It is in a window, but the window has no frame, no border, no title bar. But it doesn't fill the screen; there are icons around it. Never saw a program do that in Windows before.

I click "Install"

"WARNING! You are currently trying to install DOOM 3 on an unsupported Operating System (Windows 95/98/98SE/ME/NT). If you proceed with the installation you will not be able to run the game. Are you sure you want to continue to install DOOM 3?"

God Fucking Damn it!!!!!

Do one of you l33t h4x0rz have a copy that will run on Linux? Because, God Damn it, I am NOT going to buy Windows again.

POLL
I should...
Return the game 10%
Buy XP 10%
Pirate XP 20%
Pirate 2K 0%
Kill everyone I see 30%
get drunk 20%
get stoned 10%
just forget the whole damned thing 0%

Chapter 50: Crab racing at the saloon
Thu Aug 12, 2004 at 06:23:57 PM EST

Tuesday night after cursing and ranting about the spam problem and the corrupt legislators who let it happen by passing any legislation the multinationals want and refusing to pass anything that might actually be a benefit to citizenry, I opened the fridge and... damn. No beer. I hadn't wanted to go anywhere.

I went to the gas station and picked up a six pack. Yes, you folks in other parts of the world might find it hard to believe, but they sell beer in gas (petrol) stations here.

Speaking of "here", and races, before we start the crab races, one last (maybe) word about the Illinois Senate race. For those of you not in Illinois, Star Trek Borg Seven of Nine's ex-husband, Jack Ryan, dropped out of the Senate race after being caught lying to senior Republican party hacks about wanting to watch his Borg wife have sex with other men in sex clubs, which is why she divorced him.

So the Republicans, not wanting a white man to lose the Senate race to a black man, have nominated a black man to lose, Alan Keyes. Keyes has never once stepped foot in Illinois and had bashed Hillary Clinton for running in New York. At least she'd visited there once...

Those Republicans. First they can't find Osama Bin Laden in Afghanistan, then they can't find weapons of mass destruction in Iraq. Now they can't even find a black man in Chicago!

They hadn't had any Rolling Rock stocked in the cooler, so I settled for a warm six pack. I stuck my beer in the passenger side floorboard of the old clunker, and decided to cruise downtown for a cold one. But where to go?

If Duffy hadn't shut his bar down I'd have gone there and watched the sunset. This is a great time of year for watching sunsets in Illinois. Dempsey's? I barely gave them a second thought. Rier raised the price of Rolling Rock and the place was usually pretty empty on Tuesday. Not even a pretty bartender, as most of Dempsey's bartenders are guys these days. Hell, half the reason I used to go there was the pretty bartenders.

The Firehouse has pretty bartenders, but they usually get them from that God damned Frankie's Bar, where they charge import prices for Rolling Rock. I was getting tired of arguing with new bartenders from Frankie's who wanted to charge me as much for a Rolling Rock as for a Heineken. I'm starting to think that the firemen who own the Firehouse are as bad to work for as Frankie's employees have told me he is. Otherwise, why so much turnover?

Boone's came to mind. There are always young pretty bartenders there. Well, maybe not supermodels but at least the bartenders are neither male nor butt-ugly. I was thinking I was a day early, as there have been posters up at Boone's saying that starting August 11 there was going to be crab races, and I was curious.

Linda was tending bar, and the place was doing a brisk business for a Tuesday night. Most nights except weekends the bars here are pretty empty. Boone, the owner, was at the other end of the bar. "Hmmm..." I said to Linda, "I can't decide what kind of beer I want tonight."

"Import drafts are two fifty tonight" she said.

"In that case, give me a Foster's."

Linda's a very attractive young lady. I was surprised to see her there, as last week I'd gone there for a pizza, and she'd told me she had a new job at a chiropractor's office. And now the poor girl was going through even more stress, as it seems she broke up with her boyfriend over the weekend. She was a little blue.

"If I had the slightest hint you liked old guys I'd hit on you," I said. She grinned wryly.

She went to pour someone else's drink, and Boone strolled up. "How ya doin?" he asked.

"Good," I said. "I'm looking forward to your crab races tomorrow. How does that work, anyway?"

He laughed. "I'm not really sure, we're still working it out."

"You should serve crab legs," I said. "Hey," he replied," that's a good idea! I should!"

I finished the second beer, left a tip for Linda, and went home.

Wednesday night I headed to Bread stretchers for

dinner, noting how the weather here has been weirdly awesome since the weekend. Normally, Satan leaves hell and vacations in Illinois during the State Fair so she can warm up a bit. Not this year, it's like early April. The high yesterday was 72F, instead of the normal 99+F. As I left Bread Stretchers, the breeze gave me goose bumps. I decided to drive home for a flannel shirt.

It was about 8:15 when I left for Boone's. The races were to start at 8:30.

On the way, I spied something out of the corner of my eye I'd never seen before: an Irish Leprechaun. A real live honest to God Leprechaun, about three feet high wearing a green bowler hat and coat, bright red hair, long nose and smoking one of those long Irish pipes. He looked rather stoned. I always wondered what they were smoking...

I did a double take; those Leprechauns sure are tricky. When I looked straight at him, he turned himself into a fire hydrant.

When I got to Boone's the races had already started. I sat down at the bar and Boone came over and asked me if I was racing. "sure," I said. He produced a few styrofoam bowls, each with a small crab inside, with a tiny piece of paper with a number written on it glued to the crab's back. "How do I tell a good one?" I asked. "Hmm," he said, "this guy was pretty active earlier."

Number thirty two was a monster among these crabs, with a shell nearly two and a half inches long. I gave him the one dollar racing registration fee.

Linda wasn't there, but there were two other pretty bartenders. One of them was new, I'd never seen her before. I couldn't decide if she was knockout beautiful or butt ugly. I got a beer and went over closer to the racing table, and caught half a race before a half dozen guys that looked like pro-wrestlers came in and made a wall between my table and the race. Cops? No, one guy was wearing a shirt advertising fire engines. Likely cops and firemen. Or maybe just skinhead punks, who knows?

Several races and a second beer and number thirty two hadn't been called yet. I went over and asked the announcer when 32 was up. He checked his clipboard. "Why you're next. Last race of round one."

The races were an elimination, with the slowest crab being eliminated and put back in the terrarium. I walked over to the racing table.

The tabletop was white, with a red ring around the outside about four inches thick, and a red circle in the middle about a foot in diameter. Bright, big red letters said "Boone's Saloon" and "Crab Racing". When not in use, the table top served as an advertisement. A bright, and rather warm, light hung from the ceiling about three feet above the center of the table. There was a circular plastic "fence" around the red circle, probably a used gallon ice cream container with the bottom cut out.

The race starts when the fence is removed, and ends when all but one crab is in the red ring around the outside of the table.

Two fat girls were putting their crabs in the fence. They were little crabs, less than half as big as mine. I put my crab in the fence, and it immediately went straight for one of the little crabs, who went quickly inside its shell. My crab was all over it. "I think my crab's trying to eat your crab," I told the fat girl.

"And they're off!" the announcer announced, taking the fence away.

The two little crabs, thoroughly intimidated by my monster, sat there huddled together shivering, while mine took off straight toward the fat girl, who shrieked and started waving her hands wildly.

"Hey," the announcer said, "you can't do that, that's cheating!"

But it was too late. My crab, almost to the red ring, had already turned around heading back toward the center of the table. He got halfway to the two little crabs, who freaked out and started running away from the big crab.

Straight to the finish line. My crab lost his first race. Next week, I think I'll just be a spectator.

Chapter 51: Evil-X cheered me up
Mon Aug 16, 2004 at 08:43:19 PM EST

There was too much happening Saturday for me to do a normal mcgrew diary.

The guy who owns Bootleggers, a bar south of town, decided to host three bands on his birthday. Posamist started, followed by Luke Turasky and Friends, with The Station playing until they closed at 3:00.

To make a long story short and litigation-free, there were a couple of young women there who thoroughly enchanted me.

Levi is infuriatingly ass burgers; excuse me, Asperger's in one respect – he can't tell when women are hitting on him. I mean, they're all over the guy. Later I say "Dude! she wants you! Christ man!" and he doesn't believe me.

He introduced me to the enchantresses.

I got a pizza. Nobody seemed to believe me when I insisted I couldn't eat the whole thing myself. "Don't tempt a fat man!" Levi exclaimed, and started eating.

I've noticed two things: it's OK for a man to be fat, and it's OK for a woman to be skinny. But fat women and skinny men are decidedly uncool. But fat men don't realize this.

The second band, Luke Turasky, was playing and...

"Hey," I said, "isn't that the Green Grass Pickers?"

After much debate, it was. They were one of the old Dempsey's bands, two or three owners ago.

The enchantresses disappeared about the time Levi did. Probably went to the Firehouse, where Posamist was playing later. I stuck around for The Station, who I hadn't seen in a couple of months.

So all day yesterday I was blue, thinking of the young enchantresses and how fucking old I was and how I wouldn't be able to tell if a young woman was some kind of pervert who just liked old guys. Like such a thing even exists.

I was lonely.

"I'm getting pierced," Patty said. "Mom's taking me and signing for it."

The doorbell rang like a dirge, a feeling of doom was in the air, and Patty let Evil-X in.

My God that woman has gained some weight! Fuck! Holy shit! Damn I'm glad I'm no longer married to that ugly fucking whore!

Poll:
Loneliness
just a word 7%
a chance to read 7%
a bummer at times 30%
is misspelled, I think 7%
I bet on that horse last week! 0%
what else is there? 23%
Hah, I'm getting laid, loser 23%

Chapter 52: Little Feat
Thu Aug 19, 2004 at 06:14:12 PM EST

Thirty years ago, I'm sure when they played *Don't Bogart That Joint* the auditorium lit up with the sweet smell of muggles. Not Harry Potter "muggles," but muggles in the sense of the word as it was used in 1940. If you're wondering where Rowling got that term, it's a drug reference from even before MY time.

Parking at the fair is a bitch, so I try to not drive there. Actually, I try not to go there at all, but Little Feat was scheduled to play, and I've never seen them live. I would have liked to have seen them when Lowell George was still alive, but what the hell...

So I had my daughter drop me off at the westernmost gate, nearest the concert. I paid my three bucks for fair admission and walked in. A very pretty sunset was developing.

I paid five bucks for admission to the concert itself (and you fools paid how much to see that God-awful Elton John?) and started walking up... and the sunset was just spectacular. I stopped and stood there watching for a good ten minutes as the crowd walked past, oblivious to the beauty surrounding them.

A big cloud to the west/south-west made it even more spectacular. Some fool noticed me staring at the sky and remarked to whomever he was with as he walked past "I hope it doesn't rain."

Blindness abounds. These fools will pay ten dollars to see a movie, a hundred to see a Broadway play, ten million to have a Van Gogh painting, but put God's art in front of them and they might as well gouge their worthless eyes out.

I figured I could probably see the sunset from the stands, so I walked on up and bought a beer. Three bucks for a Budweiser. Ripoffs. Damn, but I hate being overcharged.

There was a table set up with t shirts and CDs. The CDs were a little high priced, but were all signed by the band. I got a copy of the double CD *Live At the Ramshead*. Another twenty bucks.

I walked down, got a seat, and watched the sunset. That big cloud seemed to be getting closer.

As darkness fell, the Groove Daddys started playing. I hadn't heard them before either, despite the fact that they're a local bar band. They played for half an hour, putting on a very good show. I made a mental note to see them again and see if they have any CDs.

I walked down toward the stage, and something wet hit me in the eye. Was someone spitting at me? Another drop. Birds? No, it was starting to sprinkle.

ka BOOM! rumble rumble.

Fuck.

Some guy announced that they were going to wait for the rain to pass, that their radar said it was a smaller, local storm. I walked back to get out of the rain. I spotted Jeff standing by the stairs.

"I thought you guys were supposed to be playing here tonight?" I asked him.

"Yeah, we were supposed to but it kinda fell apart. Hey, everybody's here, come on up."

When we sat down, I asked Joe what happened to their gig.

"We were supposed to take the Groove Daddies' place where they're normally playing while they're here opening for Little Feat, but they only wanted to pay us half of what we normally get." Mojo Nixon's song *Where The Hell's My Money* popped into my mind for no reason whatever.

By ten o'clock, the announcer came on the house speakers, which I could barely hear. He said something about the show being canceled and refunds at the arena.

The arena is on the far side of the fair, a mile's walk away. God damned thieves run the fair, it seems. Three dollars for a seventy five cent beer, gate admission plus show admission, they don't pay the talent shit, but they claim to lose money every year.

Some Chicago politician is lining his pockets big time. Heh, some things never change.

Little Feat owes me a concert.

Poll:
Crab racing
better than horse racing 0%
better than auto racing 0%
stupid idea 50%
sounds like fun 50%
people only go to those things to watch the crabs crash 0%
other 0%

Chapter 53: The Farmer And The Dell
Thu Aug 26, 2004 at 08:11:57 PM EST

Last Thursday I opened the Illinois Typo to find a good place to hear some live music over the weekend, and... there wasn't any. Yeah, Breadstretcher's was having a Playground Heroes CD release party, but the place would be packed with snot nosed teenagers. Including my daughter.

So I copped a six pack from the gas station and went home and opened a shoutcast stream, and posted a link on K5.

Saturday morning I got up, drank some coffee, and drove downtown to Recycled Records. As I walked in the door I cursed; I had forgotten those DVDs. My damned old eyes had done me wrong and I'd bought the fullscreen version of LOTR3 instead of the widescreen, and what I thought was the now-illegal *The Exorcist* was, in fact, the second sequel. I hadn't known that they'd even made a second sequel. The first sequel was bad enough.

Oh well, I could get a couple of bucks for them some other day. Today I wanted a cassette deck. See, I have six cases of tapes, each case holding two dozen tapes. That's a lot of music I couldn't hear, and haven't been able to hear since Evil-X hocked my tape deck in 1995.

Most of you think cassettes are low quality. In fact, the very first ones were. And the very last ones were. I bought an off-brand walkman a couple of years ago for the express purpose of sampling my cassettes, and only sampled one, and deleted the file. Looking closer at the FM, or "fucking Manual" for those of you non-nerds who may be making the sad mistake of reading this book, and how did you make it this far? In this case the "FM" was a a piece of paper that came with it, and it was no wonder the sample sounded like shit, the newer walkmans have a frequency response of 1khz to 3khz. Shitty shitty shitty. Makes a low quality MP3 sound good by comparison.

So I picked up a used deck with a response of 50hz to 18khz. That's a better response than CD, with its zero to 22khz response but only a zero to 10khz undistorted response. Aliasing sucks almost as much as tape hiss.

My pig farmer friend Mike called as I was driving home. "Comin' down today?"

Well, yeah. My turntable was at his house, as I have nothing to actually plug a turntable into. And I had more vinyl to digitize. This time, I shouldn't have to take my computer along, as his wife just bought a brand spanking new Dell, dude, and paid fourteen hundred bucks for it. Mike's still pissed at his wife for spending all that cash.

On my way to Mike's farm in Columbia, I stopped by "Gange Farmer's", just outside Dupo. No luck; his pickup truck was gone. Oh well, Mike and I would have to make do with beer.

I have decided I hate Dell, and I hate XP. I go to plug Mike's stereo into his Dell, and there are five damned jacks. I put on my reading glasses to read the little squiggles... hey Mike, turn the light on, would you? I finally resolve the squiggles... and they're still squiggles. God damned fucking icons. Meaningless icons. That one looks like the schematic representation of an antenna, this one looks like a ground... WTF???

"American" company, my ass. What the hell is wrong with labeling shit in plain English, you fucking Dell morons??? Christ, but I hate globalization. None of them worked as an input.

"Where's the fucking manual?" I ask. "These things aren't marked. Well, not in English, anyway."

"Hell, I don't know. She knows where it is, she should be home in half an hour."

We ate stew and waited for his wife. She found the FM and I found... nothing. This model had a sound card, not an onboard chip, and the manual didn't say jack about the card.

Like as if your car's manual didn't tell you where the spare tire was when it's in a non-standard place, saying only "Your spare is in the trunk, unless you have an add-on spare." Well, duh, YOU ADDED IT ON! Fucktards. I hate Dell.

But the plug for "mic" in the chipbound Dells was pink, according to the almost useless manual, so assuming the card's mic input was pink as well... viola! Distorted, monophonic sound.

Hmmm. Maybe the one right next to the mic is the aux? It was.

Now to adjust the volume... where's the volume control? Not in the tray. OK, start... damn fucking Microsoft changed the Start Menu around for XP. "All Programs?" OK... drill down five menus below, just like 98. Open the volume control and... unlike 98 there's no check box for putting it in the system tray.

I copied the icon to the desktop, cursing. May Bill Gates die in poverty, and his evil lawyer parents, too. And his kids. And all his friends. And anybody else who had a hand in designing that piece of shit operating system. And especially the trolls and shills who post on messageboards that Gates is God and XP is better than sex.

Yes, I hate XP. I will NOT be buying a copy. Or even stealing one.

So I put *Demons and Wizards* on the turntable and sampled it with EAC. I opened it for editing, cut out the blank parts, marked the track skip points, and went to burn the CD and...

EAC couldn't see the Japanese CD burner, OR the Korean DVD burner.

Shit. So much for sampling. I burned the .wav file to a CD as a data file with the incredibly crappy software that came with the Dell, so I could take it home and burn it on another CD as a redbook audio CDA album.

So, so much for sampling albums today. Mike and I decide to go visit Gange Farmer. We get into Mike's car and drive off the bluff, down to Dupo.

GF was home, finally. GF asks, "got any papers?" I had come prepared, buying two books of Zig Zags before I left Springfield. "Yep," I answered, dug into my pocket... and I'd left them in my flannel shirt, in the car. In Columbia.

"Well, looks like Mike's outta luck," GF says. Mike doesn't like GF's pipe. "Wait a minute..." he remembered where he might find some papers.

Unfortunately for me and especialy for Mike, GF's crop wasn't doing so well. He could only sell me twenty bucks worth, and Mike was out of luck. But he had enough to get us both loaded.

Saturday and Sunday I worked on my bankruptcy. Wells Fargo had sent me a bill for ten thousand dollars for the car they had repossessed last year. And the mortgage company will probably send me an eighty thousand dollar bill for the house they repossessed. So I'm worse than broke.

And I still don't have a girlfriend.

Poll:
What's wrong with me?
too ugly 16%
too good looking 8%
too nice 25%
not nice enough 0%
too mean 8%
not mean enough 16%
fucking loser 8%
all of the above 16%

Chapter 54: Beer and Anti-Paxil
Fri Oct 01, 2004 at 08:06:43 PM EST

So I hopped into the jalopy and cruised down to Boone's. The band was already playing.

I drank a beer or two, said "hi" to a few folks and shook a few hands, and wound up on the bus when the band took a break. Levi turned on the stereo. They have a killer stereo in there, a Panasonic DVD player underneath a TV set on top of the same type of speakers they have on stage. I often donate CDs to the bus, and last night the *Presence* CD I had ripped from vinyl was playing.

The party had moved out to the bus, which was almost full. Someone produced a bowl, and, um, I forgot what happened. Anyway, the bus then emptied after everyone's beers did, and we all went inside to refresh our mugs.

Nobody from the band (at least that I noticed) was on the bus with us. So, I notice that Joe got in the bus with a couple of attractive ladies after everyone else had vacated it. I hadn't talked to Joe in a couple of weeks...

OK, shit, you got me. I wanted to meet the women. Joe's engaged, maybe I could get both of the ladies?

I get on and sit down, Joe says "hi". He's showing the ladies around the Posabus. The Zepplin had stopped. We're just making conversation, and I mentioned that whenever Posamist plays it's a party. One of the ladies, holding a pen and a small pad, asks "can I quote you on that?"

"Huh?"

"She's with the *State Journal Register*," Joe said. "Aw, come on," she pesters. She wants my last name (Joe had introduced me just as "Steve").

I finally relented. Damn, now I guess I'm going to be in the newspaper.

I drank one more beer and went home.

I drove down to visit friends yesterday, and as I got out of the car in Cahokia my phone rang. It was Evil-X.

"I just got a thing in the mail saying I have to go to court! What's going on here," it demanded. "Oh," I replied. "You're going to pay child support!"

"Oh no I'm not! It says in the divorce settlement." I smiled a huge grin. "See you in court, bitch." And I hung up on her.

I went inside and visited with Jeff and his girlfriend and her daughter, who was playing the original Wolfenstein on Jeff's primitive computer.

We chatted a while, and I drove out in the boonies to Brett's house, where Mike the pig farmer was partying. Only when I got there, nobody was partying. They were all on the roof, laying shingles.

One of them came down and rolled. As we were waiting for everyone else to get off the roof and join us, my phone rang again. Somebody fired up a big circular saw, I walked back outside. It was my daughter Patty.

She was livid. Her mother had called her crying, and Patty insisted that I not pursue child support, citing her mother's poverty.

She threatened to move in with her sister. X had won again, using one of her favorite weapons, my children. I walked back in. I'd missed half of the doobie.

Bret gave me a beer, and everybody but Mike went back up on the roof to finish nailing. It's amazing how fast a man can work with air hammers and other power tools. I can only imagine what it was like building the house I lost, built with hand saws and hand drills and no such thing as a power tool at all. It boggles my mind, and houses were built that way for millennia.

"What's wrong?" Mike asked. I told him about the conversation,

"That's bullshit!" he said, perturbed himself. "If she was living with her mom you know you'd be paying out of your ass!" And he was right.

We went back to Jeff's. Jeff and his girlfriend also told me I was crazy if I was going to let X win this round.

I started driving up 55, my whole day had been shot. I was angry and blue. The two emotions fought for control.

Halfway home the phone rang. It was Patty again. "Where are you?" she demanded.

"I'm halfway home. And before I hang up on you, you never cared much about my tears, when I couldn't stop your mom's insurance payments for that brand new car to come out of my paycheck when I was walking everywhere. And you didn't mind my tears when she got part of my pension. I'm going to be dirt poor when I retire, but THAT doesn't bother you. For the first time in my life I wish I'd never had kids."

And I hung up. I shouldn't have said that, but I was uncontrollably livid. True though it was at the time, it was a thing I regretted instantly; both saying it, but more so the truth of it.

Once again, the kids would help the slut have her way. And I was just damned sick of it.

I called her cell when I got home. "Where are you?"

"I'm at Mom's house."

"Yeah, well tell her if she doesn't want to pay child support she damned well better go in front of a judge and work out a deal where she stays out of my pension!!"

I went downtown and got a sandwich, and to Dempsey's for a beer. No band tonight, but I didn't much feel like partying anyway. I bent Rier's mom's ear for a while, and went home after the one beer. I was in bed by 10:30.

Patty came home about six. I thought she'd stayed at her mom's. Nope, she had been with a friend whose parents had divorced and had gone through something similar.

I guess all women are evil bitches who will use their children no matter how much it hurts them.

I argued with Patty for quite a while, She went to her room and I made coffee.

Life sucks. I hate that I ever took any Paxil, because life now seems empty, meaningless, with all my good days behind me and few days ahead, either good or bad. Don't ever take an antidepressant unless you plan on continuing with them until you die. I've never in my life thought of suicide, until this morning, when it fleetingly crossed my mind.

It's not going to happen, but if the thought could cross my mind, it would be enough to end it for others. Beware these drugs!

Chapter 55: Child Support and other scams and bars and music and
Mon Oct 18, 2004 at 03:33:50 PM EST

Evil-X has gotten herself a lawyer. And, of course, caused much other mischief.

Saturday, Patty told me she was going to her Mom's for "some kind of modeling school thing." I thought little of it, besides a vague feeling of uneasiness when the "Evil-X is up to no good" detector goes off. She left for her mom's and I drove down to Cahokia to visit Jeff.

Poor Jeff has tons of problems. His job pays shit, and his girlfriend is a certified lunatic. I mean certified, on antipsychotic drugs and SSI. She used to be a stripper, but she's gotten very fat. Probably the psycho meds' fault, but her stripping days are over unless she sheds a hundred pounds or so. Jeff doesn't mind that a bit; he likes 'em large. Jeff's no tiny guy himself.

She had talked him into seeing some kind of presentation about selling shit over the internet, and they had absconded with two hundred bucks of his money, having convinced him that the internet was the road to riches. This despite the fact that neither of them has an internet connection.

Josh was there, and they were watching a training DVD for the "selling shit on the web" deal.

"Have you checked on Jeff's amp?" Josh asked.

Jeff had given me an old car (which caught fire and burned to the ground three weeks later; see old diary entries from last year) in return for the promise of fixing his guitar amp. After my VOM exploded in my hand while trying to figure out what was wrong with the amplifier, I threw the amp in the trunk and took it to a music store in Springfield. It had been there a few weeks. "No, I'm going in this week" I told him.

We talked of Jeff's need to get a computer, or at least, find a modem that will work in an ISA slot (his PC is a 486) or a serial modem he could plug into the serial port. "Of course," I told him, "you won't be able to use your mouse. And you're going to need a phone line!"

Mike called from a park in Columbia. "Big party here, come on down." I told him I didn't know anybody, that I would feel like I was crashing the party. He talked me into it with promises that they needed someone to help eat the ton of food and drink the three kegs of beer.

Beer... I drove out. Indeed, they were glad to have another person help eat and drink, and I was more than glad to help.

Sunday morning I asked Patty how the "modeling thing" went. "Mom's going to put me through modeling school and it's going to cost a lot of money so I want you to drop the child support thing." She seemed to think that she would be guaranteed a well paying modeling career if she went through the school.

It seems the "Evil-X is up to no good" detector is working fine. "You should have called your aunt," I told her. "She went to modeling school, and they have money now, but it didn't come from modeling. Or you could have called my cousin." My cousin had not only gone to modeling school, but had a career as a model for several years. Before becoming a dental technician. Before becoming a dancer. "Kathy's not rich, in fact she stopped modeling because the dental thing paid better."

Patty convinced me that she wanted this, that it would help her music career... and I was not going to let X get over on me with this. I was going to collect child support if it actually costs me more money than I collected.

I agreed to pay for it. She went to her mom's, waiting for the phone call. "Don't worry," Patty said, "I probably won't get picked. They only pick one out of ten."

A few hours later Patty was back. "They picked me! There were only thirteen out of two hundred kids that got picked!" My heart sank, and I congratulated her.

Evil-X had convinced her that I would somehow use the modeling thing against her in the child support war. X is, as you might imagine, someone who will hit you over the head with a shovel and then sue you for damages to the shovel. The whole modeling thing was a ploy to get me to drop the child support, to get Patty mad at me. And I wasn't going to fall for it. Rather than resist the expense, I ju-jitsoed her. "I will bend like the reed in the wind," Paul had said in *Dune*, and I was determined to do the same.

Monday was a holiday, Columbus day. Tuesday after work I dropped by Walko's to check on Jeff's amp. "It's done," the spooky looking dude said. This guy is about seven feet tall and can't weight more than 120 pounds, including the half dozen piercings on his bottom lip.

"I'm going to have to run home for my checkbook. How much is it?"

"Twenty seven bucks." Wow, I was thinking a hundred, two hundred... I pulled out my wallet and paid cash, and took the amp home.

Wednesday I went to lunch at Top Cat's, and there was Patty waiting for me. "Why aren't you in school?" I demanded.

She was, she said, on her lunch and needed me to write her a check for the modeling school. Six hundred twenty dollars.

Gulp. Shit. "OK," I said, "But I don't have my checkbook with me."

"I brought it," she said.

I wrote the check. Damn. I wanted to buy a new bass guitar, a new bed, I had a few bills to pay and I needed to get a new prescription for contact lenses, since they wouldn't sell me any more without my eyes being checked again and I'd had the one in my left eye for a month and a half.

I was going to be broke as hell for the next month. Again. Crap, I'm just catching up after paying the lawyer for the bankruptcy.

"You work tonight?" I asked. "No, but I'm going to Grandpaw's with mom right after school."

Around seven I'm sitting at the computer responding to some troll when the doorbell rings. I finish typing my sentence and the doorbell rings again, quickly and rapidly, as if she's got a monster after her. "Impatient kid," I mutter, and get up and go out the apartment door...

BLAM!!! A cop comes flying, literally, down the stairs and right through the neighbor's door like an action hero in a movie. Jesus but those guys can move. And they sure can get a door open fast! The noise had been them going through the heavy, locked steel door – in seconds. The cop couldn't have gotten in the neighbor's apartment faster if he'd used a key.

Slick. They can get in your house in two seconds without breaking anything. I was amazed. "Someone here called us?" the cop asks the neighbors.

"Whoa," I say to myself as I quietly retreat into my own apartment.

A couple of hours later Patty came home and gave me the check back. "Grandpaw's paying the down payment," she said.

Grandpaw is her mom's dad. I like Hubert and still drink with him.

Wow. I'm going to have to visit the old fart with a fifth of his favorite cheap whiskey. How a fellow like that could raise a demon like Evil-X I'll never understand.

Last night my oldest daughter called. She was upset with her mother, who "takes care of" her finances for her. Seems she'd neglected to pay Leila's cable bill but had used the money to get a lawyer to fight the child support.

I went to Boone's later to see Posamist play. The band spotted me as I was getting a beer.

"McGrew!" they all yell, waving. I walked over.

"Dude," Levi says, "you're famous!" and handed me a piece of a newspaper.

It seems the local paper had done a big writeup on Posamist, and I'd been quoted. That, too, is in a previous diary. Not only quoted, but my quote was the last words in the article. There's a name for that, but I don't know what it is because I'm not a journalist.

I smiled. I didn't mention that more people will read this diary than the newspaper article I'm quoted in.

Poll:
The music streaming now is...
really sucky 25%
not bad 0%
my favorite 0%
Cool! Never heard it before! 25%
WTF is this shit??? 25%
from a major label 0%
never ever going to ever get any kind of airplay outside college radio 25%

Chapter 56: At the bar... no, not THAT bar
Mon Oct 25, 2004 at 09:17:58 PM EST

I went to court the other morning trying to collect child support. Evil-X was there already, noxious fumes rising from its blubber laden hull. Not the expected brimstone fumes, but the stench of stale cigarettes and fat old woman sweat and cheap perfume.

She had spent four hundred dollars on a shyster.

"Is there anyone who hasn't signed in?" the bailiff outside the courtroom asked. I went up and spoke to them. They still hadn't corrected the screwup the State's Attorney had made. "She'll call you," I was told.

Nobody called me. The judge was at his bench, and I went in.

There was a huge black man standing before the judge. Apparently this fellow was unemployed and hadn't been paying his child support.

He said "Look, Judge, I gots no problem with child support."

"Yes, you do," the judge replied. "You may not have a problem with the idea of child support, but you do have a problem with actually paying it."

There was some nearly subaudible back and forth between the judge and the large man standing before him, when the judge said "Do you think this is a joke, Mister Johnson?"

Mr. Johnson replied quietly, too quiet to hear. The judge repeated, "I'll ask you again, Mr. Johnson," very firmly, "Do you think this is a joke??"

"I gots no fuckin' money!" Johnson replied. "You gonna sent me to jail?"

"Would you like me to cite you for contempt, Mr. Johnson?"

"Fuck you, motherfucker!" Gasps and giggles from the gallery...

"Contempt of court!" the judge ordered. "Take him to jail."

"Fuck you!" Johnson added rather stupidly.

"That's two" the judge said.

"Fuck you! Eat shit cocksucker!"

"That's three."

"Kiss my big black ass, motherfucker. Fuck you!"

"That's four!"

"Suck my dick bitch!"

By the time he got to eight, Mr. Johnson was being led out in handcuffs. The judge shook his head in wonder. This was more entertaining than a TV courtroom drama, for sure.

Another black man came in through the door Mr. Johnson left through, wearing Sangamon County's black and gray striped jail uniform. I always thought prison stripes were only in cartoons, but I guess this *is* Springfield.

Apparently this fellow had run afoul of the judge before, ignoring a court order or something. Or maybe he, too, had called the judge a motherfucker. If so, this time he was respectful towards the judge, who asked him if he was employed.

"No sir."

"What kind of work do you do, Mr. Black?"

"I'm a cook, sir."

"A cook?"

I think he got out of jail, but I'm not sure as the State's Attorney's staff finally got around to talking to me. "We need a little further information." I walked out in the hall with her.

It seems Evil-X had stupidly lied to her lawyer, who was under the impression that she lived with my older daughter and was supporting her. I informed the State Attorney lawyer, who was representing me on the taxpayer's dime, that no, X had moved in with her boyfriend and my oldest daughter was living alone, and was being supported by SSI.

I went back in and sat down as a white fellow was explaining to the judge that he was unemployed. "Didn't you list..." the judge looked at a piece of paper, "your children as dependents on your unemployment claim?"

The SA lawyer came over and whispered to me that "he's going to ask the judge for a continuance, and I'm going to object. Did you have to take off work today?" I answered in the affirmative.

Evil-X's lawyer and the SA went to the bench. More mumbling between the lawyers and the judge, and the judge announced "I'm granting a continuance. You will be here on

December second and you will both be prepared. Am I understood?"

I was given a document with the new court date, and drove back to work. Fortunately for me, I had the presence of mind not to curse at the judge. Indeed, one should respect a judge, because you can most definitely go to jail for the crime of gross stupidity.

Now I have another worry. If X gets in front of the judge and perjures herself and the judge sends her to jail, both of my kids will be pissed off at me. As evil and stupid as the bitch is, I wouldn't put it past her.

Chapter 57: The missing diary
Wed Nov 17, 2004 at 06:37:44 PM EST

It's still missing.

The diary in question involves activities at Boone's Saloon on the night of November 4th, two days after the election.

This isn't an actual diary, but a "movie trailer" kind of thing here, the real diary is still coming.

Posamist put on an exceptional show that night, at least the first set; I have to work, so can't spend all Thursday night in a saloon. It was capped off by Plead The 5th's Levi Leach sitting in and giving a rousing rendition of the Stones' *Sympathy for the Devil*, which involved a long verbal rant about the election, capped off by some pyrotechnics which I'll describe in the real diary.

After he finished his number, he sat down and asked what I thought about it. I told him if he'd email the rant, I'd post it on an internet site that gets ten thousand hits per day.

"Sure, what's the site?"

"K-u-r-o-5..."

"Corrosion?"

"You've heard of it?"

"Heard of it??? Dude... that's a primo site!"

"They like me there..."

Levi was impressed, and I was puzzled.

This past Monday I stopped off at Demsey's for a beer. Levi and Joe (not Joe Frew, this is a different Joe) were leaving as I was walking up. "We'll be right back, don't go away," Levi said.

Rier, the owner, was tending bar. "How's everything?" he asks, handing me a Rolling Rock.

"Shit," I said. "Damned hard raising a 17 year old daughter by yourself."

Rier had his own problems, which involved the beer distributor fucking up. He had a standing order of two cases of Rolling Rock per week, and they'd only delivered a single case of Corona. "I only have two Rolling Rocks left, and you're drinking one of them!"

That was OK as I'd only planned on drinking one. Levi

and Joe walked back in.

Levi and Joe go way back, going through school together. Joe's a quiet, good natured fellow that I always thought was a little nerdy. Maybe not as nerdy as me but still nerdy.

"So," I asked Levi, "Where's that email?" He hadn't written it. "So, what'd you think of Saturday night's show?" he asked.

PT5 had played Dempsey's Saturday, and I was supposed to bring a PC and record the show. It didn't work out that way.

Jeff, down in Cahokia, had been roped into some sort of internet business, so had bought a new computer and a phone line and DSL. I was supposed to help him wire up the DSL and get him on line.

The previous Saturday we had unboxed the PC and set it up. He was dialing up until he could get his DSL. When I set up the PC (running XP, of course) he hadn't yet gotten a phone line. Unlike the fictional Jeff in the rejected "Jeff's Unhackable Computer," which I should probably resubmit, the real Jeff doesn't know shit about PCs.

I installed SBC's software, including clicking "yes, I agree." Gees, I already agreed when I was using SBC's DSL myself. I don't know if Jeff agrees or not, but at any rate, he never clicked the "I agree" button.

SBC has obviously seen my rants about clickthroughs and how I get a minor to click them for me, they added language saying the clicker must be over 18. And???

Since no company is stupid enough to let a clickthrough "agreement" go to court, since they would surely lose, Congress should write a law specifically stating that they aren't binding on anyone and be done with the charade.

I got the stuff installed and... damn, his DSL is a lot slower than mine was. And Google refused to connect. I got suspicious, of course.

"You've... been on the internet this week?"

"Yeah, Todd and his wife were here Tuesday looking at porn."

Oh, shit. My heart sank. I triple fingerd it and looked at the running processes, and it looked as if a dozen different viruses and spyware programs were all fighting for control of the machine Jeff thought he owned.

After an hour of trying to eradicate all the malware, I gave up and reformatted the drive, and reinstalled Windows (actually, I ghosted the HD from CD), Mozilla, Zone Alarm, and Road Rash. I then logged on to the internet, and downloaded updates from Norton which was preinstalled with the ghosting, and Windows updates.

Jeff was on line, finally. I was going to be late to Dempsey's, and still had to go to Mike's in Columbia to get my mouse and keyboard, as I wasn't going to drag my cordless ones to the bar.

Josh and his dad Chris were at Mike's, and they were partying. I got back to Springfield about 11:00, in time for PT5's last set, but I had given up on the recording.

What shitty writing this is today, sorry. Anyway, Monday night he asked how Saturday was and...

Everyone sort of wordlessly started going out the back door, which could mean only one thing. I headed out, too. A pipe was being passed around. Levi's guitar player, Daryl, and a couple of other guys were there.

"Dude," Levi says to Joe, "did you know Steve's one of Kuro5hin's premier posters?"

Joe looked startled. I'm sure I did too. "You've read my stuff?" I said.

"Yeah, but I didn't know it was you. It dawned on me the other day when you said you posted there. You're K5's mcgrew!"

"Uh, yeah. So you're a fan?"

Joe seems impressed. "Ever get on the front page?"

"Uh, yeah, most of my stories get FP."

Darryl and the other guys have been here, too, it turned

out.

"Wow," I said, "I didn't realize you guys were such nerds!"

Poll:
Best Springfield band
The Station 0%
Posamist 0%
Plead the Fifth 100%
Ed McCann's Rock House 0%
Ultraviolet 0%
Black Magic Johnson 0%
Ray Lytle and the Itchy Pickles 0%
The Oohs 0%
Inspected By Twelve 0%
The Mug Shots 0%
F5 0%
Other (post) 0%

Chapter 58: Found: The Missing Diary
Sun Nov 28, 2004 at 01:34:01 PM EST

Well, most of it, anyway. Bits and pieces of the month old thing have fallen out of my brain while I slept.

The diary in question concerned the Thursday night after the US elections. It hinged on a rant from Levi, who was going to email the rant so I could post the diary.

He finally sent the email, but I remember the rant being a bit longer. I'm sure I've forgotten some of the most memorable goings on of the night, as well.

I went in to Boone's, sat down at the bar and got a beer. Folks at the bar were all expressing disbelief among themselves that Bush had actually won the election, and what's more, apparently won it fairly this time.

The band had finished setting up, and was playing golf in the next room, on some video game machine. Joe came by and said "hi," and I wound up following him on to the bus. Someone was there passing a pipe around, and people were talking about how they couldn't believe that incompetent Bush had gotten re-elected.

Back inside the bar, Sarah arrived. I said "hi."

"Hi," she replied, "Can you believe that election?"

I shook my head. "Nope..."

Jeff and Joe were talking about the golf game. Not the other Joe, Joe Frew. I should find a new nick for the other Joe so fewer people will confuse Joe with "Joe".

Levi came in and said "hi" and Sarah walked over to where they were playing golf. "I can't fucking believe that cocksucker got re-elected," Levi said. "Fucking son of a bitch!"

"Yeah," I replied, "he should have been impeached and shot for treason, not re-elected."

"Are you going to stick around? At least until the break?" Levi asked. "I have a special version of 'Sympathy' tonight." Whenever Levi was at a Posamist show, which is pretty much whenever his own band isn't playing somewhere, Levi gets up and sings a custom version of the Rolling Stone's *Sympathy for the Devil*. I told him I wouldn't miss it.

Perhaps it was the smell of that special blend of pipe, but Posamist seemed to put on an even better show than usual that night.

I was sitting at a table with Sarah. "Should I get up there?" she asked. "Sure," I said. Joe asked if anybody had any requests, so I thundered "Sa-RAH!!" Other people joined in calling for Sarah, and Joe called her up there.

Sarah did "All Along The Watchtower". Then Levi walked up, and Joe introduced him as "My little brother Levi!"

Levi took the mic and started singing.

Please allow me to introduce myself, I'm a man of wealth and taste.
I've been around for a long, long year, stole many a man's soul and faith.
I was 'round when Jesus Christ had his moment of doubt and pain-
Made damn sure the pilate washed his hands and sealed his fate.

Pleased to meet you, hope you guess my name.
But what's puzzling you is the nature of my game.

I stuck around Saint Petersburg when I saw it was a time for a change.
Killed the czar and his ministers, Anastasia screamed in vain.
I rode a tank. Held a general's rank, when the blitzkrieg raged and the bodies stank.
Pleased to meet you, hope you guess my name, oh yeah
Ah, what's puzzling you is the nature of my game, oh yeah

I watched with glee while your kings and queens
Fought for ten decades for the gods they made
I shouted out, "Who killed all those Kennedys?"
When after all it was you and me.

Let me please introduce myself, I'm a man of wealth and taste.
And I laid traps for troubadours who get killed before they reached Bombay.
Pleased to meet you, hope you guessed my name, oh yeah
But what's puzzling you is the nature of my game.
"So what's everybody think of this election???"
The crowd yells and boos.
"Yeah, that's what I thought. We've put our lives in the

hands of the stupid man again... and they wanted us to vote???? They said you have a choice. You can change the world. Your opinion matters. Well, this is my fuckin' choice."

He held up a lighter and his voter registration card, and set the card ablaze, holding it high. Loud whistles and cheers, applause. Remember, Bush lost in a landslide in Illinois. He's not the most popular politician here.

Just as every cop is a criminal, and all the sinners we are saints!

Lets just say they call me "Levi" cause I'm in need of some restraints.

And if you meet me have some courtesy, have some sympathy, and some taste.

And forget all of your George Bush politics, cause I'm laying your mother fucking soul to waste!

"Best show 'evar'," I thought.

"We're going to taka a short break," Joe says. Levi comes by the table. "What'd you think?"

Chapter 59: Evil always wins
Sun Dec 05, 2004 at 02:07:55 PM EST

"All rise."
"Be seated."
The judge didn't look happy.

A black man stood before the judge, some words were exchanged, and the man left. The court reporter (or whoever it is that does those announcements) read another docket number, and another black man stood before the judge.

The fellow had apparently been ordered to look for work and was told to bring in documentation that he had turned in two job applications per day. The judge wasn't buying his protestations that he had left his list of prospective employers at home.

The man was jailed. The judge seemed pained, and protested to everyone or no one, or perhaps God, that he didn't like sending people to jail but sometimes they left him no choice. He coughed. "I'm calling a recess to, uh, get some cough medicine."

This seemed like an ideal time to use the rest room. As I searched for it, I spied Satan, the Evil-X, lurking at the far end of the hall. It looked especially dour. I was hoping it hadn't paid its lawyer and didn't have one anymore.

It didn't say anything, it just sat there. I finally found the restroom.

As I came out, the lady from the State's Attorney's office was looking for me. "Her attorney claims that she's paying for your oldest daughter, and..."

Finally before the judge, the State's Attorney lawyer was so nervous she was shaking. I realized this was her first case.

Sigh. No child support for me. X's slimy lawyer had convinced everyone that X was too poor to pay child support.

So that ends it. If I'm not too unlucky I won't have to deal with X any more.

Chapter 60: Dempsey died
Wed Dec 08, 2004 at 09:01:58 PM EST

"We're putting a new bar in," Rier said a month or two ago at Dempsey's, his tavern. "We're taking out this big, round one and putting in a bar that will stretch from here to down there. Ought to give us a lot more room."

A couple of weeks later, I was in Dempsey's, and one of the off-duty bartenders had a t-shirt that read "MoJo's."

"Only a few more days of Dempsey's," Rier said. "I'm changing the name, too," pointing at his barkeep's shirt.

"Mo' Joes?" I said. "That's what you're going to call it?"

"Yeah."

"Or is it," I said, looking at the pretty female bartender (the on-duty barkeep) "the Spanish pronunciation? Mo' Ho's?"

She blushed. The off-duty bartender laughed. Rier made a face.

A week ago Saturday, Inspected By Twelve was playing. Good band, I should make them the Rudies.US "song of the week." Can't do it right now, though, as I have the two Quake Christmas MP3s there, "I Saw Mommie Killing Santa Claus" and "Rudolph The Four Legged Stroggie", both sung by my then 12 year old daughter. So as I have extremely limited space these days there's no room left for 12, they'll have to wait until next month.

Rier looked wistful. "This is it," he said. "Dempsey's last night. No more Dempsey's!"

"As long as you have mo' hos," I said. Rier made a face. "Mojo's!" he said.

Last week as I was driving down Monroe, I noticed that the awning outside Dempsey's that was also its sign was gone, and the door was propped open. I parked and stuck my head in. Rier was inside with some workmen. The big round bar was gone, the place dirty, dusty, and ugly.

"Wha's happenin'?" Rier said.

"Just seeing how it's coming along."

"The bar's gone!" Rier said.

"Well, yeah, you said Saturday was the last night."

"No, the bar!" he exclaimed, gesturing to the big empty space where the bar had been.

"So, when do you get the new one?"

Dempsey's closing had a bit of an effect on me. It was responsible for my trading my nerdy, out of style coke bottle glasses for contact lenses. I recounted the story in another diary last year. Or was it the year before? At any rate, there are a lot of new K5ers since then.

It was a drizzly spring night, and as was my custom then, I walked downtown to have a couple of beers and listen to a little music and lost one of the lenses to my glasses behind a heavy cooler.

At the time, I hadn't met Rier, and he hadn't yet bought Dempsey's. I was still living in the big house on 7th street, so I could walk downtown and get as shitfaced as I wanted without worrying about a DUI.

I miss those days. Now I have to drive, meaning I have to limit myself to a couple of beers.

That's one more reason the mcgrew diaries aren't as good as they used to be. I'm not quite as tame when I'm drunk. I stopped taking the Paxil right before my house was foreclosed, and was in a really, really, really shitty mood for a couple of months. I mean, it's bad enough getting off of an antidepressant, but getting off of them when life is kicking your ass will really spoil your mood.

At the time I got off of the Paxil, I wondered if my writing would suffer, especially since the muse seemed to have left as well. It seems to have; but giving it more thought, I don't think so.

My old long abandoned site was "The Springfield Fragfest", so named because the online game *Quake* involves running around in virtual nightmare scenes, shooting people and running from people who are shooting at you. These games were called "frag fests", and getting killed was called "getting fragged". I understand the actual term "frag" came from Vietnam, where tossing a grenade at your Commanding Officer was known as "fragging" him. The Fragfest was fairly popular in its day, back before all you millions got on the internet. Lacking any inside knowledge of "teh game industry", rather than news I ran "nooze", which was a rather warped perspective on computer gaming news reported elsewhere, as well as the goings on with other Quake web sites. Often I would have the then excellent, now utter crap *PC Gamer* magazine's mascot, Coconut Monkey, battling Stroggs. Often I battled Stroggs myself, sometimes in a Coconut Monkey Quake skin. Sometimes, of course, in a Kenny skin or a Baal skin or even a Santa Clause skin.

As an example of what "nooze" was, there was a fellow named "Nacho." I'm not sure if he's the same Nacho that posts here at K5; I don't think so. At any rate, one post had me visiting him and his friend "Tikki God," who was complaining about how the shambler pissed all over everything. I'd have to look the post up, but I had them smoking something that smelled funny, and shooting rockets at Tikki's shambler (a "shambler" is one of the monsters in the Quake game) because it pissed on the couch. Or something. At any rate, gamers ate it up, and I very often got links from Blue's News, Planet Quake, sCary's, and just about everybody except Old Man Murray, who was always jealous, mean, nasty, and hilarious.

The Fragfest was especially popular in December when the Christmas page ran. The Germans especially liked it, site logs showing as many folks coming from German sites (.de) as dot coms. I used to call the Germans "Danes" just to see if anybody would correct me. Nobody ever did.

As long as I was having fun writing, people were having fun reading it. And then life started kicking my ass and I stopped being amusing and got all grouchy, and my audience left in droves. Later when things in my real life got better, the writing improved again and a lot of the old fans came back. Not all of them, though...

At any rate, if life would stop kicking me in the ass my writing would probably improve, as it did with my old site. That won't likely be any time soon, as my daughter has become a nightmare. And no, I'm not going to go into detail. But things will get better. They always do. Everything seems to go in circles.

But I digress... I do that a lot, don't I?

"So when do you get the new bar? When do you reopen?"

He said a couple of days.

Last night I was sitting at home, flipping through 72 channels of worthless, uninspired, boring drivel and decided to drive down town to see how Demps... er, MoJo's was coming. Besides, I ran out of beer.

I had planned on stopping if they were inside working, but the new awning said "MoJo's," the lights were on, and the beer lights in the window were on as well! MoJo's was open for business, it seemed.

Rier was behind the bar, Kat was tending, and a half dozen or so folks sat at the bar, including Rier's investment banker, who had sold him the bar in the first place.

Rier saw me come in and waved.

"Hey," I exclaimed, "*Mojo! Buenos Noche! ¿Que pasa?*"

Rier made a face.

"Rolling Rock?" Kat asked. "Hmm," I said, "I've been getting back to drinking Busch, 'cause the price of Rolling Rock has gone through the roof."

"Not here," Rier said, "It's still two and a quarter just like all the other domestics!"

A year ago, a six pack of Rolling Rock at the gas station was twenty cents more than a six pack of Busch. Now a twelve pack of Busch is twenty cents more than a six pack of Rolling Rock, and with my daughter running up hundreds of dollars worth of cell phone bills every month I can barely afford Busch.

"Oh, come on," Rier said, "Have a Rolling Rock."

Indeed, he only buys the stuff for me and maybe two other regulars.

His banker was drunk.

A coconut monkey sat near the ceiling behind the bar. I eyed it warily. "Is that a nice coconut monkey or a mean coconut monkey," I asked the drunken banker, remembering the PC Gamer's Coconut Monkey fragging my ass mercilessly when playing Quake.

"That's MoJo!"

I guess I got home about 8:30, having bought a six pack of Rolling Rock on the way home. I opened one, sat down, and fell asleep in the chair before even sipping any. I woke up and went to bed a couple of hours later.

How disappointing MoJo's was. Rather than having mo' hos, there weren't any hos at MoJo's at all!

I'll be back tonight to hear *The Station* play. Perhaps there'll even be a few mo' hos.

Chapter 61: Killer
Fri Dec 10, 2004 at 06:21:52 PM EST

Wednesday night I walked into the bar for little rock and roll. "Dude, you got that kill?"

"Uh, yeah," I said.

Darryl and "Joe" were there. Not Joe Frew; Joe Frew is on his honeymoon, having just gotten married Saturday. "Joe" is just a nick for a fellow who doesn't want to be famous among his fellow geeks, and if I'm wrong, Joe, say something and I'll use your real name here.

MoJo's was busier than a bar has a right to be on a Wednesday night. But that's expected, as The Station is still the house band there. If you've never heard them, you're missing some of the most original rock and roll music I've heard so far this century. If you're nowhere near the American Midwest, you can hear some of their 1993 shows in lossless .shn format at Archive.org. I pray the record companies don't discover them and fuck them up like they did to Reel Big Fish, whose latest CD, produced by Brittney Spears' label, sucks elephant ass.

The Station has one CD out, *All That Lies Between*, and is working on another one.

"We can't go in the alley to smoke, Rier's dad is here tonight." Alleys are America's 21st century smoking parlors. Were we able to use the alley we could sneak our drinks out the back. But as it was, we would have to time it so everybody's drinks were gone at the same time. Tricky.

Somehow it was managed. Darryl said he was just going to sit there and hold the couch. Yes, now there are two bars in Springfield with couches. Is that a New York thing, a west coast thing, or a European thing? Or is it, like eating horseshoes, a strictly Springfield thing?

We walked out, across the street to the Illinois State Library; excuse me, the Gwendolyn Brooks Illinois State Library, where Levi had lost his car.

"Oh, here it is" he said.

"Where's Joe?" I asked. Levi looked around. "Guess he changed his mind." We got in the car and Levi drove off. I lit up.

Back at the bar and Joe was really, really disappointed. "Didn't you see me chasing you?"

"No. But then, I wasn't driving and I guess Levi wasn't watching his mirrors."

"I chased you all the way down Capitol Street!"

Joe looks sort of like The Three Stooges' "Curly," only without actually looking stupid. Joe's your typical computer geek; overweight, with stubble on chin and head. The picture of him running down Capitol street, on foot, after Levi's car was amusing as hell to me.

We went out to Joe's car and I burned another one.

Back in MoJo's, someone asked what the date was. "December 8th," I said. "It's the anniversary of John Lennon's murder."

"Really?"

"Yeah, the day after Pearl Harbor day." Which was the only reason I knew what day it was. I'd watched the news the day before, and remembered Lennon's death vividly. Lennon's death had come during a particularly bad year in my life.

While we were in the bar discussing John Lennon's murder, another murder was taking place.

The Alrosa Villa is a bar some 500 or so miles away from MoJo's, in Columbus Ohio. Damageplan was playing good old fashioned rock and roll (also known as "Metal") when a nut case named Nathan Gale went on stage and fired multiple rounds into "Dimebag Darryl" Abbot, Damageplan's guitarist and the former guitarist for Pantera. Also murdered were Dimebag's bodyguard and two other people, including another band member. Police shot and killed the murderer.

Last night at Boone's, Dimebag's murder and Joe Frew's wedding were all anybody was talking about.

I hadn't expected there to be any music at Boone's, and planned on driving past just to be sure before going to MoJo's. I'm not going back to the Firehouse until somebody cleans the fucking rest room; the whole God damned bar smells like stale piss. I almost puked the last time I was there, and I'd only drank one beer. I guess that's what they get for marking the men's room "hose" and the ladies' room "no hose".

But the Posabus was parked in front of Boones. I parked in front of the bus.

Inside was half of Posamist, Jeff and Jeff, and half of The Station, Dave and Dave.

Damn, but it was a great show, despite the fact that they had never played together before. Tim did a little guitar work, Levi did a little singing. In fact, he did some of the best singing I've heard him do. On one blues number especially, he made Johnny Lang look bad.

I almost got up there myself, but didn't. I haven't played in front of more than a handful of people at once in years. Maybe it's time to start back up?

I hated having to leave and go home. Does anybody have a few spare million I can borrow for a few decades so I don't have to work any more?

Somebody had a laptop wired up to the sound board, so there's a chance you might get to hear it. Lets hope so, last night's once in a lifetime show, "The Statiomist's" only performance, was killer.

Chapter 62: A Christmas Present from God
Mon Dec 27, 2004 at 09:35:47 PM EST

MoJo's sucks on Saturdays.

We did Christmas on Friday. It was my sister's decision, since she's the grandma now and we do Christmas at her house.

It makes me feel old to think that my little sister is a grandma with a four year old grandson. At any rate, the girls went down to Belleville with me and saw their aunt and uncle and cousins and grandma.

I drank Sangria and made my youngest daughter drive home.

Saturday Evil-X had the kids, so I drove down to Dupo to see Pot Farmer, then to Cahokia to visit Jeff, whose girl friend was spending Christmas in Wisconsin or somewhere. Mike was there, and Josh and his dad showed up and partied later, too.

I got back to Springfield around 10:00 pm, and decided to drive downtown and see if I could find any music. I wasn't very hopeful, it being Christmas and all. Damn, but it was cold.

Half the bars in town were closed, and I didn't see any bands inside the open ones. I decided to go to MoJo's for a beer.

Saturdays appear to be Disco Night at Mojo's. There was a disk jockey, a black fellow playing rap, hip-hop, and other disco-like "music."

The place was pretty empty. When it was Dempsey's they had a band on Saturdays and you could never, ever get a seat at the bar, and were lucky to sit at all. There were two empty bar stools, and only two tables with people at them.

A girl whose name I never learned, having never formally been introduced, waved from her table and said "hi." I didn't recognize any of the people she was with, and it looked like a double date, so I said "hi" and sidled up between the two empty seats at the bar.

" 'Sgoin' on, dude?" Rier asks. "Beer?"

"Yeah," I reply. I gave a dirty look toward the disk jockey, who continued to pump out bad music. "Not very busy tonight" I said, hinting that maybe Rier should stop with the disk jockey bullshit and get a band on Saturdays.

"No, but they're drinkin'!" he said. And disk jockeys are dirt cheap compared to bands.

I sat down. Rier asked "Seen Levi?"

"No," I said, "Haven't seen him since... Thursday night, here."

A thin, attractive young lady with jet black hair and a black leather jacket staggered in, said "hi" to the rather unattractive young lady sitting next to me and gave me a dirty look. I'd seen this woman somewhere, probably in a bar. "I'm sorry," I replied to her frown, "did I take your seat? Here, you can have it back" I said, moving down a stool. She frowned, and smiled, and sat down and ordered some kind of whiskey drink.

A year or two ago I would have hit on her, but I've pretty much come back down to earth and realized that there's less than a snowball's chance in hell that I'll ever take any of these pretty women home. A year ago I'd have been fruitlessly buying both of them drinks.

God but the music sucked... I'm drinking this one beer and leaving. Damn, I'd rather be by myself with headphones than listen to this dreck sitting next to a pretty girl.

A pretty girl who kept turning around and giving me funny looks, like she expected me to hit on her. There was something about this drunken woman that bothered me... for the first time in a long time, I was actually afraid to hit on her! Not afraid of the guaranteed rejection; I am too damned old for these women, after all, but afraid that she wouldn't reject me and I'd wind up with another broken heart.

Damn. I realized that I've crossed another bridge, that I've started getting used to being by myself again and liking it. And afraid that the first time I get laid will be my last day of freedom.

I must have had my not so ugly as usual face on that night. Two young couples came in, the men staggering. One of the young ladies spied me watching, and I smiled at her. She smiled back and winked. The thin young woman next to me saw it, and stared at me again.

"Another?" Rier asked.

"OK, just one more... the music sucks but the scenery is nice."

I couldn't hear the ladies' conversation over the poor excuse for music, and didn't really want to. I couldn't help overhearing, though, when they started arguing, and the thin attractive women next to me said "age doesn't matter."

Boy, did my ears perk up! I waved to Rier and told him the lady needed another drink. "You buying?" she asked. "Sure," I said, "why not."

But I didn't pursue farther, this woman scared the willies out of me, and I couldn't figure out why. Then it hit me – she gave the same vibes I got from Evil-X the night I met her.

I finished my beer and went home, shivering. And not entirely from the cold.

Chapter 63: Racism on Martin Luther King's Birthday
Tue Jan 18, 2005 at 07:06:58 PM EST

Like many other American drones these days, I had Monday, January 17th off for Martin Luther King's birthday. I had planned on sleeping late.

I was in for a rude awakening.

Bam! Blam! STOMP STOMP STOMP stomp stomp SLAM!
Slam SLAM thump thump slam SLAM!

Shit. That damned crazy bitch upstairs isn't going to let me sleep late today. I rolled out of bed, went to the kitchen to start the coffeepot and headed to the bathroom.

Thump thump STOMP STOMP!

"God damned bitch," I muttered to myself as I left the bathroom. I fired up the computer to hear a few random MP3s as I finished my coffee. My stomach was still upset despite having emptied my bowels. Maybe I should eat something? I've been unintentionally losing weight since I stopped taking the Paxils. I had gained 40 pounds, going from 125 (Yes, I was very thin) to a more normal 165 pounds, but I fear getting skinny again.

I ate a pastry with my coffee. It was starting to get light outside.

SLAM! BANG BANG THUMP!

After feeding my daughter's cats (she doesn't come home much lately) I shut off the tunes and fired up the TV, and watched some History Channel show about a jockey who had won the Kentucky Derby twice around 1900 but who wasn't allowed to race here "because of his skin color" after the sport became more popular.

At least, that's what the historians are saying. They also said in the show that racism is keeping black jockeys off of horses today.

Racism? Er, didn't they pass laws against that sort of thing about 40 years ago?

As I watched, my mind drifted back ten years to a conversation I had with a black woman as we stood outside the workplace shivering and smoking. Yes, it's completely legal to discriminate against smokers, regardless of their race, gender, or sexual preference. One of the questions my landlord had asked was "Do you smoke?" and if the answer had been "yes" my rent would have been much higher.

This lady was complaining to me about racial discrimination, the smoking discrimination completely passing her by. It seems she had been in some store the night before, and the salespeople had followed her, watching like a hawk, as if she was going to steal something.

"I wish I had that problem," I had told her. "I need a clerk and I can't find one."

In 1900, the time of the black Kentucky Derby winner, American society was incredibly racist. After all, it had only been a few short decades since blacks were thought of and treated as animals; bought, sold, and worked like horses or dogs without pay. They were property, just like the horses and dogs. You don't pay your dog, you feed it and water it.

A black friend once informed me that this was the reason black people find being called "boy" so demeaning, "nigger" so insulting and either word incredibly hurtful. In the early 1800s a man would go into town and buy a horse, a few head of cattle, a nigger, maybe a dog or two. Here boy!

My take on it was this happened a century ago (at the time I knew this particular fellow), that I had never owned a slave, nor known anyone who had ever owned a slave, or known anyone who had ever been a slave, or known anyone who had known anyone who had ever owned or been a slave. Delroy agreed, and said that's the reason black people throw the word "nigger" around so much.

I almost never ever hear a white person use the word "nigger." It's hard to be in a crowd of blacks without hearing one of them use it. Pot? Kettle? Dead horse?

Hypocrites?

I shut the TV off and sat there, thinking about race relations and the black friends I have had over the years. A car stopped outside my apartment with its radio on. Jazz wafted through the walls. I looked out the window and spied a black woman going in the building next door as her car idled outside with its radio blaring. Five minutes later it and she were gone.

BLAM BLAM BLAM!!!!!

It was my door. The peephole cover flew five feet across

the room, the door was being beaten on so hard. I had no doubt who it was; the crazy bitch from upstairs, who hates white people and wakes me up at 5:30 AM on my day off stomping on my ceiling and slamming doors.

"GOD DAMN HONKEY MUTHAFUCKA SHUT THAT DAMNED MUSIC DOWN YOU MOTHAFUCKING SONABITCH! GOD DAMN GOD DAMN GOD DAMN!"

"Go away" I said.

"GOD DAMN MOTHERFUCKER CRACKER SONOFA-BITCH TURN THAT DAMNED MUSIC DOWN!"

You want to end racism? Act like a human being. That goes for all of you, whatever your race.

I turned the MP3s on and cranked it up as loud as it would go, steam seeming to come out of my ears.

A fitting tribute to Dr. King, I thought.

Chapter 64: The Angel's Mother – Chris at Christmas
About a year later...

Christmas is such a heartbreakingly lonely time.

Many if not most believe the Paxil Diaries are fiction. I can't blame them; my whole life has been pretty unbelievable. This one will likely not be believed by anyone at all, but it's true nonetheless.

I had met Kim and Vickie and their sister Valerie a month or two earlier at George Rank's, a bar I frequent often, one that more women my age go to than any other bar in town I know. I was the only one there when they came in.

Valerie was almost anorexicly thin, and I had been smitten. I'm a fool for skinny women.

This was yet another unwritten and unbelievable Paxil story. Valerie was very, very attractive and somehow, I'm not exactly sure how, she wound up with her legs draped over my lap very pleasantly, with me massaging them.

"Steve sure is smiling big," Vickie said to Kim.

"Of course he is," Kim said, "Valerie has her legs on his dick!"

Valerie said she had a tumor, and gave me her Saint Jude medal. Saint Jude is the Catholic saint of hopeless causes; I know this from the movie *The Untouchables*. So fitting, my loneliness was hopeless indeed. I'd long ago given up ever finding a girlfriend, or even getting laid.

I was sure I was finally going to get lucky, until the bar owner came in and the three abandoned me for the monied man. I had yet again gone home alone after having my hopes raised high. I found out later that Dave wasn't the least interested in any of them.

But this isn't the story of the three lovely ladies, I digress. Sorry, I'm bad about that. Back to the Angel's mother...

The Angel's mother gave me back one of my most important possessions, one that had been stolen from me.

When a man's wife cheats on him, it is a wound that is hard to heal. It rips and tears his self confidence, leaving his soul in tatters. The first time the Evil-X cheated on me was barely into the second year of our marriage. Despite the pain and wounds to my soul, I forgave her.

By the time all that was left of the wound was a scar, by the time I had managed to repair the rips and tears to my self confidence and self esteem, she did it again.

It happened over and over. By the time the marriage

ended twenty seven years later, my soul had no more flesh left, only scars. My self confidence was in horrible ragged tatters. I took Paxil and drank far too much.

The Paxil took away the pain of my soul like morphine takes away the pain of a flesh wound. But like morphine, the Paxil has its downside and I gave it up a year and a half later, and bore the pain as the wounds to my soul healed naturally.

A year after the Paxil stopped, my tattered confidence was still tattered. A very young woman stitched a few threads of my esteem back by asking me out. I met her at a Posamist show at the late Eleven West, and she called me the next day. No, there is no use looking at the Paxil diaries for the story as I didn't write that one either.

She saw me not as a prospective lover but as a prospective friend, and our relationship has been a platonic one, even though I would gladly lay her down if she wished. But that friendship restored my confidence enough to at least ask a woman on a date, and although she may feel as she's using me, helping heal my tattered soul was worth far more than the money I loaned her that I don't expect to get back.

She restored a few threads of my confidence, a gift that was invaluable. Gifts for the soul are worth more than Bill Gates' entire fortune. I was finally well enough to ask a woman on a date.

No real date materialized, but the women I asked were kind in their rejections. Most gave excuses; one said yes then stood me up, giving the lame excuse that she was too old to go to a rock show and besides, was afraid of being hurt again, as she had been through two bad marriages and feared heartbreak more than she feared loneliness. One was going through a divorce and promised she'd go out with me when it was final; we'll see, I guess.

And then one night last summer, there was a woman I had worked with who moonlighted as a bartender. I asked her out.

She laughed in my face.

The tattered threads of self confidence I had worked so hard to regain were completely ripped away. I could no longer get up the nerve to ask anyone out again. I was resigned to loneliness, a forlorn life free of sex and companionship. My flesh ached for flesh, but I couldn't bear the possibility of such cruelty again.

Christmas eve day I visited family at my sister's house (she's a grandma now) with my oldest daughter, and that evening sat alone in my little apartment feeling sorry for myself. I was in misery, and I prayed to God for my loneliness to be lifted.

No sooner than I said "amen" than the phone rang. It was my young platonic girl friend, and she was lonely, too. We decided to go out and have a few drinks, and I picked her up and went to one of her haunts, a bar where she knew everyone but I knew nobody. I had some fun nevertheless, and my loneliness was lifted, my prayer answered.

Yes, unbelievable but true. Miracles happen.

Christmas day I watched "Jesus Of Nazareth" on the History Channel, alone in my little apartment. My youngest daughter hadn't been able to attend the family Christmas the day before because she had to work 12 hours, and came by and exchanged hugs and presents later in the afternoon. She brought reggae, the blues, and Jerry Lee Lewis on CD, Cream's farewell concert on DVD, and the guitar strings I had asked for. She was thrilled with the new Nintendo DS I bought for her. It turns out that her boyfriend has one, and they can now play video games together with the Nintendo's wireless link.

She left for work, and as I was listening to Lightning Hopkins and Bob Marley I got the lonely blues again. I had been reminded by the History Channel that Jesus had said not to pray for stuff, because God knows what you need before you do, so I said the Lord's prayer. I then decided to go out and find a place where I wouldn't be so alone.

I went to George Rank's, about the only bar open, and there tending the bar was the woman who had laughed in my face.

I wasn't exactly nice to her. The owner was there, and we told blond jokes with another fellow who had a list of them in his pocket.

The cruel bartender had been a blond before her hair went gray. This was pretty gratifying to me, as you might imagine.

Then my phone rang. It was my oldest daughter; her TV had quit, she wanted her nerd father to come over and see what I could do about it. I left for Chatham, got her TV going, and searched for somewhere to buy dinner. No room at the inn? Hell, they were all closed for Christmas. I went back to the bar I had been drinking and laughing in earlier.

As I pulled in, an attractive young woman and two men were getting into the car in the space next to mine to leave.

I went inside, and the stool I had been sitting in was still empty. There was a woman named Chris I had known at that bar for a couple of years sitting there by herself. When I had seen her before, she was always with someone. Her ex husband, or her boyfriend; one of the two.

Chris was likely a beauty in her youth, before she lost all her teeth. But she was still thin and short, with pretty brown (probably dyed brown) hair, and I'm a fool for thin short women, as I think I said before. I'm also a fool for women who don't wear makeup.

She was wearing no makeup, and was crying.

Chris has some mental and emotional problems, and hadn't been taking her medication. Her live-in boyfriend's children were driving her crazy "running around the house nekkid" and she had needed to get out. I wiped her tears, and actually had her laughing at one point.

She was about fed up with the boyfriend, a fellow twenty years her junior who had no job, who was leeching off of her and who she was about to throw out "after the holidays."

We talked some more, and she said she had always

thought I was married, as when I'd go to the bar I'd drink one or two beers and leave. "Do you think I'm pretty?" she asked.

She told me she was attracted to me the first time she saw me, and I asked if she would let me buy her dinner the next day. She'd love to!

The bar phone rang, and Nellie the mean old bartender yelled "Chris?"

It was Chris' daughter, who wanted her to come home. "She's coming here," Chris said, disappointed.

A few minutes later the woman I had seen leaving as I got there came in. It was Chris' daughter. Chris introduced me her daughter, Angel.

I bought Yaeger Bombs for Angel and myself and we toasted her mother, who was drinking draft. I bought Chris another beer, and one for me, and we all talked. Chris had a skin infection on her hands and hadn't been able to wash her hair in a couple of days. Angel had planned to do it for her mother the next day, and they were going to get their pictures taken.

I told Angel of the date I had made with her mother, and promised to get her mother home safely when we were done at the bar. Angel and I exchanged phone numbers, as Chris had no cell phone. She was to call me when they were done with the festivities, and I told Chris if I didn't hear from her by six I was just going to show up at her house.

I promised Angel again that I'd get her mother home safely, and she left after a second bomb.

Kim and Vickie came in. The bar was filling up. I got a bag of peanuts, as the kitchen was closed for Christmas of course.

I had looked the Saint Jude medallion up on the internet, and found that it was worth twenty or thirty dollars. I didn't feel like I could accept a gift like that from someone I had just met, and tried to get Vickie (or was it Kim?) to give it back to Valerie for me.

She said I couldn't give it back, but I could give it to

someone else.

I gave it to Chris. I thought she needed it more than I did.

Kim and Vickie and Chris and I talked, and Kim turned out to be a beautician. She put makeup on Chris' face and put her hair in a young style pony tail. My hand was resting on the back of Chris' chair, and at one point my hand was lodged between Chris' and Vickie's breasts.

Heaven on earth! I certainly had good will to all God's creatures at that moment! God, but what a merry Christmas it was! I wasn't even mad at mean old Nellie any more, who was getting increasingly angered at my attitude to her, but what in the hell did she expect? In my heart I forgave the heartless old bitch. Hell, if Evil-X had walked in I might have even been pleasant to her.

I had a wonderful time, and when last call came, none of us could believe it was so late. Chris and I got in my old junker, and it was cold in there. We snuggled up, and kissed passionately.

As I drove her home I told her that I hadn't had sex in three years, and she didn't believe me. "Three years? What, are you gay?"

I pulled up in front of her house, and we sat in the car and kissed goodnight. And I won't go into more detail about what else.

But at the verge of sinning on Christmas, God sent Angel out to the car.

Yes, I went home alone yet again. Alone, but happy.

I'd finally found a girlfriend.

The End

www.ingramcontent.com/pod-product-compliance
Lightning Source LLC
Chambersburg PA
CBHW031613160426
43196CB00006B/113